CU00819291

Discussion Materials

Tales of a Rookie
Wall Street Investment Banker

Bill Keenan

A POST HILL PRESS BOOK

Discussion Materials:
Tales of a Rookie Wall Street Investment Banker
© 2020 by Bill Keenan
All Rights Reserved

ISBN: 978-1-64293-408-3
ISBN (eBook): 978-1-64293-409-0

Cover art by Cody Corcoran
Interior design and composition by Greg Johnson/Textbook Perfect

This is a work of nonfiction. All people, locations, events, and situations are portrayed to the best of the author's memory.

Post Hill Press
New York • Nashville
posthillpress.com

Published in the United States of America

To anyone who's worked in plastics
....

Disclaimer

The following discussion includes forward-looking statements that are subject to uncertainties[1] and factors[2] which are difficult to quantify, and therefore I have italicized everything to lend credibility to the suspect rationale. Forward-looking statements that wildly misrepresent what I'm trying to conceal can be identified by words such as "future," "anticipates," "estimates," "the," "and," and "a." Differences, fabrications, and outright lies include, but are not limited to, the entire document. I do not undertake any obligation to publicly update or revise any of the materials found herein provided this becomes a big hit and Oprah recommends it to her book club. Given certain individuals and companies prefer to remain a going concern, I hereby acknowledge some characters are composites, and names—humans, companies, and otherwise—are pro forma for God only knows what type of adjustments. The idea is to instill equal parts boredom and anger at the outset so you skim the rest of the document and miss the real risks buried deep in footnotes and incomprehensible legalese. Also, this is the smallest font I can legally use.

I am acting as the exclusive advisor and writer of this book (the "Book"). I will gladly accept any and all accolades with respect to the Book's success. However, I absolve myself from any liability ~~if and~~ when shit flies into the fan. The information and projections found herein must not be reproduced in any electronic or physical form and must not be communicated, disclosed, or distributed to any other person in whole or in part except strictly in accordance with the terms of the confidentiality agreement. None of this applies if you're an analyst who's been told by your managing director to get a hold of the document. In that case, it is permissible to use your smartphone to capture as many dog-shit JPEGs of the document during a company presentation and/or photocopy as many pages as possible at the hotel front desk.

Some more stuff about the Financial Services and Markets Act 2000 (Financial Promotion) Order 2005 (as amended) and Article 49(2) (a) to (d). Good luck tracking down what that means. If you've made it to this paragraph, kudos, though something is clearly wrong with you. You may be suited to be an investment banker.

---

[1] See footnote 2.
[2] See footnote 1.

Prologue

Then the forty-fourth floor's overhead lights flick off. They do that when no one's walked down the hall for fifteen minutes. My dual computer monitors save me from total darkness.

"And William, have you tried disabling iterative calculations in the options—"

"Yeah, did that—doesn't work. You can call me Bill. What's your name again?"

"Kamaliyyah."

"Any other ideas, Cam?" I adjust my headset and take a sip of my Red Bull. After dinner, the only thing keeping my eyelids from drooping is a steady drip of caffeine—natural or synthetic.

"I assume you've checked your circularity switches—" he begins.

"Yep."

"…and run the troubleshooting utility and cleared the cache—"

"Cleared cached config, cleared cached workspace. I tested the RT servers, the AC connectivity, uninstalled then re-installed all the add-ins."

"You'll be receiving an email from me in the next couple seconds. If you could reply, please attach your spreadsheet, and let me know which tab you're having the issue with."

I follow his instructions, though I don't need his explanation. I know the drill.

"It's the fifth tab—'PF Financials.'"

The line is silent as Cam gets to work while I pick up the mini Nerf football on my desk and fire it across the floor, just missing the stack of deal toys lining my VP's cube—a vice president at the bank and the dictator of my life.

"No circular references…add-ins seem to be running properly," Cam says, more to himself than to me. "Let's see…"

"The tab to the right is reffed out too, but I redid all the formulas. Doesn't make sense."

"Let's have a look…do you mind…can you give me a few moments? I need to use the restroom."

"Sure." I exhale as I say it, loud enough to convey my disapproval of his not having a catheter at his desk.

Rose made the rounds early tonight, around 10:45 p.m., when I was still eating dinner. The smell of old sushi and soy sauce nauseates me, even though I threw my dinner in the trash of the vacant cubicle across the room. Raku Restaurant opened a week ago and has a good deal on tuna rolls—four for under the bank's twenty-five-dollar dinner allowance. Fifty percent chance I'm gonna get sick, but it's a risk I'm willing to take.

The investment banking job description that was hammered into me during the never-ending business school recruiting circus flashes in my mind: "Exceptional problem-solving abilities; keen interest in global markets; superior financial analysis skills; strong team player." Someone forgot to mention "graphic artist" and "ability to get people in India to unfuck up your shit."

I finish off my Red Bull.

"Sorry about that, Bill. Can you provide any context on this spreadsheet?" Cam's back. Thank God. Allah too.

"Can't really tell you."

"Of course. I shouldn't have asked—private information."

"Nah, didn't mean it like that. I don't really know what type of transaction it is—just got an email tonight with no context."

"Okay, I think I see what the problem is," says Cam. My pulse quickens. "The most recent version of the document has a link to another spreadsheet that is probably deleted. The earlier version of the document isn't linked to it. I'd like you to try deleting all the cells on the fifth tab below row 113. That should get rid of the broken links that are causing the problems."

I do as told. "Still reffed out." My eyes dart to the bottom right corner of my right computer monitor: 2:54 a.m.

"Have you tried disabling macros?" he says.

"Twice."

"There's one other thing you could try."

"Anything."

"Have you tried restarting your computer? In many instances—"

I don't respond, but instead emit a condescending scoffing sound. You'd have to be an idiot not to have closed Excel and restarted the computer.

"You know what," I say. "Forget it. I'll figure it out."

"I'm happy to stay on the line."

"No, I'll figure it out."

"Is there anything else I can help you with?"

"Nah. Have a good night or afternoon, rest of the day." I rip off my headset, hang it on the cubicle divider, and restart my computer for the first time since I can remember. When I reopen Excel fifteen minutes later, the problem is fixed.

Thanks, Cam.

I grab my keys and wallet off my desk while I attach the updated file to a new email and send it off to the rest of the deal team, whoever they are.

I log out before anything else can pop up on my computer. I don't bother retying my shoelaces; I sling my suit jacket over my shoulder and jog down the hallway to the elevators.

But you're never free. As I enter the elevator bank, my Black-Berry buzzes on my right thigh. I reach into my pocket to retrieve the device and withdraw it to find the tiny red light blinking—over and over and over: one new email.

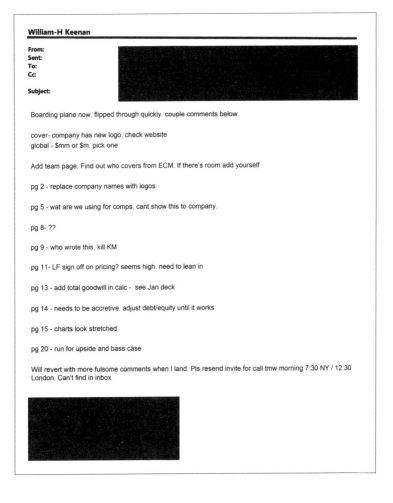

William-H Keenan

From:
Sent:
To:
Cc:

Subject:

Boarding plane now. flipped through quickly. couple comments below

cover- company has new logo. check website
global - $mm or $m. pick one

Add team page. Find out who covers from ECM. If there's room add yourself

pg 2 - replace company names with logos

pg 5 - wat are we using for comps. cant show this to company.

pg 8- ??

pg 9 - who wrote this. kill KM

pg 11- LF sign off on pricing? seems high. need to lean in

pg 13 - add total goodwill in calc - see Jan deck

pg 14 - needs to be accretive. adjust debt/equity until it works

pg 15 - charts look stretched

pg 20 - run for upside and bass case

Will revert with more fulsome comments when I land. Pls resend invite for call tmw morning 7:30 NY / 12:30 London. Can't find in inbox

1

Stripes and Solids

I'd gotten used to wearing pants with a drawstring, so the suit and tie already put me in a bad mood.

"Which deal are you guys using for BANK?" asked Dark Gray Suit as he frantically shuffled through the papers in front of him, a collection of *Training the Street* and *Breaking into Wall Street* study guides.

"Burger King's acquisition of Tim Hortons," said Navy Suit, sitting at the head of the table.

"What was the purchase price?" said Dark Gray Suit.

"Eleven billion—seven billion of cash, four billion in stock," said Navy Suit as he leaned back in his chair.

"Eleven point four billion USD, or about twelve-and-a-half CAD," chimed in Dark Gray Suit #2, his eyes glued to his laptop computer screen.

"And it was all about inversion, right? Tim Hortons is headquartered in Toronto, and since Canada has a lower corporate tax rate—"

"Twenty-six and a half percent," said Dark Blue Suit.

"Right, so it's lower than in the US, which makes re-domiciling the combined entity in Canada attractive." As he said it, his eyes scanned the table for reassurance. "Wait, was BANK lead left? Or were they co-bookrunners with BANK?" Seconds later, he darted across Watson library to a Bloomberg Terminal.

"He's fucked—the deal was more about realizing cost synergies than the tax thing. Plus, BANK wants to hear about stuff that isn't front-page news—need to show them you've done some research." Navy Suit fixed his cufflinks and brushed a piece of nonexistent lint off his sleeve.

"Good call. What transaction you using?" asked Navy Suit #2.

"Got a debt offering that I found—didn't get a lot of press but heard from a buddy that it got BANK a lot of respect on the Street."

"What company was it?"

"Look up your own shit."

"Keenan, what deal are you using if they ask?"

"Probably that Burger King one," I said.

"You're interviewing with BANK next, right?"

"Yeah," I said.

"Dude, pretty sure they didn't advise on that deal. You can't use that as your example if they weren't involved in the transaction."

"I heard that place is a real sweatshop," added someone.

"So do you have a backup deal you can use?" Dark Blue Suit asked me. "Keenan?"

But I was busy reading the most recent headline on NHL.com about a former junior hockey teammate who at age twenty-eight was getting called up to the Vancouver Canucks to make his NHL debut. After toiling in the minor leagues for nearly seven seasons, he was about to realize his childhood dream—and mine. Equal parts envy and pride rushed through me as I stared at his picture on my computer screen.

"They're going to love you with the hockey background," said Navy Suit #2 as he peered at my screen. "Plus, you already got sick banker hair."

I didn't have banker hair. It was hockey hair. But he was right: it was sick.

Four months ago, a day after my first class at Columbia Business School, recruiting for investment banking started. There were nights spent in "banker circles"—six-plus students standing in a circle, holding half-empty, watered-down vodka sodas with crooked nametags pinned to suit jackets, listening expectantly to some banker. One student would ask how BANK thought about the effects of low interest-rates or increased regulation on M&A activity, at which point the Oracle of Nowhere would regurgitate—using mainly acronyms—a highlight reel of the deals he'd worked on, most of which we would have seen "on the front page of the *Journal*."

"We were sole advisors on TTZ's LBO of a major CPG company. Bought them out at seven times LTM EBITDA." Which of course begs the question: WTF?

We would nod in unison and pretend to know what the hell the guy was talking about, and then it was onto the next question. Rinse and repeat. Periodically, I'd take breaks to hit on the HR women; they'd pretend to know what investment banking was, and I'd pretend to care what they were saying.

When the banker had exhausted his shtick, he'd dole out business cards to the group in the circle. "Any questions, don't hesitate to shoot me an email." Rest assured, no one hesitated. After grabbing another drink and finding a new group of first-year students to serenade, it was a mad dash to write down some identifying features of the banker. "Short, bald, TTZ seven times deal???—ask Xinchen in corporate finance class on Monday." These would be key in drafting up our thank-you emails to be sent the following day, no earlier than 9:00 a.m. and no later than 5:00 p.m. according to the head of the investment banking club at school.

The thank-you emails—holy shit. Crafting those tailor-made responses to everyone who handed me a business card at countless events took up more time than studying for any test—and I tried in school this time around. I pulled an all-nighter composing a batch of thank-you emails one night. I'd be lucky to get a response with "tx."

Then there were the informational interviews. We'd sign up weeks in advance to schedule a fifteen-minute conversation with a senior investment banker. Setting up these humdingers involved typing phrases like "nice to e-meet you," "pick your brain," and "look forward to connecting"—phrases that make you rethink life.

After e-meeting the senior banker, we'd set up a time for an "informational." After regaining cell service following the subway ride downtown to whatever bank, we'd receive an email from a secretary explaining how something important came up, and the banker needed to reschedule. When we finally had the informational interview, it was a fifteen-minute, one-on-one session in which the banker fellated himself, glanced at our résumés, then left them on the table after we thanked him profusely for his time. Informationals, however, were useful in that they helped eliminate the prospect of working at a boutique bank. My first and only informational at these smaller investment banks, which focus on advisory services, involved thirty minutes (the guy literally had a timer) of technical financial questions. Within sixty seconds, he had quizzed me on the accounting of JV net income and the treatment of inventory step-ups on a pro-forma balance sheet. He never asked my name. From there on out, I had narrowed it down to bulge-bracket banks.

But as painful and tiresome as the recruiting process was, it finally came to an end. And it's not like anyone had forced us to go through it. For the most part, I gave banking a shot for the same reasons most did: to earn some stripes, learn about how businesses work, and hopefully start down a path of freedom paved by financial independence. Investment banking was also the first industry to start recruiting—no doubt to entice wayward individuals like myself who felt urgency to explore careers but had little idea what they wanted to do. You didn't choose banking; banking chose you.

I stood up from my chair and scanned the library, each of the dozens of tables more frenzied than the next. "Gotta take a leak, boys."

Navy Suit #2 retrieved his iPhone from his inside jacket pocket. "It's 11:27. You only have three minutes."

Two hundred seconds later, I was back at the library table, which was now empty aside from Navy Suit #2.

"Where's your interview?" he asked.

"J-17." We both stood up as I looked for the room on the perimeter of the library.

"Your top button is undone," he said. I buttoned it and cinched up my tie.

"Thanks, man. Good luck." I whacked him on the shoulder.

He looked down as I made my way across the library where introductions were already underway in front of all twenty-five library private rooms. With my matte black binder, I covered the small piss-stain on my crotch and moments later arrived at room J-17.

"Good to see you again, Bill." I shook hands with Stripes and met his colleague, Solids.

We took our seats at the rectangular table, me on one side and Stripes and Solids on the other. I'd been involved in plenty of odd-man rushes in my hockey days, but never had I been on the business end of one.

"Since we've had a chance to get to know one another over the past few months, I figured I'd let Solids take the lead." Solids reached under his swivel chair and adjusted his seat up. Like a kid at a barber shop, his feet were now dangling a few inches off the floor.

Solids had a head of hair that resembled a barren hay field with a low yield after a rough winter. It wasn't a huge shocker that BANK didn't have him on the front lines as part of the recruiting team—he probably wore a cape at some point in high school. So much for Darwinism.

"Stripes has told me a little bit about you, and I've had a chance to look at your résumé." Solids held up a piece of paper which I'm pretty sure wasn't my résumé, then continued, "But I thought it would make sense for me to give you a rundown of my background first. Sound good?" I nodded and prepared to zone out. He said something about reverse mortgages for a bit, then went on about his voracious curiosity for finance and something about loving numbers at one point. I did, however, catch the fact that Solids, like Stripes, held the title of vice president. Don't get too impressed—there are hundreds in each bank. As he listed the transactions he worked on, I tried to pinpoint the industry he covered:

"So you know the retail space?" I asked.

"Enough to be dangerous," he replied.

"Would you say you have an expertise in the chemical sector?" I said.

"Enough to be dangerous," he replied.

"So look," said Solids. "I think we have a lot in common from what I've seen and heard, but it would be great to hear more about you." I gave him a sixty-second rundown of my pitch, which walked through my résumé and how my life had taken a series of twists and turns that led to investment banking being the obvious next step. There was no room for uncertainty.

Solids leaned back in his chair and did a lot of head nodding, while Stripes excused himself from the room to take a call.

"I also see you've been writing a book?" said Solids, half statement, half question. "Is it a novel? Tell me more about that."

"It's a memoir about my time playing hockey."

"How long did it take to write?"

"The actual writing was about two years, but trying to get an agent took another year, then getting a publisher was another—"

"It's so funny—sorry to cut you off—but I've coauthored a few pieces of research published in the *Journal of Financial Economics* that I wrote when I was working for the New York Fed after college. It's important to have those outside interests."

Stripes returned to the room and sat down. "Sorry for that. Got a deal that's live—big consumer name you'd know," he said.

"Look," said Solids. "Here at BANK, we like to think we have a culture that differentiates us from some of the other big firms on the Street. We work hard and play hard." Solids glanced and exchanged smiles with Stripes. "When it comes down to it, we only have one rule which is the 'no asshole rule.'" If I had a dime, even a nickel, for every time I heard a banker say that, I wouldn't need a job.

Stripes nodded his head, then leaned in and rested one elbow on the table. "As an athlete like yourself, I can promise you we know how to have a good time. There are a bunch of veterans at BANK. Actually, we're working closely with a former Marine on this deal that we're hoping will close by end of the month."

Stripes did CrossFit, an activity he brought up in all of our previous conversations—the push-jerk was his favorite exercise, but a recent lower back issue had hurt his most recent attempt to beat his PR. "And we've talked about this before, Bill. We're not about face time here at BANK, and we think that really separates us from some of the other places you're probably interviewing with." Stripes was right about that one: he'd told me a bunch of times throughout recruiting that face time wasn't a priority. The only issue I had is that up until three weeks ago, Stripes had been working at a different bank and reeling off the same spiel.

"With that, I have to put on my interviewer hat—wish I didn't— and go through a few questions." Solids opened up the notebook in front of him and removed a sheet of paper. "We'll start with a few résumé questions, then finish with some technical questions. Sound good?"

"Not really," I wanted to say, but I didn't. Instead, I went with, "perfect."

"Super. We love candidates with unique backgrounds, and you certainly are in that category. But obviously, without any real work experience, you're one of the more unique cases we've had in the business school recruiting process."

"I have to say I'd consider playing hockey real work experience. I realize it didn't involve sitting at a desk in front of a computer, but I was hired and earned a salary—and got fired, just like a real job."

"Fair enough," said Stripes, as he nodded cautiously.

Solids buried his head and scribbled something onto the sheet in front of him. After a few seconds of silence, he lifted his head. "Can you tell us about a time when you worked as a member of a team and had to resolve a key issue?"

"Absolutely." This was the "Is he a team player?" question we'd been told would be asked. I'd played on hockey teams since I was five and had spent the three years between college and business school playing professionally in Europe. Being on a team had defined my identity. "When I was playing in Sweden a couple years ago, I had a teammate from Latvia who spoke no English. A few weeks before we started—"

"Let's push pause on this for a second," said Solids. "We love the hockey angle and want to hear more about it. But do you have any examples from other relevant professional experiences? Or from your time at business school so far?"

Hockey was my only work experience before school. I could have manufactured some garbage about an assignment I'd worked on with my classmates, but we hadn't even finished our first semester and aside from getting consensus about what unlevered beta we should use on our corporate finance class cases, there wasn't much in the way of 'resolving key issues.'

Seconds passed, and I saw Stripes remove his BlackBerry from his pocket, check it, then place it on the table. Solids didn't move—he just eyeballed me.

Having trouble keeping straight Solids and Stripes? Imagine how I felt.

"I'm sure teamwork played a large role in your hockey. Can you tell us about what made you pursue it after college?" Solids said.

"I loved the feeling of winning and scoring goals." It's a feeling everyone should be able to experience.

Neither wrote anything. They both looked at me, waiting for more explanation, but that was the only answer I never had to rehearse.

"Can you tell us a little bit about how you see transitioning from playing sports to a career in investment banking?" asked Solids. For people like me, career-changers, recruiting firms loved drilling into our reasons for "transitioning."

"I think there are plenty of transferable skills that will help me in banking."

Moments passed before Solids piped up. "It looks like you played on a number of teams—bounced around a lot. Can you speak a little bit to why that was the case?"

"I got hurt once, traded once, and cut by a couple teams. I went where there was an opportunity to contribute."

They still didn't write anything, but Solids checked his BlackBerry.

"I spent the summer after my senior year backpacking through southern Europe with some college roommates, so I'm sure we can swap some similar stories," said Stripes. He then jotted something down.

"You have a tremendous opportunity at school to explore a number of industries, so what is it about investment banking that makes you certain this is what you want to do?" said Solids.

"I've always been interested in how businesses work, and the idea of being a strategic advisor to some of the biggest and best companies in the world is really exciting to me. I think banking combines a quantitative element with a need to be a superior problem-solver, all in a fast-paced environment." Once again, these were sound bites I'd rehearsed *ad nauseum*. Stripes bought it, but I could tell Solids needed more stroking. "The deals you guys work on are front-page news in the *Journal*, the deals that move markets. It's exactly the work environment I want."

A smile grew wide on Solids's face as he nodded, laid his pen down, and leaned back in his chair. "That's exactly it. We're not making headlines every day, but when we do, it's the first thing you read when you wake up."

Solids turned to Stripes as if to give him the go-ahead to fire a question my way. "I remember you mentioning natural resources is one of the industries you were interested in." Stripes looked at me in search of confirmation. My slight nod belied the neon sign flashing in my head that read, "*OH FUCK.*"

Stripes continued, "What are your thoughts on where oil is headed?"

"Like any other commodity, the price is going to depend on supply and demand. On the supply side, I think OPEC will probably keep production going to try and damage the economies of certain rivals, specifically Russia. With demand...." A brunette outside with a little sundress caught my eye. "On the demand side, I...we're going to see...." I could feel the first bits of sweat inching down my forehead. *Was that girl from Columbia? How had I never seen her on campus? Undergrad, maybe?* I exhaled slowly, returned my eyes to somewhere in the middle of the table, and went through my mental emergency interview checklist—when in doubt on these subjects, reference the following terms: accounting → taxes; corporate finance → leverage; marketing → customer lifetime value; operations management → bottleneck; miscellaneous → diversity; and economics....

"China," I said. "China is going to play a large role in demand, but with projected GDP growth slowing down, I don't think there will be enough demand to have a material impact on prices. With those dynamics in mind, I think we'll see it around forty dollars per barrel for the foreseeable future."

They both jotted down some notes as I peered out the window, but the girl was gone. All I saw now were two students, walking and laughing, though the size of each of their backpacks was nothing to laugh about.

"Any favorite classes this semester?" Stripes asked. There was one correct answer.

"Corporate finance," I said. And I wasn't even lying. It wasn't the content of the course though, but the way our Chilean professor pronounced the "b" in "debt," and how he replied to every statement made by my classmate Brad, a former Marine who still used military time, by politely stating, "You have all the right words but need some work on the order."

"What'd you think of the Calaveras Vineyard case?" asked Solids, a Columbia Business School alum who for some godforsaken reason still remembered the case studies in first-year corporate finance class.

"Yeah, definitely an interesting one," I said trying to buy time.

"How'd you approach calculating the WACC with all the uncertainties?" Solids asked. He had me on the ropes. And if the guy really wanted to know so badly, he should have asked the Norwegian girl in my study group who did the case. Beads of sweat gathered on my forehead.

"I remember a lot of those case studies ran together," said Stripes, saving me as he shot a smile in my direction.

"Okay. We're going to get into some of the technical stuff now—shouldn't be too difficult, so don't worry." Solids clicked the top of his pen and tilted his neck to one side, then the other. "Could you walk me through how you'd get from net income to free cash flow?"

This was a layup—it was in every single study guide and something we'd been told to prepare for from the first day of recruiting. If I could avoid putting myself to sleep mid-explanation, I'd get the check mark.

"Starting with net income on the income statement, I'd add back interest expense, multiplied by one minus the tax rate—"

"And why one *minus* the tax rate?" said Solids.

"Interest is tax-deductible." I said. He made a mark on his sheet, then motioned me to continue. "Then I'd add back depreciation, subtract capital expenditures, then subtract investment in working capital."

"And why would we be interested in a company's free cash flow versus, say, its EBITDA?" Solids clicked the top of his pen twice, then poised himself to write while his eyes fixed on my mouth.

"EBITDA may be easier to calculate for back-of-the-envelope calculations and is a decent proxy for operating cash flow, but the biggest issue is that it doesn't take into consideration capital expenditures or working capital needs. Free cash flow, on the other hand, does, and so it is really the best gauge to understanding how much cash a company generates, which can then be used to buy back shares, pay dividends, make acquisitions, or pay down debt if it has any." I'd rehearsed that for weeks and was in such a groove that I decided to go off script. "Because the unlevered free cash flow is the best calculation for the cash a company generates, it's those cash-flow projections that are used in a discounted cash-flow model to calculate a company's net present value." They both scribbled down more notes.

"Well that leads us into my next question," said Stripes. "If I said, 'Here, Bill. Here's a million dollars. You can either take it today, or you can wait, and I'll give you 1.11 million dollars next year,' which would you take?"

This was another question we'd been prepped on repeatedly. When I first heard someone ask it, my reaction was, *what dumbasses are dishing out a million bucks willy-nilly? No wonder the economy has been in the shitter.* But the concept they were testing was "present value"—a dollar today is worth more than a dollar tomorrow. The reason is that a dollar today can be invested at a "risk-free" rate in a government security, and therefore can be worth more after a year than a dollar that you kept under your mattress. However, the wrinkle in this case involved using that risk-free rate (in this case, a treasury bill with one-year maturity) and discounting $1.1 million to today's value. I didn't have a clue what that specific interest rate was, but I knew for sure that it wasn't much more than zero percent. Think about the interest you earned in your savings account around 2015—it sucked.

Anyway, the point was that if I invested one million bucks at just above zero percent for one year, I wasn't going to be close to having 1.1 million bucks at the end of the year—to get there I would have needed a 10 percent return.

That's when it hit me.

Prior to business school, my knowledge of investing was limited to watching *Shark Tank* reruns on CNBC. But in my corporate finance class, I'd done a project with a heady guy who'd worked at a hedge fund prior to business school, and he told me about his most recent investment idea. He was one of those guys who said he picked up Benjamin Graham's *The Intelligent Investor* in high school, and "it just made sense." Plus, on his LinkedIn profile he had CFA, CPA, NAACP, AARP, and a bunch of other initials next to his name, so he had some credibility, at least in finance.

"I'd take the one million dollars today," I said. Solids immediately reached for his BlackBerry and started typing with a smirk on his face.

"Could you walk us through your reasoning?" said Stripes. As Solids placed his BlackBerry back on the table, Stripes's BlackBerry vibrated.

"Sure. I'd take the million bucks and buy shares of Atlas Properties, which is a REIT that owns commercial properties in the US. The stock just got hit because there was confusion about litigation regarding one of its major tenants. It's currently yielding eleven percent, so assuming they don't default, I'd have one-point-eleven million dollars at the end of the year."

"And what if the price of the security dropped?" said Stripes.

"Well, I won't sell the position, so it would only be a loss on paper."

"Can you talk more about the risk associated with this?"

"Well, the company isn't overleveraged, and they have raised their distribution consistently over the past twelve quarters. Of course there's market risk, but I'm twenty-eight years old, which I think is young enough to take some risk. Plus, I know I'd learn much more by getting involved rather than spending a year on the sidelines."

Solids pressed the middle button on his BlackBerry. "We need to wrap up, but before we do, I wanted to ask if you were involved in any more of the clubs here. I see the investment banking club on your résumé. Are there any others?"

There weren't.

"Yeah, a couple others," I said.

"Could you tell us about one, ideally where you hold a leadership position?"

The last real leadership position I'd had was as an assistant captain of the Swedish team I played on in my last year of pro hockey, a position I was elected to by my Swedish teammates. But Stripes and Solids had already put the kibosh on anything hockey related.

"I'm the VP of events for the Energy Club," I said. I felt slightly bad for lying, but I needed to stay in the game. Holding a leadership position for a club in business school consisted of signing up electronically to join the club, paying the fifteen-dollar initiation fee per club, then volunteering to organize some event during the semester. Following through on the event wasn't even required. If you volunteered to organize an event where a friend who happened to be Asian came to speak to the club, you'd hold a title like Co-Chairman of Asian-Pacific Relations.

"Terrific...terrific. That's great," said Stripes. "I was actually VP of finance for the Energy Club." Solids checked his watch, and the three of us stood up.

"We'll be in touch," said Stripes.

I shook hands with both of them and exited the room.

From the corner of my eye, I saw Helen, one of the few female students recruiting for banking, booking it toward me.

"I totally screwed up my last interview at BANK. I'm effed," she said.

"I'm sure you nailed it," I said.

"Definitely not."

There were circles of students forming at every corner of the library, no doubt debriefing and comparing notes on their interviews. I just wanted to get out of there and piss away the rest of the day at my apartment.

"A bunch of us are heading to Tito's on Broadway for some margaritas. Come."

"I gotta return some videotapes," I said.

"Videotapes? Who even has a VCR anymore?" This had been a common occurrence through business school—classmates taking my comments at face value.

"It's a line from *American Psycho*. It was a joke." What wasn't a joke was that going to Tito's for some *cervezas* and frozen margs wasn't on my to-do list, so I had to come up with something convincing. "Seriously, though, I gotta help my sister move this afternoon, and I promised I'd head to her place right after interviews."

"You can come for one," she said, batting her eyelashes.

Behind Helen, I saw a clock hanging on the far wall that read 12:36 p.m. "I told her I'd be there by twelve forty-five, and it's all the way in the East Village. I'll let you know when I'm done though."

"Okay. Text me later." She started to walk away, but then turned around. "By the way, how'd your last interview go?"

But I was already gone.

* * *

I'm sure some of you are wondering, which firm did Stripes and Solids work for? Others of you couldn't give two shits, but I'll tell you anyway: BANK. I also interviewed at BANK, BANK, BANK, and even BANK. The interviews all took place that week and went like the one I described, more or less.

They also all resulted in the same outcome: Thanks for your interest in BANK, but we won't be making you an offer.

Who did get offers? The first week of school, I was studying in Watson Library when I spotted a classmate across the table from me. I recognized him, but we hadn't yet formally met. I was battling through our first microeconomics problem set and had spent the better part of the past couple days trying, with little success, to understand Vickrey auctions.

"Hey man, you take a crack at this microecon p-set?" I asked. He looked up from the book he was reading, Dale Carnegie's *How to Win Friends and Influence People*.

"I took a look at it yesterday." He looked to his left and right then leaned in close to me, his expression growing more befuddled. "And I got a little worried."

"Same shit," I said as a wave a relief overcame me.

He cast another wary glance around the room, then continued. "It was just, like, it seemed so easy, I was a little worried I was missing something, you know what I mean?"

Given that this guy looked like his only sexual encounters occurred with something that could be deflated and stored in a closet, I suppressed my primal instinct to dropkick him in the neck. Anyway, he did banking recruiting, listed "comedy" as an interest on his résumé, and got twelve offers.

It wasn't disappointment I felt when the final rejection call came, but relief. I'd given it a shot and now had the time and a little more education to explore other industries—there were marketing firms, retailers, consulting firms, start-ups and many more. As I sat at my desk on a Thursday afternoon and considered which of those career paths might be worth looking into, my cell phone buzzed. I reached into my pocket—"Unknown Caller" read the caller ID.

"Hello?" I said.

"Bill. It's Tripp Witherspoon. I'm a managing director at BANK."

"Hi Tripp. How are you?"

The only Tripp I remember meeting was myself when I decided to try out using the name in third grade, since my name has the suffix "III." That experiment lasted all of a day: that night I showed up at hockey practice for the New Jersey Rockets and told the first teammate I saw in the locker room, "Call me Tripp." He didn't, but he did cross-check me in the face in practice and call me a pussy.

"Plenty busy with a few live deals, but busy is good in this business," said Tripp.

I opened up my Excel spreadsheet, where I'd compiled contacts I'd met throughout banking recruiting, and hit Ctrl+F, then searched "Witherspoon"—nothing. A LinkedIn search came up empty too.

"I'm calling to follow up on your interview last week. I know you received an email the other day letting you know we wouldn't be able to extend you an offer, but we've done some reshuffling." He went silent for a few seconds. "We'd like to make you that offer to join BANK this summer."

"That's great news. Wow...wasn't expecting that."

"It'd be super for you to meet a few more members of our team, but I thought it would be fun for it to be in a venue you're more used to."

"Terrific."

"We have ice time Saturday night at 11:30 p.m. at Chelsea Piers and would love for you to join."

Midnight on a Saturday? Sounded horrible. "Sounds great," I said.

"Afterwards, a group of us head to the Chelsea bathhouse for a few spritzers and some guy time."

"I got class really early—a review session Sunday morning, so not sure—"

"Come on, Keener. It'll be fun." It was my good friend and old junior-hockey teammate, Derek, who was working in investment banking at Deutsche Bank.

"Son of a bitch—shocked you could pull off that douchey voice."

"Spent enough time with you—wasn't hard to pick up."

"By the way, can't even imagine trying to lace 'em up now. You even know where your equipment is?"

"Bottom of the Hudson. What're you up to?"

"Trying to get motivated to go to the gym."

"Pretend like you're going to do cardio, then end up lurking around that hip machine the broads always use?"

"Sounds right."

"Well get the workouts in now, 'cause when you start working here, you won't have any time for that shit."

"Start up where?"

"You by your computer?"

"Yeah."

The line went silent, then I heard him typing. "Place is more ridiculous than you could ever imagine," he said.

A new email popped up in my inbox. I opened it and saw a thread of over thirty emails with the following subject line: "Re: Bill Keenan—Columbia." Scrolling through the responses, it was clear Derek had slowly convinced the decision makers in the bank that they needed to hire me. He wore them down, just like he used to wear down a team's defense to set me up in a scoring position on the ice.

"They emailed me a few days ago telling me to fuck off along with the rest of the banks," I said.

"Well you can blow me later," he said. Few things in life rival a well-placed friend. "Now onto more important shit. Did you see who got called up to The Show a few weeks ago and is now a top four defenseman on the Canucks?"

2

Orientation

The air in the 60 Wall Street auditorium was ripe with the smell of cold brew as conversations buzzed among the summer interns. As I surveyed the room—a sea of side-parts perched on dark gray trimmings—the decision on where to sit had been made for me. Despite my being thirteen minutes early, only a few empty seats remained—all in back.

After settling in my seat, I took a sip of my Starbucks, then placed it on the floor below me. It was ninety-three degrees outside and felt about the same inside, but everyone's suit jacket was still on. Conversations among neighboring interns were animated, with lots of hand gesturing and nervous laughter.

My buddy and former teammate, Derek, who had helped get me the job, had since left the bank. "It was time," he had told me cryptically.

An outstretched hand emerged in my direction as I surveyed the auditorium. I looked to my left to identify its owner.

"Hi. I'm Zhe," he said, nodding his head and smiling as we shook hands. "Zhe," he repeated. "Like nin-JA." He had answered the question that my face was asking.

"Bill," I said. I tried to think of something cool to say that had my name in it but came up empty.

"Summer associate?" he asked. I nodded. "Me too." Zhe's head nodding picked up steam, and his grin transformed into a full-blown smile. He raised his iced coffee to his mouth and took a sip.

The incoming Deutsche Bank intern class was comprised of analysts who had just finished their junior years of college and associates who had just finished their first years of business school.

I checked my watch—7:50 a.m.

"My apologies," Zhe said as his right elbow inadvertently nudged my left arm. In his lap, Zhe furiously scribbled something, then turned the page of his notebook to a blank sheet and continued writing. The internship hadn't even officially started and I was already behind.

"What school are you studying at?" Zhe asked after closing his notebook.

"Columbia. Here in the city," I said.

"Columbia! Are you in the value-investing program?"[1]

"No," I responded. Zhe looked deflated.

"But I have a friend—"

"Your friend is in it?" Zhe said with restored hope.

"Yeah, a friend of a friend, I think, just got accepted into it," I said. Zhe nodded. "How about you? What school are you at?" I picked up my Starbucks and re-caffeinated.

"University of Chicago. We have three students in internship here. What are your summer rotations?"

"FIG and Industrials," I said. "You?"

---

[1] The preeminent program that built on the investment philosophy Warren Buffett was taught when he was a Columbia student. Once admitted to the business school, interested students had to apply for admittance in the value-investing program, a process more rigorous than the business school admittance process itself.

"TMT and leveraged finance. TMT is my number-one choice though," Zhe said. I liked that he pronounced the word "finance" with a long "i," and not the douchey way, "fuh-NANCE."

"You work in tech before business school?" I asked.

"I was at Apple working on the DevOps engineering team, helping with the deployment and maintenance of our Hadoop and NoSQL clusters. Were you working in anything related to FIG or Industrials before school?"

"I was a hockey player."

"Oh! Very non-traditional background. Hockey," Zhe said, readjusting his body toward me. "With the stick and ices?"

"Exactly."

"Did you play in the NFL?"

"Never made it to the NFL. Played over in Europe for a few years."

"Is that good?"

Before having to explain to Zhe that I was about as close to making it to the NFL as I was to playing in the NHL, a sturdy woman approached the stage. Zhe reopened his notebook and removed a pen from his inside jacket pocket. The woman on stage tapped the microphone twice, then began speaking, officially signifying the beginning of my investment banking career.

Now, some of you might be wondering why I was considering joining an investment bank after how I described the recruiting process. Others might be curious as to what exactly Hadoop and NoSQL clusters were. I will attempt to answer one of those questions.

After stopping hockey three years prior, I was at a loss, moving back into my parents' apartment at twenty-seven years old. Without hockey, there was a huge void I had never experienced in my life, so after months of deep thought and watching television, I decided to return to school to spend six figures trying to fill that void. I knew I missed competing, but the answer for choosing a career didn't come easily. But I had to pick something, and quick, since internship recruiting started the second week of business school. From what I understood, investment banking attracted smart, competitive individuals—often younger people who, like myself, weren't certain what they wanted to do in the long-run but saw this as a good way to keep moving forward. Plus, my parents had both done investment banking and part of me wanted to prove that I could do what they did. These might not be great reasons to do something, but without really knowing what I wanted to do, they were enough to give it a shot.

Nearly every banker I met through recruiting said that the first couple years could take a toll on one's personal life. I had no girlfriend, and I hung out with the same two friends from college every weekend. Sure, the soup kitchen in Harlem I worked at on Saturdays and the pediatric hospital where I did candy-striping on Sundays would probably miss me, but those were sacrifices I was willing to make.

And the internship was only a ten-week commitment. The goal was to secure a full-time offer at the end of the summer, at which point there would be plenty of time for reflection and more TV watching to determine if banking was the route to go. Offers could also be shopped and would increase one's value in the second-year business school recruiting track.

"What an interesting day for you all to begin your internships here at Deutsche Bank," the woman on stage began. Knowing nods of muted agreement filled the room.

"Incredible timing," Zhe whispered to me as he made a mark in his notebook.

"Today marks not just a new chapter in your careers, but also the first career chapter for many of you. It also marks a seminal day in the history of Deutsche Bank, as you all know from today's news release," the woman continued.

As the introductory speech continued, I spotted a copy of the *Wall Street Journal* in Zhe's briefcase. I pried open the folded-up copy of the paper just enough to read the front-page headline:

"Deutsche Bank Appoints John Cryan as New CEO to Replace Jain, Fitschen."

As I wondered what impact this change in management would have on me, if any, a woman from the compliance department was introduced to mild applause.

"I see a lot of the tops of your heads, so I'd ask that everyone put away your cell phones and give me your undivided attention." I "liked" one more Instagram picture of a girl who didn't know my name, then I slipped my phone in my pocket.

Alright, I ripped through a few more Instagram pictures then turned my attention to the compliance director.

"Which brings me to my list of no-no's. No taking home price-sensitive information under any circumstances. Your managing director wants to go over a pitch book on a Saturday, so you decide to bring home a copy Friday night? I don't think so. Don't do it. Each group has its own supplies closet, so it's okay to take home a pen or Post-its or an extra stapler, right? Or I'm out of paper at home so I'll just take some from the printer at work. That's no big deal, right? Wrong." She paused and turned the page of her notes.

"Emails," she continued. "Everyone, I'm sure, has heard of the *New York Times* test—only write in an email something you'd feel comfortable having published on the front page of the *New York Times*." One should be so lucky to appear in the *Times*, let alone the front page. A moment passed as she slowly walked to the other side of the stage.

"And absolutely no attachments should be sent from your work email to your personal emails. This is automatically flagged, and you will be contacted by compliance. It's not something you want to have to deal with. Here's another one that recently came up: photo-copying documents on work premises for an outside charity you're involved with. We are big supporters of charities here at Deutsche Bank, and you will have ample opportunity to work with the many, diverse charitable causes we support, but do you think this is an example of something that is permissible?" She scanned the room. "I see a lot of heads shaking. Again, prime example of a no-no."

Zhe was taking this down for the both of us. I leaned over toward him and said, "Think we can use the toilet paper at work if we ate breakfast at home?" Zhe considered it for a moment, consulting his notes, then shrugged.

"Understanding the regulations governing the lines of communication internally is vital for everyone in this room. There are strict rules against information that can be transferred between the public and private sides of the bank. For those of you joining the investment banking division, you'll have access to proprietary information that is never to be shared with your colleagues in equity research, even if you're covering different industries. As most of you probably know, this is the Chinese Wall that was put in place to prevent conflicts of interest within banks." She took a sip of water. I'd heard of the Chinese Wall she was referring to, but there was no doubt that the most formidable Chinese Wall was the one I encountered in the front row of my corporate finance class that year.

"Pleading ignorance to any of these infractions will not absolve you, and be warned, the ramifications are severe." She looked around the room one last time. "Good luck. We're excited to have you all join the Deutsche Bank team on a day that marks an exciting, new chapter in the firm's history. I'd now like to introduce our building's chief of safety, Tom McNamara."

Tom approached the stage. He wore a short-sleeved, button-down shirt and had a ring of keys hanging from the belt loop of his Wranglers. He removed his glasses from the breast pocket of his shirt, propped them on the bridge of his nose, and eyed his clipboard.

"I'll keep my spiel short and sweet. Got issues with the HVAC system down here in the basement, trying to get resolved, but rest assured, the A/C is pumping on all the floors you'll be on. Fire-safety protocol: we got two types of alarms, single and double action. If I do my job properly, and Lady Luck's on our side, none of you will be pulling any fire alarms. In the event an alarm is triggered, there are two evacuation stairwells: A and B. Your floor will determine which one you use. Use precaution—back of the hand to the door and check for heat. Handle hot to the touch probably means trouble. Most importantly, if it's smoky, any type of smoke, get the hell away from the door and check the alternative stairwell door. Smoky behind that one too, well…." McNamara pushed his glasses up to his forehead. "Don't wanna be the first truck to arrive on the scene that day. I've been in fire safety almost thirty-five years, twenty with the FDNY. Bottom line, don't try to be a hero. Let the professionals do their jobs."

Tom was true to his word, keeping it short, but the same can't be said of the next guy up from Global Banking, who droned on for half an hour, praising Deutsche Bank's flat culture, after which he outlined the new management-reporting structure and how all of us had upwards of one hundred bosses, more or less.

"I'd like this to be interactive, so please ask any questions," the man said. "I've been with Deutsche Bank for almost two decades, over a decade as a senior managing director, so I have a lot of knowledge about the firm and its processes that can help you all." Whether it was a collective decision among interns to deny this guy a chance to spout off his firm knowledge, or possibly the diuretic effect of the coffee we were drinking finally kicking in, no hands shot up. "Going once," he said squinting his eyes and scanning the audience. "Twice…three times…well, my email is readily available, so feel free to ping me should questions come up. I'm certain they will."

In one motion, I stood from my seat and kicked over my iced coffee onto Zhe's briefcase. I would have gone ape-shit if it had happened to me. Zhe smiled.

"This happens," he said, removing some napkins from his coffee-doused briefcase. "Here." Zhe reached into his back pocket, removed his wallet, and handed me a Starbucks gift card. Zhe's patience and grace dumbfounded me. That would have been enough to ruin my day, and quite possibly my entire summer, yet he found a way to reward me for my carelessness. I needed to stay close to him.

As we followed the mass of interns out of the auditorium and up the escalator to the lobby, I checked the piece of paper I had outlining where to report for my first rotation in the Industrials group: forty-fourth floor. There were typically two coverage groups on each floor.

"What floor you on?" I asked, hoping TMT might be the group that shared floor space with Industrials on forty-four.

"San Francisco," he said. "Just here for orientation today. Tomorrow morning, they fly me to California for the summer." We shook hands and parted ways.

Shit.

My ears popped as the elevator ascended the Wall Street skyscraper.

"Forty-fourth floor," said the automated voice. Removing the newly-issued company ID card, I waved it in front of the small detector device. *Click.* I opened the glass double doors and was met with a rush of cool air to my face.

It may have been day one for interns, but it was another Monday for everyone else. Managing directors occupied the large offices on the perimeter of the square floor. I walked slowly around the interior square loop. Most of the MDs I spotted through their glass windows were having animated phone calls on speaker, or maybe they were talking to themselves. Some looked to be howling in laughter, others howling in rage. Cubicles, four deep, were arranged on the interior of the floor, though there was no telling what level of seniority the occupants of a given cube were, aside from making an educated guess based on the quantity/color of hair that could be seen popping above the sterile, gray separators. After further consideration, a better proxy of seniority may have been the number of deal toys[2] arranged on the cubicle dividers. I took a

[2] Small trophies bankers have manufactured following a deal closing—trophies they give themselves. We'll get to them later.

full lap around the floor, noting that most of the bankers I saw were speaking into headsets with measured voices accented with pangs of panic.

I spotted my new home: cube 44-014. I sat in the swivel chair and stared at the two black monitors in front of me. Next to the keyboard was a packet labeled "Deutsche Bank Summer Internship Materials."

"Is that EBITDAR or EBITDAX?" said a disembodied voice in a cube somewhere behind me. I was familiar with 'EBITDA.' But EBITDAR? EBITDAX? School was over.

"No, we need IBES consensus. Does the footnote show which brokers are excluded? Then fuckin' figure something else out. I don't know what to tell you," said another voice.

"Why the fuck won't this update?" said the guy in the cube behind me. He slapped his mouse on his desk a few times then picked up his headset and dialed a number.

"BAML banks the shit out of those guys," said one of two guys as they walked by my cube.

"Memory insufficient to collate job?" said a pint-sized woman standing in front of one of the floor's countless printers.

There was an intensity to the environment, like I had stepped onto the ice of a hockey game from the stands midway through the game, except I wasn't sure what position I was playing, and my stick was the wrong curve. And suddenly it hit me: I wanted the full-time offer.

Throughout recruiting, the one line bankers had repeated was, "Once you get your internship, the full-time offer is yours to lose." I didn't want to lose it. Maybe it had something to do with wanting to feel that energy that radiated from those around me. Maybe not. It didn't matter. I felt a passion on the floor, and even though it was more secondhand than my own, it was there.

Mine to lose.

I thought about the orientation speeches: "Don't be a hero," the fire safety chief said. "Don't bring home pens or Post-its," warned

31

the compliance director. What derailed me in the interview process was trying to get creative, making a case for investing in a stock instead of taking the sure thing. I didn't heed the advice I had been given prior to interviewing: "Don't go off script." Securing the full-time offer seemed a matter of *not* doing a bunch of things. Fall into line, and don't stand out. Don't give them a reason *not* to hire me. Like a steady, stay-at-home defenseman, going unnoticed meant you were playing well. I thought of the time-tested advice my first junior-hockey coach gave me before a game-deciding penalty shot: "Don't fuck it up."

I'd keep my head down, my headset on, and in ten weeks, the full-time job would be mine. At that point, I could make a judgment on what to do with it, but for now, "Don't fuck it up," I thought, as the surge of confidence raced through me and I powered on my computer and monitors.

An urgency ran through the maze of cubes on forty-four. Conversations, both on the phone and in person, were short, direct, and demanding: "Send me that real quick." "Go get Joel real quick." "Open that folder real quick."

And apparently, the person who last occupied my cube shaved over the keyboard; the number of whiskers between the keys was staggering.

Before encountering my first stumbling block, which was figuring out my log-in credentials, my desk phone rang. I considered for a moment putting on the headset—it seemed to be the thing to do—but I decided against it since there was no headset. So I picked up the receiver.

"Hello? I said.

"Is this William?" asked the voice.

"Yes," I said. "This is Bill."

"Swing by my desk." *Click.*

The log-in screen was now loaded on my computer monitor—*Enter User ID.* Since everyone on the floor was seated, I thought maybe if I stood up and lingered around my desk, the person who had called would recognize the lost intern and wave me over. I weaved slowly in and out of the maze of cubicles on the forty-fourth floor. Twice. Phones rang. Headsets were put on and ripped off. Keyboards chattered. But no one wrangled me in.

Returning to my cube, I eyed the digital display on my desk phone. Six minutes had passed since the call. I could already see the assessment of me at the end of the summer: "Next up: Keenan, William. Guy's not punctual. Asked him to come by my desk on day one, took him ten minutes. Easy peasy. Axe him. Moving on...."

Maybe I could find a clue in the packet that had been left for me. Inside were colorful brochures of young bankers' smiling faces—Asian, Indian, black, white, male, female—faces that bore little resemblance to the panicked faces that surrounded me. As I sifted through the propaganda, I found one sheet outlining day one's schedule. The Industrials group-specific orientation started at 10:00 a.m., followed by a series of on-boarding training modules, including how to set-up our email; Microsoft, PowerPoint, and Excel best practices; FactSet training; and a host of compliance briefings. But alas, no seating chart. I looked at my desk phone— seven minutes had passed since I had been summoned.

Then I noticed the "call log" button. I hit it twice and identified the mystery caller—Greg Kim. Since the guy in the cube adjacent to mine was one of the few people not talking into a headset (though he was wearing headphones plugged into his computer), I sought his help. He had a slender frame, and thin, brittle hair. As I leaned back in my swivel chair to peek at his computer screen, I could hear DJ Khaled's "All I Do is Win," feat. T Pain, Snoop Dogg, Rick Ross, and Ludacris, blaring on his headphones. I tapped him on the shoulder, and he turned to me, staring for a moment with the music still thumping before finally removing an ear bud.

"What's up?" he said, averting his attention from the series of colorful column-charts on his screen.

We introduced ourselves. "You know where Greg Kim sits?"

"Over in the corner, in front of that conference room," he said.

I stood from my chair and looked in the direction he was pointing. "Thanks. He just called and asked—" I looked back, but the guy had turned his attention to his computer—the column-charts were gone, replaced by an array of pie charts. Both earbuds were in as he bobbed his head again, nearly imperceptibly, to the beat.

I adjusted my tie and walked to Greg Kim's desk, feeling a sense of accomplishment for some reason, like figuring out where he sat was worth a degree of praise.

"Greg," I said, extending my right hand. "Bill Keenan, sorry it took me a few minutes to find you." Greg remained seated as we shook hands. His thin, pale pink tie with either a Windsor or half-Windsor knot (fuck if I know) was draped over his right shoulder. As if suddenly aware of it, he returned it to its normal position, where it then hung in front of his crisp, white Oxford button-down.

"How you feeling?" he asked, smiling at me, then returning his attention to his email inbox.

"Great," I said. "Excited to get started."

"Super," Greg responded, elongating the *u* sound as he typed at his keyboard. "Here it is." He double-clicked on an email. "So here's the deal: DB has been working with a big energy company, about three billion in sales, called QRT—they do drilling, midstream, refining, everything. Three senior guys on their management team—CEO, CFO, and some other guy—recently decided to leave to start their own company. They're still in the initial stages—looking to round out the rest of their team and finding investors. We've set up a bunch of meetings for them with some of the big private equity shops here—Greek God Capital, Lakecrest," he looked back at the email open on his monitor, "and Carlview Partners."

I nodded along, suddenly wishing I had brought a pen and piece of paper.

"These three guys liked what we did for them when they were at QRT, so we'll have the inside track to lead all their deals once their new company gets off the ground. Should be some nice, big fees for the bank. That's the good news," he continued.

"Great news," I chimed in.

"Bad news is the two guys from our Houston office in the Natural Resources group missed their flight here this morning."

I shook my head, then felt Greg's eyes zero in on me. "So I'm glad you said you're feeling good. You're filling in for them today and will be taking these guys around to the meetings."

"Wow," I said. We had been told during recruiting that you never knew what to expect each morning when you came to work—guess it wasn't some BS line. "You coming with me?" I continued.

"I'm jammed on this sell-side that just blew up," he said matter-of-factly.

I nodded like that made sense. "Who's the other person coming?"

"Just you," he said. "Know how to order a black car on our intranet?"

"No."

"Get your company AmEx?"

"Not yet."

"Your email setup and BlackBerry activated at least?"

My throat tightened. "We have group orientation at 10:00 a.m. Think someone explains all that to us then, so no, I can't even log in to my computer yet and haven't got my BlackBerry."

Greg leaned back slowly in his chair then rocked forward, placing his right hand on the desk, tapping his index finger. After a few moments, he unplugged his BlackBerry from its charger and handed it to me. "Password is three, two, one, three, five. I'll let the Houston guys know you have it. They'll get in touch with you by emailing me. The VP down there is Jeff Sullivan, so any emails you see from him will be for you."

A stream of sweat trickled down the center of my back. I was waiting for Greg to crack a smile and tell me this was some "welcome to banking" joke they'd pull each year on an intern.

"You know I'm just an intern, first day...I mean, part of the intern class...." I trailed off.

"Yeah, I wouldn't mention any of that to the QRT guys. As far as they're concerned, a full-time Deutsche Bank banker is taking them to these meetings, which will determine whether they can get their company funded or not." He glanced at his computer monitor. "You better get moving. First meeting is in Midtown, Fifty-Seventh and Park Avenue, in forty-five minutes. Here's Jeff's number." He handed me a piece of paper. "I'll tell him to shoot you an email with some more info so keep the BlackBerry on you at all times."

"The password...three, two, one, two, five, right?" I asked.

"*Three* five," he said. "Three, two, one, *three*, five." I wrote it down on the piece of paper with Jeff's number on it and inhaled deeply.

"Breathe," Greg said. I exhaled. "And smile. These guys know their stuff but will be nervous, so your job is to keep them calm and confident, regardless of how the meetings go. Keep it light, be yourself."

"Anything I should bring?"

"A notebook, and not one of those spiral-bound ones—looks amateur. Find something leather-bound. Ask around if you don't have one handy. Can also check the supply closet."

"Okay," I said.

"And last thing...most important: keep your receipts."

"Receipts," I echoed. "Got it."

"If you don't have them, you won't get reimbursed." Greg checked his watch. "You should get going. Probably gonna be fighting traffic up the FDR."

As I walked toward the double-glass doors that opened to the elevator foyer, I saw the rest of the Industrials intern class shuffling into the forty-fourth-floor conference room.

"What'd that guy want?" asked one of the interns as we passed each other. The fact I was wearing a tie and still had my jacket on gave away my intern status. "Looked like a pretty intense convo for first day on the job."

"He asked me to take this management team around to some private equity firms." I regretted my answer the moment I finished speaking. I could see the disdain in my fellow intern's eyes. Despite what we had been told, history had proven that not every intern would receive a full-time offer.

"What management team? Which PE shops?"

"Energy focused. Forget the names of the firms," I said.

"Energy? So upstream, or midstream, or what?"

I nodded.

"Both?"

I nodded again. "Yeah, think so."

"If they're upstream guys, must be looking at acreage in the Utica and Marcellus shale. Nat gas can't stay at these prices forever, but who knows." I give him credit—in thirty seconds, my fellow intern had managed to rattle me even further, highlighting how ill-prepared I was to represent the firm in this task.

"Yeah, well, I gotta get going. I'll see you in a bit," I said.

"Enjoy chauffeuring them around," he said as he disappeared into the large conference room.

In the elevator bank, I waited for one of the six elevators, periodically lifting my arms to see if the sweat had seeped through my undershirt, dress shirt, and suit jacket. The BlackBerry vibrated against the right side of my chest. I removed it from the inside pocket of my jacket and saw a new email, most likely from Jeff, the guy in Houston. "Please enter password," instructed the tiny screen on the phone. So I did. "Incorrect password. Four attempts remain." I re-entered the password. "Incorrect password. Three attempts remain." One of the elevators dinged, alerting its arrival on the forty-fourth floor. I entered the empty elevator, simultaneously removing the crumpled piece of paper from my pocket on which I had written down the password. But the sweat from my hands had smudged the ink, and I couldn't make out the final number." A tidal wave of panic washed over me.

"Going up," announced the automated elevator voice.

3

Full-Time Intern

"I'll be damned," said Beaux as he stood by the floor-to-ceiling glass window of Greek God Capital's forty-third-floor conference room that overlooked Central Park. "That *is* the building from *Ghostbusters*." Between his white suit, white facial hair, and brow-line glasses, Beaux bore an uncanny resemblance to Colonel Sanders.

Beaux walked slowly to the far end of the room. "And, well, shoot." Beaux tapped the glass window. "That there is the Natural History Museum, innit, Crock?"

"If it is, we'll drop you off later. You belong in it," said Marshall Crockard, Lulu Energy's CEO, as he remained seated, leafing through his notes. Marshall had an average build and a smile that made you want to trust him.

The well-heeled secretary who had escorted us in ten minutes earlier poked her head into the room.

"The team will be in shortly. Can I get you gentlemen anything to drink while you wait? Perrier, Smartwater, iced coffee?"

"Tap water's fine," said Beaux. Marshall nodded in agreement. Next to Marshall sat Waylon Betts, Lulu's CFO. By far the largest of the three, Waylon hadn't said a word since introducing himself to me in the lobby. The hair he lacked on his head was more than made up for by a bushy, white biker-mustache, which gave him a perpetually somber appearance.

My BlackBerry buzzed. In the forty-seven-dollar cab ride uptown, I had managed to come up with the correct password with only one attempt remaining, according to the warning sign. Part of me wanted to see what would've happened had I exceeded the number of incorrect attempts. I'd spent the first few minutes of the cab ride Googling things like the current prices of natural gas and WTI oil, but then became preoccupied instructing the cabbie on which route to take uptown in order to avoid the traffic that was unavoidable.

The secretary returned with a pitcher of ice water. Marshall poured a glass and offered it to me before pouring himself a glass.

"Gentlemen," said a voice, as the door swung open. "Sorry to keep you waiting." Two Greek God Capital guys walked in the room. The speaker was in his mid-forties with a carefully coiffed comb-over, a well tailored navy-blue suit—punctuated with a cardinal-red tie—and shiny, brown loafers. Behind him was a replica, but ten years younger.

Marshall sat to my left, Beaux to my right, and Waylon to his right. On the other side sat the two Greek God Capital guys. Hands were shaken, then in one motion, each person removed a business card and slid it across the table. As we all returned to our seats, the Greek God Capital guys organized the three new business cards in front of them.

"Let's see," said the older Greek God Capital guy. "Looks like we have Marshall Crockard, CEO." Marshall raised a few fingers in acknowledgement. "Waylon Betts, CFO." Waylon nodded. "And Beaux Bridges, CGO."

"Present," said Beaux.

"CGO," the younger Greek God Capital guys repeated. "Chief…."

"Geologist Officer," said Beaux. "I do the rocks; these two beside me take care of the rest."

"Great, great. And you are…" said the younger Greek God Capital guy, once again trailing off as he scanned the three business cards, then returned his gaze to me.

"Bill Keenan from Deutsche Bank." I reached in my wallet then made a face. "Looks like I forgot to bring my business cards."

"Work with Jeff in Houston?" asked the older Greek God Capital guy.

"Yeah," I said. "Back and forth between here and Houston."

"Haven't seen him in a while. He still up to no good down there?" The Greek God Capital guys shared a chuckle, then looked at me for confirmation.

"Indeed. Jeff's up to his usual shenanigans." Despite my limited flexibility, I had a sudden urge to kick myself in the neck.

Marshall reached into his briefcase and removed a pile of spiral-bound packets, handing each of us a copy.

Both Greek God Capital guys removed pens from their jackets and scribbled down the date and names of each Lulu guy. "I think what makes most sense is for us to provide you with a little background on ourselves. Then, Marshall, happy to have you dive in and tell us about the company," said the older Greek God Capital guy.

"Works for us," said Marshall.

"So I'm a managing director in Greek God Capital's energy-investment group, been here a shade over five years. We run just around $20 billion and invest across the energy-value chain." I found myself instinctively taking notes like I was in class. I wasn't sure if it was unprofessional-looking or not, but knowing that I wouldn't be saying anything for the rest of the meeting if all went to plan, it was one way to show I was engaged. "Before joining Greek God Capital, I was a principal in TTZ's energy group, up on the forty-fifth floor, same building."

"We sold him on the shorter commute," said the younger guy. I wondered how many times they had done this routine. Over the next thirty minutes, both Greek God Capital guys traced their careers, in impressive detail, back to their days as investment bankers. By the time they were through, I had more or less transcribed each of their résumés onto paper.

Marshall had barely gotten to the second page of his ten-page deck when he was interrupted by the older Greek God Capital guy. "Sounds like you guys have some great ideas for, uh," he flipped the spiral-bound handout Marshall had distributed, "Lulu Energy Resources," he continued, before removing his phone from his pocket. "We have a twelve o'clock downstairs, so we're going to have to push pause on the discussion here. But let's be in touch."

Everyone stood. Hands were shaken, once again, after which the two Greek God Capital guys made a swift exit.

"Be in touch, my ass," said Beaux as the door to the conference room shut, leaving the four of us alone.

"That one guy saw our vision. Could've used another fifteen minutes to show 'em nuts and bolts," said Marshall, trying to buoy the group's flagging confidence. "Wouldn't be surprised if we get a follow-up call from them wanting to dig deeper, know more about our plans," he continued.

I turned around and noticed the two sets of Lulu business cards the Greek God Capital guys hadn't even bothered to take.

Waylon brushed his mustache with his thumb and index finger, elongating his dour expression. He still hadn't spoken since we met in the lobby. As Beaux and Marshall checked their phones by the door, I scrambled to pick up their discarded business cards off the table and shove them in my pocket. But when I looked up, Waylon's eyes met mine. He didn't say anything. He didn't have to.

* * *

There wasn't much time to mope. The next meeting at Lakecrest was in twenty minutes. After signing in at the Madison Avenue lobby, we rode the elevator up to Lakecrest's offices on the thirty-sixth-floor.

"Not a bad photo," said Beaux as he inspected the black-and-white security picture on the temporary ID badge we had all been issued in the lobby.

The view in the conference room wasn't as interesting this time, so as we waited, Beaux whipped out his flip phone and played *Snake*, achieving a new high score. Marshall made some notes on a legal pad while Waylon sat silently.

The meeting lasted just over an hour and progressed in a similar fashion as the prior one. Marshall was able to get through nearly half the ten-page deck this time, and the Lakecrest investors probed more into the details, like what size investment Lulu was looking for and what the company's "secret sauce" was. But despite both Lakecrest guys pocketing the Lulu business cards at the end of the meeting, there wasn't any talk of staying in touch.

"Went better'n Zeus," said Beaux as the elevator descended to the lobby.

"Zeus?" asked Marshall.

"That last place," replied Beaux.

"Greek God Capital," said Marshall.

"Zeus, Greek God Capital, same nonsense. That's the problem with these damn places. These city slickers think they're immortal."

"I knew this was a mistake coming here," said Waylon. It was the first thing he'd said aside from a few grunts of confirmation during the meetings.

"That last guy—the tall one," said Marshall.

"With the frosted tips?" said Beaux.

"That's the one. It was like listening to an introduction to horizontal-drilling class from a professor who'd never drilled a hole in his life."

"Not to mention he kept talking about the poor economics of drilling in the Permian Basin, only 'bout a thousand miles from where we're looking to develop."

The collective morale in the elevator was plummeting faster than the elevator itself. My BlackBerry had been vibrating non-stop over the past hour. There was an avalanche of emails for Greg, so I scrolled through to see if any were sent from Houston Jeff. There was one which read: "All good? Keep mood light and confidence high."

"Where to?" said Beaux as we stepped outside into the scorching June sun.

We had three hours before the final meeting at 5:00 p.m. Deutsche Bank had paid for the team to stay the night at the Pierre Hotel on 61st Street.

"How about some cold drinks at the hotel?" I offered. The guys shrugged their approval, and off we went.

The Pierre is a palatial hotel located on Fifth Avenue just north of Central Park South, teeming with a who's who of people who think they're somebody and people who aren't anybody. A rush of cool air greeted us through the revolving doors.

"I gotta hit the head. Find a table," Beaux instructed.

"I need a nap. I'll see you in a bit," said Waylon, before walking to the elevators.

Marshall and I settled into a booth in the corner of the sprawling lobby bar.

"How long you been with Deutsche Bank?" said Marshall.

"Not long," I said. "How'd you guys come up with the name Lulu?"

"Beaux had a poodle named Lulu. Passed about a year ago. We wanted a name that meant something to one of us so we went with that."

"He's a character. Wish there were guys like that at the office," I said, suddenly realizing I didn't really know anyone at the office.

"Beaux is one of the best petroleum engineers in the country. Thirty years drilling wells—Bakken, Powder River, Woodford, Arkoma, Barnett, Utica, Marcellus, Eagle Ford, Niobrara—you name the basin, this guy knows every rock and formation, and more importantly how to produce at the lowest cost. But Beaux is Boone County, Arkansas, through and through. Me and Rich are small-town guys too. How 'bout yourself? Where you from?"

Marshall yanked slightly at the knee of his suit pants, then crossed his right leg over his left, revealing black Nike gym socks. Before I began exploring investment banking as a career during business school, wearing black Nike gym socks wouldn't have even fazed me, since that's exactly what filled my top drawer at home. But during the recruiting process, I'd undergone a gradual transformation. I noticed how bankers judged those students who had rubber-soled shoes, wore reversible belts, or didn't have collar stays. Looking the part was as crucial, if not more so, than playing it. The only way to be taken seriously was to adapt and conform. But ultimately, without guys like Marshall, Waylon, and Beaux, investors wouldn't have companies to invest in, and bankers wouldn't have companies to advise. They represented what most people wanted but few people had the guts to do: give up a safe career at an established company and create something from scratch.

I suddenly had an overwhelming urge to show Marshall I was more the athletic-sock-with-dress-shoes guy than a younger version of the private equity guys. By gaining credibility, maybe I could help the Lulu guys more. But explaining to Marshall that, while Beaux was inspecting the *Ghostbusters* building from Greek God Capital's conference room, I could see my childhood home on the Upper East Side wasn't going to help my cause.

"Here in New York. What town are you from?" I said.

"Wheeling, West Virginia," Marshall said. I smiled as a surge of energy raced through me.

Beaux arrived at the booth just as a waitress came to take our order.

"Jack and Coke, please," I said.

"Now you're talking my language," said Beaux. "Make it two, and mine a double."

"Iced tea," said Marshall.

"What'd I miss?" said Beaux.

"Just telling our banker about Nail City," said Marshall.

"You ever go to Nailers games?" I asked. Marshall readjusted in his seat, and for the first time since we met, I felt I had someone's attention.

"Brother's got season tickets. I get to a dozen or so every year. How you know about them?"

"Who's the Nailers?" asked Beaux.

"Minor-league hockey team," I said. "Play in the ECHL. I skated with them a few years back in pre-season." It was only a partial lie. I'd been invited to pre-season camp with the Wheeling Nailers but decided to play in Europe instead.

"Dang, I knew you looked like a hockey player," exclaimed Beaux. "With that slicked back hair. Missing any teeth?"

"Not anymore," I said smiling. "You guys come up here often? To New York?"

"Try to avoid it, but it's part of the deal when you're looking to get funding," said Marshall.

"Too much noise and hullabaloo," said Beaux. He paused as a leggy brunette in white jeans strutted by. "But the city does have some scenery worth checking out."

"Problem is, most of these investors want to tell you how much they know about these basins and horizontal drilling instead of listening to the guys who actually lived their whole lives there and are drilling Monday to Sunday," said Marshall.

My BlackBerry buzzed. A new email from Houston Jeff: "Carlview Partners just cancelled final meeting. All done."

"How long we got till this last meeting?" asked Beaux. "Feelin' good, Crock. Third time's a charm."

"We got a little time," I improvised as the waitress returned with our drinks. I could see a resurgence in energy. It was a numbers game, finding someone to give these guys a shot. If I could buy some time, I thought, maybe Houston Jeff could come up with something.

"How big an investment you guys looking for? That Lakecrest guy said they usually do about hundred-million-dollar checks for these ventures, right?"

"One hundred million is a hobby," said Marshall. "We've heard that before. That was his way of saying he wasn't interested. Need two-hundred-million minimum to secure the right leases, equipment, crew, and the rest."

"What time's our flight outta here tomorrow, Crock?" asked Beaux.

"Four-fifty a.m. Earliest they got," said Marshall.

"Perfect. Can go right from the bar to the airport," replied Beaux, slapping his palm on the table.

"He'll be sound asleep before ten o'clock," Marshall said to me.

My BlackBerry buzzed again. Another email from Houston Jeff: "Get to DB's Midtown office, 345 Park Ave. Set up a video conference meeting with Derry Capital at 4:00 p.m. Probably a throwaway meeting but need to go anyway." I ran a quick Google search to figure out who the hell Derry Capital was.

Waylon appeared.

"Quickest nap I ever seen," said Beaux.

"Maid was cleaning the room," said Waylon.

"Still got bed head," said Beaux as he stood and rubbed Waylon's bald head. Waylon responded with a gentle, backhanded swat to Beaux's gut.

"Perfect timing," I said. "Last meeting just got moved up an hour so we should head over."

The guys didn't probe when I informed them the meeting would be over video conference rather than face-to-face. And they didn't seem to realize the final meeting was with a different firm than previously scheduled. All they knew was they had another opportunity to explain their vision to a potential investor, and that's what they did.

Whether it was because Derry Capital was based in Houston, or good fortune, or some combination, the meeting went far differently than the previous two. Instead of extolling their own backgrounds, Derry let Marshall run the show while Beaux jumped in to talk operations and Waylon piped up to talk numbers. Once the Lulu guys finished their presentation, Derry asked pointed questions.

Q: "How many horizontal wells did you spud while with QRT?"

A: "Seven hundred and seventy-six in the Marcellus/Upper Devonian, and 1,347 in the Huron/Berea regions."

Q: "Why the Marcellus shale?"

A: "Thirty-two percent CAGR in production since 2008 with 23.3 Tcfe 3P reserves."

Q: "Why should we invest with you guys?"

A: "Eighty-plus years of combined relevant experience. Marshall grew up in the region we're targeting and has personal relationships with leasing agents and local officials which will keep costs to a minimum."

The meeting extended fifteen minutes past the hour of originally allotted time. As the four of us exited DB's Midtown building, the sun's heat had subsided and was replaced by a cool summer breeze that swept down Park Avenue. Marshall, Waylon, and Beaux all removed their jackets and loosened their ties.

"Want to grab some dinner with us?" asked Marshall.

"S'posed to be a real good BBQ place few blocks west of us," added Beaux.

I'd almost become numb to the incessant vibrating of the Black-Berry. And as much as I wanted to join them, I was still on my first day and felt I was losing ground on securing a full-time offer each moment I wasn't at my desk.

"Think I need to head back to the office, guys. I appreciate the invite," I said.

"We'll be down in Houston in a couple weeks. Probably will stop by the DB office. Hope to see you there," said Marshall.

We parted ways, and I hailed a cab.

"Sixty Wall Street," I said.

When I arrived back at the office around 6:00 p.m., my desk was just as I'd left it. I went largely ignored the rest of the night, aside from a few furtive glances from the other interns, whose faces confirmed that word had spread about my whereabouts.

While my fellow interns were busy (or at least appeared busy) cranking away on their computers with lowered heads and hunched shoulders, I had missed the group orientation and was still unable to log in. I spent an hour tracking down the correct number to call, then another hour on the phone with the help desk as they informed and misinformed me on how to get my computer and email operational. Around 9:00 p.m., as I got familiar with the various drives and programs we'd been told to explore on our computers, Greg Kim stopped by my desk on his way to the bathroom.

"How'd it go?" he asked, more because my cube was on his way to the bathroom than out of any real interest.

"Great, I think." I exhaled slowly. "Thanks for giving me the opportunity." Part of me wondered if there was a particular reason he'd asked me to go, or whether I was just the first name on the intern list he had been handed. I never found out.

"You missed a bunch in orientation, so find another intern either tonight or tomorrow and ask them to catch you up to speed." My enthusiasm turned to dread as I suspected few, if any, of my fellow interns would be thrilled at the idea of helping "catch me up to speed."

Greg started walking away, then spun around and doubled back. "Also, Rhonda is out for the day, but when you have a minute, drop your receipts off at her desk and she'll walk you through how to get reimbursed." He tapped the top of my cube with his palm, then disappeared into the bathroom.

I didn't need to dig into my pants pocket to realize I'd forgotten to take my receipts, though I did remember signing them all: the forty-seven-dollar cab ride uptown, the fifty-four-dollar drinks bill at the Pierre, and the thirty-five-dollar cab ride back to the office. I opened my wallet, hoping through some magic the receipts might materialize. They didn't, though the five-dollar Starbucks gift card Zhe had given me that morning helped ease the pain.

I'd been an investment banker for one day, and I was already poorer.

4

246, 135, 10

I arrived early Tuesday morning, the second day of the intern-ship, and was greeted with an email informing me of my first official project: Deutsche Bank had a specific color palette it used in all its presentations to clients. Recently, the bank had changed their company-wide shade of orange. In the Microsoft PowerPoint color-settings feature, the old orange code was 255, 165, 55, while the updated code was 246, 135, 10. My task was to go through all folders in the auto-and-transportation drive and change relevant graphs, charts, and boxes from the old orange to the new orange. There were over a hundred companies in the drive with multiple pitch books in each folder. I wondered if my performance on day one had sealed my fate: Would I now be singled out to complete tasks like this, since I couldn't be relied on for more important projects?

Nearby sat another summer associate who seemed good-na-tured and looked more like a substitute teacher than a banker.

"Got your first project yet?" I asked as we crossed paths in the hallway.

"Yeah, you?"

He responded in a hushed voice. "I did." I could tell he was reticent to give details unless I did first.

"Basically gotta go through a bunch of old client books and change stuff from one color to another color."

A smile of relief emerged on his face. "Honestly, I'm happy to hear you say that. I mean, that's brutal, but listen to mine—you meet that Indian managing director yet? Kind of wiry looking—"

"Hair plugs?" I said.

"That's the one. Apparently he used to be really fat, like obese. Someone told me he got that gastric-bypass surgery like Al Roker. Anyway, I have to go through all the old pitch books for the clients he covers and change the photo of him from the fat version to the thin version."

"But aren't those just face shots? And like an inch big?" I asked.

"0.92 inches long, 0.37 inches wide," he responded.

But the truth was, we interns weren't qualified to do much more than these menial tasks. Paying dues was part of the process, as was not saying a peep about how boring it could be. Around us sat full-timers who had at some point been in our position. Now they appeared to be wheeling and dealing, so my goal remained to keep a low profile and not give them any reason to take away the full-time offer.

"Then you'll create a zip file for link manager and save it to the hard drive. But for Pete's sake, whatever you do, do *not* paste the tombstone as a JPEG!" said the woman who taught our formatting boot-camp class later that day. The session lasted long enough for me to know how vital formatting would be for the job, but it was over hastily enough that I picked up almost nothing.

Then there was the day where I spent the better half of the morning and afternoon constructing a "rose page." With no guidance, aside from seeing a "spider chart" that resembled a spider, I assumed the structure of the rose page was supposed to look like a rose. Things were cleared up once I delivered my first draft and was informed over email it's a "rows" page.

To keep us sane and instill the hope of more excitement come full-time status, the bank organized plenty of events each week: drinks on Stone Street, dinners at Cipriani's, wine tastings at Capital Grille—the good life. Most events ended the same way: full-time bankers showing off their loud mouths and crimson-stained teeth, while we interns clung to the hope that the full-timers would remember our names. I was cornered on three occasions by the same senior banker who, unsolicited, explained his mantra to me: "If you don't think you're the most important guy in the room, why would anyone else?" I feigned enthusiasm as best I could at these outings, hoping that maybe it would become real at some point. The amount of booze at these events was staggering, though it still didn't excuse a managing director in the leveraged finance group from shot-gunning a beer at the Seaport one Friday and then exclaiming, "If any of you interns recorded that and put it on social media, I'll make sure you never work in finance again." I guess the bank figured if they could keep us sufficiently sauced throughout the internship, we'd either be too drunk or too hungover not to return full-time.

To show us that Deutsche Bank wasn't solely interested in its standing in the almighty "league tables,"[1] community-service events were organized. T-shirts with "DB Cares" across the back were doled out before we made the trek to P.S. 27 on the Lower East Side to volunteer at a summer camp on a muggy July afternoon.

I was paired with Yaleesha, an eight-year-old from Alphabet City, and tasked with helping her create an imaginary world with a piece of purple paper, three markers, four popsicle sticks, gold glitter, some cotton balls, scissors, and a half-eaten glue stick.

"Who's that," I asked as Yaleesha drew a stick figure with glitter eyes.

---

[1] A chart, wildly susceptible to quantitative manipulation, which shows how much greater Bank X is relative to other banks.

"That's one of my brothers," she responded, tilting her head then using some cotton to make his hair.

"How old?" I asked.

"Ten."

"Any sisters?" I asked.

"Thirteen," she said.

"Wow. Know how old they all are?"

She shrugged. "No. They live with their dads. Can you give me the glue stick?"

To repay me for helping her assemble her imaginary wonderland, Yaleesha taught me the "Stanky Leg" later that afternoon during the dance portion of camp.

But the dance party didn't last long. After five weeks in the Industrials group, it was time for my rotation in the Financial Institutions group (FIG), which was more of the same mundane tasks interspersed with me watching YouTube tutorials on how to use the OFFSET formula in Excel. The rotation was highlighted by the occasional invitation to join an MD in the conference room and sit silently as he spoke to a client. Banking had its own language, but I had more difficulty picking it up than others, it seemed. I'd take notes during these calls, knowing full well that no one would ever read them. While questions were encouraged, it was also a way to show the full-timers just how lost some of us interns were. Investopedia replaced Google as my preferred search engine.

Conversations between interns as they crossed paths during the day were all the same: "Dude, I heard Raj's getting *crushed* in Healthcare…everyone in TMT is getting *crushed* this quarter." It was a badge of honor for some reason to be getting *crushed*. It seemed like it was happening to everyone; and if it wasn't happening to you, you were doing it wrong. Was I getting *crushed*? I couldn't even tell. And if you stayed past 3:00 a.m. one night, all that mattered was working it into every conversation you had the next day.

The summer internship culminated with a case study, a thirty-minute presentation each intern would give to a panel of bankers that exhibited all we had learned over the summer, from formatting to valuation to sales. Again, the idea wasn't to blow them away with our industry knowledge, but rather to show we had the raw tools to be full-time employees. Presentations were held on the penultimate day of the internship. This was not so much an opportunity for someone to shine, as an opportunity for someone to royally fuck up and show he didn't belong.

I'd spent progressively more time working on my presentation as the weeks passed. By the final week of the internship, we were expected to work solely on them. Full-timers were instructed to offer minimal guidance to ensure a level playing field. We received a single sheet of paper with very few instructions. Our client was Doddridge Coal Company, and the presentation was an M&A pitch. In our deck, we were expected to give a brief industry overview, choose a minimum of three and a maximum of six valuation metrics, then provide a concluding recommendation. I honestly didn't know whether we were supposed to value Doddridge or potential acquisition targets (or both). I had general ideas based on stuff I'd worked on over the summer, but the lack of clarity for a novice in this world was staggering. Through eavesdropping on a conversation two other interns had in the bathroom, I learned that the goal was to pick a couple of possible acquisition targets and value those, then decide which company Doddridge should buy.

Sitting in the small waiting area outside the forty-fourth-floor conference room, I rehearsed my opening remarks and my transition into the industry-overview section. Then the conference-room door opened. The intern who had just presented emerged. He looked like he'd just been told he was adopted. And this guy had his presentations bound in official DB format—dark blue cover, section dividers, black back, the works. My presentations were in color, but hand-stapled. A head popped out of the conference room. It was a vice president in the Industrials group with whom I had interacted a handful of times.

"Ready," he said. I couldn't tell if it was a question or statement. It didn't matter though. I was on the clock.

I walked into the conference room expecting to see two or three bankers. There were seven, all seated on one side of the long table. I sat on the opposite side and was immediately relieved I had printed those extra few copies of the presentation. I mumbled some greetings, then went into my opener, which I'd rehearsed all morning.

"Thanks for joining me today as I present why Apple should buy both Amazon and Google." The room went silent. The junior bankers were baffled. Most of the senior bankers were preoccupied with their BlackBerries, but I spotted one managing director crack a smile. At least he would remember me.

"Just a joke," I said as I distributed seven copies of my presentation, keeping the eighth and final copy I'd made for myself.

"Thanks, Bill. The floor is yours," said one of the senior bankers.

I flipped to page one, the executive-summary page, outlining the four sections of the presentation. "Today, I'd like to talk about strategic opportunities for Doddrid—"

In one collective motion, the heads of all seven people across from me lowered so their scalps were facing me while their hands furiously rifled through my deck until they each found the first pages of numbers, the quantitative valuation pages, the pages I knew least about and hoped to breeze through. A series of pens clicked in succession as lines, circles, and question marks were scrawled on nearly every deck I could see.

I'd assumed the thirty-minute presentation would be comprised of me babbling for twenty minutes, then a light-hearted Q&A for five minutes, followed by some informal talk for the final five minutes, possibly about plans for the rest of the summer.

I had barely finished my first point on the executive-summary page when a voice barked out.

"Why don't EBITDAs on page five and seven tie?" I looked up to identify the speaker.

"These adjusted or unadjusted figures?" asked another person. My head darted to the left.

"Bust," said the first voice, as he drew a huge "X" through one of my valuation-output pages.

"Pretty bearish on your coal price assumptions. How'd you forecast them?" said a more senior guy.

"Why are you using forward estimates for your credit metrics?" asked someone else.

The pens were losing ink quickly. One guy stopped, shook his pen, then was forced to retrieve new ammo from his inside pocket.

I was getting fisted from every possible angle, even digitally when I heard a voice chime in over the speakerphone asking about my thoughts on future coal prices, given recent political reform.

I wanted to cry. Later that day, I'd hear from another intern that someone did cry during his presentation.

I addressed the questions I could and ignored the ones that flew over my head. I felt like I was drowning, struggling to gasp for air, before someone was pushing my head back under the water.

As I doggy-paddled along, the firing squad of questions slowly subsided. I could feel my time running short and knew I needed to end on something positive, really anything to counteract what had taken place in the previous half hour. A vision of Marshall, Beaux, and Waylon came to mind. I knew their composure during those meetings was rooted in their expertise, a key facet I lacked. But then I remembered how Marshall had harped on the subject of "legacy liabilities" in all three meetings. The PE guys always responded favorably when Marshall got on the topic. I remembered Marshall noting how all old natural-resource-based companies dealt with these legacy liabilities, but I never understood the details.

The room was silent.

"And I'd be remiss not to mention..." I began, as I considered if this was really such a good idea. "Legacy liabilities," I said cautiously.

A senior banker made a note. Two other bankers made eye contact with each other, in a good way. Liabilities, by definition, were something one's responsible for, a burden. Overall, they seemed negative.

"Legacy liabilities," I repeated, this time more confidently. "Certainly something to consider here." I held my breath.

One guy checked his watch. "Alright, think we can stop here and debrief," he said.

Thank fuckin' God.

"So how'd you think you did?" one of the senior guys asked.

I felt physically incapacitated, exposed, and plain stupid. Not wanting to show any more weakness but hoping to demonstrate some pride, I mustered up, "Okay."

"You held it together. It's not easy. We've been doing this a long time, and you kept your composure and looked confident," he said. I felt anything but confident. "Can't be expected to learn everything in one summer. The quantitative stuff takes some time—but that was a good catch, noting the limit those legacy liabilities are going to put on Doddridge's ability to make an acquisition."

I was right—they were bad.

"As far as presentation skills," he continued. "Formatting looked good—color schemes, right sized font, pages not too cluttered."

"Thanks," I said.

"From a delivery perspective, here's one point to remember. When you're thinking about structuring the deck, you want to think about it in three main sections: First section—tell 'em what you're going to tell them about. Second—tell 'em. Third—tell 'em what you just told 'em." His assessment was corroborated by a few nods from fellow bankers. "Don't expect anyone to make conclusions on their own. Spell it out—this isn't literature." I made a note.

"Last thing I'd add," said one of the vice presidents as he flipped to the cover page of my presentation, entitled "Doddridge Strategic Opportunities." "Our mission at Deutsche Bank is to show clients that we are a fully integrated bank, so regardless of the type of pitch—M&A, financing, what have you—the goal is consistency. So the title of all our decks is the same—'Discussion Materials.'"

"I thought since the deck—"

"No thinking. All decks—same title: 'Discussion Materials.'"

* * *

Decision day.

Word quickly spread through the summer associate group-text chain that most interns were asked to report to the human-resources department Friday afternoon, while only a handful of interns were summoned at 7:30 a.m. While most of the summer had been anything but clear, it was all but obvious that those asked to report in the early morning were not offered full-time roles. So when I walked into my appointment at 3:30 p.m., I had a good feeling. I was officially offered a full-time role to join the bank after graduation. It was a flood of relief—relief the summer was over, relief I hadn't fucked up too badly, and relief knowing I could hang up my suits and return to wearing sweatpants once school resumed in the fall.

After meeting with HR, I returned to the forty-fourth floor, where it was business as usual. I half-expected congratulatory back slaps from the full-timers, but there were none. Though my internship was over, their work continued. As I cleaned out my desk, I spotted one of the Lulu presentation books I'd kept. Six months later, as I studied for my second-year business school exams in the same library where I'd been interviewed for banking jobs, I would receive a phone call from Marshall Crockard. I had some difficulty explaining why my DB email had been deactivated, but he quickly changed subjects. Lulu had received a $250 million equity commitment from Derry Capital, the last PE firm we had met over video conference. Marshall invited me to a Nailers game if I ever found myself in Wheeling, West Virginia—beers were on him. It made me feel like I'd contributed that summer, and I swelled with pride. That feeling of accomplishment was quickly eliminated when Professor Singh posted our final grades for Applied Statistics.

Meanwhile, on the last day of the summer internship, as I continued packing up my belongings and cleaning out my cubicle,

Doug, the intern who looked like a substitute teacher, drifted over. He kept his keys and DB badge on a lanyard, which he was anxiously twirling around his finger—one way until it was securely wrapped around his index finger, then the other way. He looked lost.

"Congrats, man," I said extending my arm with a closed fist. He reached out with an open palm and clasped down on my fist before realizing I was looking for a fist-bump.

"Thanks, you too." He sat in the empty chair beside me as I continued tossing various training manuals I'd accumulated over the summer into my duffel bag. "So," he leaned in closer. "You think you're gonna take the offer?"

"Hard to say. Seemed like some interesting stuff happening. I feel like we only got a glimpse though. Like they didn't show us everything."

"That associate that sits by the door," he said. "He's there all day. When I come in the morning, he's there. When I go home, no matter what time, still there. It's like he lives here." He stood from his chair and did a 360-degree turn, ensuring everyone around us was sufficiently engrossed in whatever was happening in his own cube. Then he sat back down and, using his heels, wheeled his chair closer to me. I could smell the coffee on his breath, accented by the tangy scent of a wintergreen breath mint.

"You're all up in my grill. What's going on?" I said, giving him my full attention.

Then he asked the question I'd been too fearful to pose all summer: "It's just...I still don't get it...what *is* investment banking?"

5

Choose Your Own Adventure

L et's take a step back and distinguish between two financial terms that are tossed around: the sell-side and the buy-side. If you already know the difference, good for you—feel free to skip to chapter six.

Sell-Side

The most common example of a sell-side firm is an investment bank. Whether they're selling financial products, research, or advice, investment banks are in the business of sales though they don't own what they sell. Further clarification on "investment banks" and those who work in them is coming in a few paragraphs. Relax.

Another example of the sell-side is independent-research firms. Typically, these firms churn out research reports on companies, ultimately advising their clients to buy or sell a given company's stock. The key to this business is making noise if and when you're right. Flip on CNBC and you'll hear an interview with some guy pounding the table about how great an opportunity it is to buy

Company X's stock—there's nothing he's more certain of than this. Take a look at the bottom of the screen or at the banner in the background of the screen where his firm's name will be displayed. If the word "research" appears in the name, this guy—by law—can't even buy the stock he's so certain is the world's greatest buy. His value is in having conviction in his opinion. You may ask, *What happens if the stock of that company plummets to zero?* Who cares? The research guy moves on to his next great idea, making more noise and dismissing his prior idea that was dead wrong. If you can get one or two of these ideas to hit and have the platform to promote it when you're correct and the resources to squash it when you're wrong, you'll be in good shape.

The typical progression, at least at the junior level, is to learn the financial trade on the sell-side, then apply those skills at a buy-side fund. This, then, begs the question, how useful are the products sold by the sell-side if it serves primarily as a training ground for buy-side professionals? Would you heed the advice of a coach who never played the sport himself, who never had his ass on the line?

Buy-Side

This is where fortunes are made. The buy-side includes hedge funds, private equity funds, venture capital funds, and any other fund where capital (fancy word for money) is put at risk. Unlike the sell-side, buy-side investors have to come up with the idea, then take it one step further by actually putting money on the line. While buy-side funds typically raise money from outside investors, these money managers are often required to invest a healthy chunk of their own money into the fund. To say someone works at a hedge fund tells you very little, aside from the fact that the individual is a part of a firm that invests in some sort of asset, or really anything.[1]

---

[1] The original premise behind hedge funds was to hedge their investments so the fund would perform well regardless of market conditions. However, as investment strategies have become more aggressive, many hedge funds no longer use hedging techniques to protect against downturns.

Among hedge funds, strategies and investment horizons vary enormously.[2] One hedge fund may use proprietary algorithms to take advantage of tiny price discrepancies in stocks, where investments in positions can literally last fractions of a second. This type of quantitative strategy requires expertise in mathematical engineering. On the other side of the spectrum are "long only" funds, which typically market their managers as long-term investors who perform fundamental research on publicly traded companies, combing through financial statements and performing an extensive review of the company's business and industry dynamics. Often, these managers will take large positions (invest a shitload of money) in a few stocks, with the goal of realizing compounding returns over three to five years, and in an ideal world, never selling. While success on the sell-side means convincing clients you have great ideas (and getting them to do deals), success on the buy-side involves having the market prove you correct. This isn't to say that buy-side investors don't make as much noise as sell-side firms. If, instead of "research," the word "capital" is in the firm's name of the guy being interviewed on CNBC, you're hearing from an investor whose fund probably already has a stake in the stock he's discussing.

Investment Banking

The definition of "investment banking" has always eluded me.

I had a college roommate who got a job doing "investment banking at Merrill" after graduation. He tried to explain his job to me, but I preferred the image of him stuffed inside a Bank of America ATM, distributing cash to individuals in multiples of twenty or fifty dollars. Then there was the guy I met at the

---

[2] As do how funds make most of their money. Historically, collecting a percentage of their outperformance accounted for the brunt of the money hedge funds made. More recently, as funds' assets under management (AUM) have grown, taking a yearly management fee accounts for a larger chunk of earnings for more established firms that can rely on past performance to attract new investors' capital.

beginning of senior year, who, fresh off his investment banking internship at Goldman, was at a party and told one of my teammates that he would crush him with his wallet. He didn't, though my teammate did take down the Goldman kid's girlfriend that night. I got in there too.

My understanding of "investment banking" evolved marginally over the next few years. By the time I entered business school, I'd read several books that purported to answer the question, spoken with "investment bankers" who hop-scotched around the answer, and ultimately Googled "investment banking" and got through the first three paragraphs of a Wikipedia article.

Inside investment banks, in addition to the investment bankers, there are lawyers, public-relations teams, human-resource professionals, and an IT department. These people work *at* investment banks. However, there are only three discrete jobs that qualify one as an "investment banker": sales and trading, research, corporate finance.[3]

One commonality among the three investment banking jobs is that they require the investment banker to act as an agent (remember, sell-side) rather than a principal. Investment bankers make fees by selling either securities, research, or advice. Success (at least financially speaking) is not measured by being right or wrong, but by generating activity. In other words, despite having the word "investment" in their titles, investment banks do not act principally as investors, though much of their marketing material will claim they invest in their employees. Aside from that, the skill sets and day-to-day duties for "investment bankers" vary greatly across the three roles.

Below is my attempt to distinguish between the three "investment banking" jobs.

---

[3] There's another group called "capital markets" (both equity capital markets and debt capital markets) that is somewhere between the sales and trading and corporate finance divisions. The capital markets teams constantly evaluate the market and help the corporate finance team execute deals at the most opportunistic time. Given that they are on the private side, I'm considering them a part of the corporate finance division.

Sales and Trading

The sensationalized world Michael Lewis helped perpetuate in *Liar's Poker* was drawn from sales and trading.

Salespeople and traders are lauded for their quick thinking under pressure. It's why there's the perception that competitive college athletes do well in the industry. There are few other requirements needed to thrive. I know because the only job offer I had after I stopped playing hockey was in sales and trading. "It's like a locker room!" they told me. But as I spent more time on the trading floor of various banks, it felt less like being in a locker room and more like being around the guys who didn't make the team.

If she says she works "on the _____ desk," and you didn't even ask—that's sales and trading. The massive fines you read about in the paper—that's sales and trading too.

An important distinction is the function of traders on the buy-side (at investment firms) and the sell-side (at banks). Buy-side traders take a position in a security, and if they're long, they buy a lot and hope the price increases (if short, then the opposite). Sell-side traders, on the other hand, don't give two shits where the security's value goes. As agents, the sell-side traders make their money by taking a commission on the trade itself. Another distinction is between salespeople and traders: salespeople are the ones yelling on the phones, while traders are yelling at their Bloomberg Terminals.

Once upon a time, banks employed proprietary traders (prop traders), who took principal positions in securities, which great when the market was soaring but less great when everything tanked. When banks did away with prop trading due to the massive losses it created, many of these traders went to start their own hedge funds, where they would use the same trading strategies they had used at banks. They made themselves and their investors good money in bull markets, and when the tide turned, they'd close up shop, hide out a couple years, then open a new fund employing the same strategy under a new name.

Sales and trading doesn't typically recruit MBA students. Business schools teach accounting and corporate finance, not how to make big bets based on tidbits of information and intuition. When the chairman of the Fed farts, traders can sniff out the implications. When Melania slaps away Trump's hand, it implies political turmoil in the US, interest rates spike, oil plummets—"Go long, frontier markets," say the traders. And while they might err in their long and short calls, a quick analysis of a bank's trading floor can be a good litmus test for a bubble in the financial markets—if over half of the seniors on college lacrosse teams have sales and trading jobs lined up, it's probably time to bury your USD under the mattress.

Research

Research analysts[4] spend their time combing through publicly available information to provide views on a given company's stock (equity analyst) or debt (credit analyst). Their research is then used to help inform (and misinform) investors on how a particular company's financial instrument is trading in the market. They do the legwork, then it's up to the sales and traders to push those views on clients. Each bank has a lead research analyst for an industry—someone covers media companies, another covers industrial companies, and so forth. These analysts only cover securities that are publicly traded. For equities, that means the company has sold a portion of its stock to the public market and thus must file quarterly and annual financial reports. Some companies may choose to keep their equity private but will issue public debt, in which case they are required in many instances to publish their financials too. But with tens of thousands of publicly traded securities, how do banks choose which companies they will cover? The big-name companies will be covered out of necessity, but often, if a bank advised a

---

[4] In the research world, the term "analyst" refers to the most senior person. This should not be confused with the corporate finance analyst, which is an entry-level position for individuals right out of college.

company on its IPO, there will be an understanding that the bank's equity research analyst will then cover that company (and issue a STRONG BUY). Who in a bank works on executing these IPOs, debt issuances, and other transactions?

Corporate Finance

Corporate finance people are companies' trusted advisors. Of the three divisions, corporate finance is on the private side of the "Chinese Wall," meaning that it has access to material private information that the public side of the investment bank (sales and trading and research) does not, or at least should not. Corporate finance bankers advise companies and their management teams on all types of transactions: raising capital (debt and equity) for companies; advising companies on both mergers and acquisitions (M&A); and overall strategy and shareholder relations. There's other stuff too—keep reading.

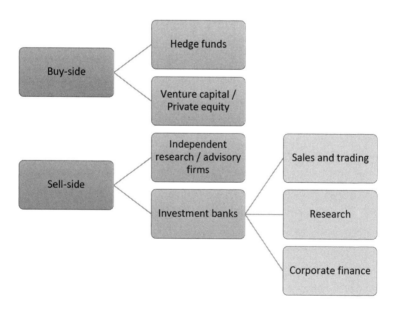

6

London Doldrums

"And why are banks typically valued at a price-to-book rather than, say, price-to-earnings or an EBITDA multiple?" Hands shot up all around me as Rupert stood, hands clasped behind his back, and surveyed the room of incoming associate bankers. I'd been reluctant to participate in class since week one, when Rupert posed the question, "How do we forecast interest expense?" to which I responded, "As a percentage of sales." It warranted the tidal wave of laughter from my classmates that ensued. Even though I quickly recovered by explaining it was in fact the debt schedule that informed interest expense, I had decided to keep my mouth shut in class from then on. Occasionally I did that thing where I'd raise my hand right as the smart kid was called on. After the question was answered correctly, Rupert would immediately ask if I had anything to add to which I'd respond, "Was gonna say the same thing."

"Mister Keenan, you've been relatively quiet the last couple weeks. Would you like to take a stab at it? Why are banks valued on a P/B rather than P/E ratio?" Rupert walked slowly toward me. The expansive room situated in the heart of London seemed to be closing in on me.

"Sure," I said, slowly lowering the monitor of the laptop in front of me. The prior summer, I'd spent half of my internship in the Financial Institutions group and had done one project on a bank. But that was a year ago. I vaguely remembered creating price-to-book charts but was never explained the rationale behind them.

"Would you care to share it with us?" Rupert continued. I looked across the room and spotted Diyor, an Uzbekistan native and recent MIT Sloan graduate. Even as he slouched in his chair, with his arms folded across his chest, head drooped on his right shoulder, and eyes shut, his six-foot-six frame ensured he was still the most noticeable among the class of forty-five associates. Diyor wasn't on his own page—the guy was in a different book, so much so that Rupert never deemed it necessary to call him out in class. Probably a smart move.

"Yeah, the banks," I began. "Banks generally use price-to-book since they don't usually own their buildings, so depreciation isn't a big—" Snickering from the Wharton crew in the front row interrupted me. I could hear side conversations starting behind me. Seating was alphabetical by last name—I was in the second row, which meant I was close enough to the instructor to have a clear view of the board with limited distractions, but far away enough to know how far behind I was relative to my classmates. Rupert tilted his head to his right slightly and scrunched up his face.

Diyor's snoring grew audible. Without opening his eyes, he raised his hand to his face, rubbed his nose, then adjusted his head gently onto his left shoulder, wiping the drool from the side of his mouth.

"Can someone help Mister Keenan out? Gaurav?" said Rupert.

"It has nothing to do with depreciation," said Gaurav, the ringleader of the Wharton crew. He rotated his torso from his front-row seat, just far enough to catch eyes with me. Then he returned his attention to the front of the room. "Banks and other financial institutions are valued on a price-to-book basis since, by nature of their business, their assets are mark-to-market, and so you'll see most banks trade around their book value."

Rupert beamed. "Thank you, Gau—"

"Regarding banks not owning their buildings, Bill was correct, partially. Deutsche Bank, for example, did a sale-leaseback in 2007 in which it sold its Sixty Wall Street building to an investment firm, then leased back the space. This type of transaction is usually done to untie cash invested in a hard asset for deployment into other assets. It also provides the building's seller with beneficial tax deductions."

"Well said, Gaurav," said Rupert. Raj extended a lowered fist and Gaurav pounded it. In my prior life, I would've dealt with Gaurav in the following manner: cross-check to his face, followed by me skating to the bench while my biggest teammates cleaned up the backlash from the shit storm I created. But there were no sticks and no teammates in this world. I was unequipped and exposed, and I couldn't do anything about it except write down what Gaurav said in my notebook so I wouldn't fuck up this question again.

Diyor emitted a half-grunt, half-snore as he readjusted in his seat, slowly opened his eyes, and consulted his Patek Philippe watch. Diyor waking up in class always meant the same thing.

"Before we adjourn, today's trivia question," said Rupert as the room stirred in anticipation and he held up the prize, a stainless steel Nalgene. "In USD, what is the aggregate-dollar-amount investment banks have been fined since 2008?"

"One hundred billion," shouted someone.

"Including banks that have since gone bankrupt?" asked someone in the first row. Rupert nodded.

"Hundred and fifty billion," exclaimed someone behind me.

"Forty-seven billion, five-hundred million," said the girl beside me after some quick math on Excel.

"Two hundred billion," shouted someone else.

"One dollar, Bob," said a voice somewhere to my left. I couldn't identify the speaker, but I desperately wanted to hug him.

A Wharton kid won the Nalgene.

"That's it for today," announced Rupert. "Remember to submit your homework before midnight or you will not receive credit. And please make sure to beauty save[1]—get in this habit, as your VPs will appreciate it once you begin full-time. I know this is the last week of training and I've introduced a lot to you over the past six weeks, but bear in mind the final exam is Friday, and this week's homework assignments will serve as a first-rate review for what you will see on the exam."

"We can bring a cheat sheet, right?" asked a Wharton kid.

"One-page cheat sheet is permitted," said Rupert.

"Double-sided?" asked the same dipshit.

"That's fine, but no magnifying glasses."

"Can I bring an analyst?" I asked. It went ignored.

Everyone packed up his laptop and training manuals—save Diyor, who traveled with only a briefcase containing a legal pad that had never been written on. Rupert continued, "And remember, your group managers will be sent your scores, so I suggest you all," Rupert's eyes met mine, "take this seriously."

The group of associates, with our matching Deutsche Bank lanyards containing our ID cards draped around our necks, shuffled from the classroom to the dining area just as the dinner buffet was being served. After a month straight of either cockles or Beef Wellington, I'd grown sick of the limited dinner selection, so I settled on a plate of bread and some cold cuts before finding a seat at one of the large round tables.

"You guys start studying for the sixty-three or seventy-nine yet?" asked Phuc, a diminutive Vietnamese guy and recent grad from Dartmouth's Tuck business school. The series sixty-three and

---

[1] This involves having selected A1 (the "home" cell) in Excel when you save a document so when it is re-opened, the document will open here rather than to another random cell.

seventy-nine were the regulatory exams all incoming corporate finance analysts and associates needed to pass to be licensed to work.

"No, no, no," said Vikram, a University of Chicago grad, as he shoveled mashed potatoes in his mouth. "Need to focus on the final exam first." Vikram popped open a can of Coke. I'd seen days when he'd guzzled three cans before noon. I vaguely remembered Warren Buffett proudly declaring that he drank five Cokes a day, but Vikram was on the wrong end of the genetic lottery, and if his chronic stress didn't give him a heart attack before the age of forty, then diabetes would no doubt be on the horizon.

"Did you even bring the study guides for the sixty-three and seventy-nine?" asked Phuc.

"Of course. I'm going to read them on the flight back to New York. Then we have three days to cram for the seventy-nine and another week for the sixty-three. But the final exam on Friday should be the focus now," said Vikram. He took a sip of his Coke. "I heard from my friend at Credit Suisse that they cut the bottom fifteen percent of the class from training—rescinded the offers." Vikram scanned the table for reactions. He lived for this type of drama.

"I heard that from my buddy at MS too," said one of the Wharton guys. "Makes sense if you ask me—I think bottom twenty percent was cut there." Vikram nodded in between sips, almost excited at the prospect.

"What's on tap this weekend?" asked Wade, one of the associates who'd be working in the Houston office. "Last weekend in Europe. Need to blow it out." He surveyed the table. Wade had spent the previous weekend in Ibiza. Or at least that was the plan. His flight from Heathrow Friday night was delayed, which pushed his arrival to Ibiza to Saturday afternoon. The lost luggage upon arrival set him back another half-day. All in all, about a thousand-dollar weekend and all he had to show for it were a couple of blurry photos on his iPhone outside Club Amnesia and a few made-up stories about Lindsay Lohan dancing near his table at Club Space. Now *that* is investment banking.

"I'm organizing a trip to Stonehenge Saturday morning," said Phuc as he dabbed the sides of his mouth with a napkin. "There's a bus that leaves every hour on the hour starting at seven a.m. If we leave early enough, we can also check out Avebury. It's another twenty miles north, but worth the trip—it's a World Heritage Site, and visitors have free access to the stones! I called yesterday and set up a great group deal for bikes."

"That could be fun," said Vikram. "My wife is visiting with our son. Maybe we'll tag along."

"I was thinking we check out the bar scene in Shoreditch," said Wade. "Picked up some absinthe at the duty-free shop last weekend." Wade's eyes met mine.

"Heard Shoreditch has some good spots," I said. I felt bad for Wade. He was one of those guys who felt compelled to always wear a backward hat when he went out socially due to his baldness. I hoped he'd make a lot of money.

"British babes galore, from what I hear," Wade said. I'd been in Britain for six weeks, long enough to know that if there were British babes, they weren't in Britain. "You in, Keenan?" he continued. "We can get you on our Tinder Social and get to work tonight. Here." He handed me his phone. "Me and a couple of the guys already set up an account. Check out our latest match."

I scanned the first three pictures. "You matched with this group?" I said. "They're all guys."

"Go to the last pic," Wade said as he leaned over and swiped at the phone. "See that hottie?"

"She's in the background of the picture—doesn't even know she's in it," I said.

"I know." Wade tapped the phone. "But these guys obviously know where the hot chicks go. So how 'bout it? You want in? Send me a pic of you, maybe a hockey one or something."

"Unfortunately, already planned a trip this weekend," I said.

"Where to?" said Wade.

"Stockholm."

"Awesome!" said Phuc. "I've heard the Vasa Museum is a must-see."

I wasn't going there for the museums. I'd set up dates with a few girls—five girls to be exact (three of whom I actually knew). I figured two or three would bail, but it seemed like the right number to ensure my last Friday and Saturday nights before work started would be fun.

"And the Nobel Museum," I added. Phuc nodded as he crammed some Beef Wellington in his mouth.

"I'm really nervous about this exam on Friday, guys. I think this needs to be our focus, and we can worry about museums and Tindering come Friday afternoon," said Vikram as he shook an empty Coke can, then put it on the table. "I talked to Rupert after class—said he sends the results directly to our group managers. He didn't know whether they'll rescind offers, but—"

I stood up and hightailed it to the garbage to bus my tray. I couldn't take Vikram's constant exploration of worst-case scenarios. I knew the discussion would eventually circle back to the fact his wife had decided to give up pursuing a career in medicine despite graduating from Northwestern University Feinberg School of Medicine, and now he was saddled with her med-school debt, his business school debt, and the cost of having a two-year-old child.

Typically, after dinner I'd stick around and plug away on that night's assigned homework for a couple hours, after which I'd spend thirty minutes asking Rupert or the teaching assistant pointed questions to demonstrate that despite my relative underperformance on the weekly quizzes, I was putting in the effort. It was like when I was sucking at hockey and not scoring goals, I'd spend extra time after practice doing self-imposed wind sprints and working on my shot, hoping the coaches would take notice—they didn't. Anyway, with training in its sixth and final week, the teaching assistant, a current senior associate at Deutsche Bank, was busy "shooting a couple over[2] from the tips with rented wrenches" at the Old Course at St. Andrew's, Muirfield, or Royal Troon. Meanwhile, Rupert had advised us that his evening office-hours would be limited in the final week, since he and his husband needed to oversee the flagstone re-laying of the Gloucestershire rectory they had purchased a year earlier in England's bucolic countryside. This is all to say that I had good reason to bolt early and work on my homework from the comfort of my sprawling, un-air conditioned, three-hundred-square-foot room at the King Street extended-stay living facility.

The walk back to our lodging was a fifteen-minute stroll from where daily training was held. The final rays of the warm August sun beamed through the large glass windows of the building, temporarily blinding me as I rode the escalator down to the ground floor and exited onto Cabot Square in Canary Wharf. Across the street stood a large figure barely visible in shadows created by large scaffolding, his face obscured by a puff of smoke: Diyor. He raised his vaporizer to his mouth once more, inhaled deeply, then slowly emitted another large puff of smoke. He was going to be joining the San Francisco office in September, but today, he disappeared into a black town-car with tinted windows. Destination unknown.

Aside from the training, the past six weeks in London had been a whirlwind of team-building activities, speeches, and networking sessions at royal-sounding venues, all designed to help mold a sense of unity among the newest class of Deutsche Bank employees—a group totaling over a thousand recent graduates.

The team-building activities were a finance version of ropes courses.[3] One person would take charge, a few others would fall in line, and the majority would linger on the sidelines and judge those who participated. The speeches proved more engaging—each week, a couple members of Deutsche Bank's management team and

---

[2] Would've been even par if the caddy hadn't clubbed him wrong on last two holes, resulting in back-to-back three putts.

[3] An outdoor excursion where, at some point, you'll find yourself wearing an oversized helmet crookedly on your head, multiple belts crisscrossing your crotch, and yelling "Belay on!" while flashing a thumbs-up.

board of directors visited training to deliver impassioned speeches about our ability to have a positive impact on the company's future, which was in question after recent headlines implicating the bank in numerous scandals stemming from the financial crisis. CEO John Cryan flew in from Frankfurt to deliver the final speech of training. Strobe lights danced across the packed banquet hall at the Inter-Continental as U2's "Beautiful Day" blasted over the loudspeaker. As the lights dimmed, I half-expected to see a hooded Cryan, bouncing from side to side, making his way to the stage trailed by a group of stone-faced, muscle-bound lackeys holding his title belts. I had to resist the urge to stick out my hand for a middle-five from my aisle seat as Cryan strode to the stage wearing a dark blue suit.

He was no prizefighter, but the dark, puffy bags under his eyes and the wrinkles that zigzagged his face told the story of a CEO who was in the midst of battling to keep his bank afloat. Unlike the bank's previous CEO, Anshu Jain, who had a sales and trading background, Cryan took a job as an accountant after college and spent the majority of his professional career in the corporate finance division of banks, focusing on financial institutions. If there was someone who knew the ins and outs of running a bank, it was Cryan.

He began by outlining "Strategy 2020," his five-year plan to return the bank to profitability. But that was where his finance-related material ended. Instead of another rousing speech about the promising future of DB and our role in it, he focused his message on the importance of maintaining a balanced life as we began our careers. He noted the recent promise he made to his wife that he would *only* work six days a week this year. He then reeled off a list of German composers he listened to while in his garden exploring the green thumb he'd recently discovered. In his concluding Q&A session, he demonstrated that rare ability to answer questions in clear, simple language while simultaneously making the individual who asked the question feel like a genius, even the kid who asked where DB's stock price would be in year. We were in good hands.

But despite the reassurance and comfort Cryan instilled in DB's newest employees and our nascent careers, a void remained, a void I'd felt since training had begun but had been unable to fill.

As I stood in Cabot Square, the summer sun sunk slowly on the horizon as the palatial buildings cast looming shadows on the narrow sidewalks. Waiting for the stationary, illuminated red guy to turn into a walking green guy, I spotted a girl through the glass window of a coffee shop across the street. She looked to be right in my wheelhouse—cute and nearby. She had Eastern European features, and her dirty blonde hair was in a high, messy bun as she flipped the page of her magazine, oblivious to the American guy still standing across the street even though the little guy had turned green.

I threw my shoulders back, then took the stray strand of hair that had been strategically dangling over my right eye and tucked it behind my right ear. Our eyes would meet through the window, and she'd smile, a slight nod of the head inviting me to sit with her. I'd march in, my presence putting her damn near cardiac arrest, and then I'd blow her away with unparalleled wit and charm as passersby glanced through the window, wondering what on earth this guy was saying to this girl to keep her laughing and playfully slapping his arm.

But before any of that happened, I needed to wait for the traffic to stop, since I had now missed my chance to cross the street. Thirty seconds later, I took a cautious step into the crosswalk, initiating this inevitable chain of events. Halfway across the street, as if in slow motion, she lifted her head from her magazine and looked out the window—our eyes met. I stopped and smiled. Then she sneezed before returning her attention to the magazine. A car honked. I hustled to the safety of the sidewalk.

I went through my usual routine of rationalizing why I shouldn't approach her—I was leaving London in a couple days so I'd probably never see her after this week; she was reading a tabloid so she was probably stupid; and she had weird ears, which wasn't true, but I needed to identify some physical flaw. As I went through the checklist, my thoughts returned to the void I'd felt since coming to London. It had grown each week, and I hadn't been able to pinpoint its cause—but I knew my jokes weren't as sharp, and it was cause for concern since my new colleagues rarely, if ever, understood them. I couldn't remember the last time I had landed a joke worthy of a mental self-backslap. Prior to training, I would have said I was objectively around a ten in both cool and funny on a scale from one to ten. Now if you were to run a regression of my coolness on my funniness, R-squared would be for shit and the p-value would be really high or low or whichever one demonstrated statistical insignificance.

I looked at the girl through the window. Best case scenario, I thought, would be her noticing me through the window, scrawling her number on a piece of paper, then pressing it against the glass window—most efficient at least. I played out the scenarios in my head of what would happen if I went in there and talked to her— only one made me smile, and it wasn't one that ended with me getting her number. It was the scenario where I said everything I shouldn't say, forcing her to take a fake phone call, leaving me alone and defeated. What made me smile was that I knew I could turn it into a story that my friends would like. And then it hit me—how to fill the void. I didn't need some girl from a London coffee shop, and I didn't need her number (which I *definitely* could've gotten).

What I needed was a friend.

7

#REF! Me

"You have twenty minutes remaining," announced Rupert as he erased the "45" on the dry erase board and replaced it with a "20." He sat back down in his seat at the head of the classroom and returned to *Architectural Digest*.

"Fuck me," I said, mostly in my head as I repeatedly tapped the F9 key on my computer, which is as useful as repeatedly tapping the elevator button when it's already illuminated. In the front row, the Wharton crew had already finished the exam and were now drawing attention to themselves by crunching on granola bars and whispering to one another about the deals they were browsing on *Mergermarket*, the *TMZ* of investment banking.

The exam was a culmination of all the concepts Rupert had taught us over the past six weeks: accounting, valuation, forecasting, and financing. While business school had given us a solid financial-analysis foundation, Rupert had taken everything to another level. We had three hours to complete the comprehensive three-statement model, which tested all concepts in some capacity.

The goal was to forecast five years of financials for a company whose name he had inexplicably obscured from the assignment—as a former banker himself, Rupert adhered to the banking maxim: blatantly omit information to create a veil of importance. Every public company in the US discloses audited financial statements each year (and unaudited financials each quarter). There is a ton of useful (and useless) shit in these filings, which can run upwards of 400 pages. As bankers, our focus was on the company's three primary financial statements: income statement, cash-flow statement, and balance sheet. Using the company's historical figures as a base, we referred to the assumptions Rupert provided, and were tasked with building a five-year forecast of all three statements. Despite the complexities of the test and the nuances that go into modeling it out, checking the "integrity" of the model was simple.

Does it balance? If the balance sheet balances, you're golden. If not, then fuckin' A. The balance sheet is a snapshot of a company's financial health at a given point in time. A company's assets must equal the sum of its liabilities and equity. The assets are on one side of the balance sheet and show everything the company has, including cash, inventory, equipment, receivables, and the like. The other side of the balance sheet shows how all those assets are financed, either in the liabilities section (through debt, loans, and so forth) or through equity (owners who invest money). Thus, we get the equation: A=L+E. Due to the way the model flowed, the balance sheet was last to be completed. Therefore, Rupert simply had to check the balance sheets of the five forecasted years and ensure in each year that A=L+E. Checking was made even simpler with the following excel function: =(IF(logical_test,[value_if_true],[value_if_false]). In this case, the "logical test" is whether A=L+E. If it does, the given cell will display the "value if true," which was input as "OK." If it doesn't equal ("value if false"), the cell will show the difference between A and L+E. In the Excel template Rupert provided, the row with the "IF" function was already input so it would automatically populate as we modeled out the forecasted years. Passing the exam meant that the row of cells at the bottom of the five fore-casted balance sheets (row 230) looked like this:

OK	OK	OK	OK	OK

Mine looked like this:

(34)	######	#REF!	#REF!	#VALUE!

Had they all been numbers, I'd have been in better shape to identify the root of the problem, which most likely would've been me neglecting to drag over a set of assumptions in the income statement. But these cell errors were cause for concern and an emergency trip to the bathroom.

"Shit," I said, noticing the darkened pee stain on my gray suit-pants as I washed my hands at the bathroom sink and blotted a wet piece of paper towel on my pants, exponentially increasing the size of the darkened area.

"Gotta push up on your grundle," said someone I soon identified as a fellow associate who'd just entered the bathroom. He paused on his way to the urinal, raised his hand, and made an upward motion with his middle finger. "Two pushes usually do the trick," he continued.

I considered the advice and acknowledged it with a nod as he continued to the urinal. I finished washing my hands, splashed some cold water in my face, then returned to the classroom where I passed the Wharton crew, now loitering in the corridor along with the majority of the group who'd also finished the exam.

Only a handful of associates remained in the classroom, including Vikram, who had empty Coke cans peppered around his computer. Unlike Vikram, I didn't buy that the bottom 15 percent of the class would have their job offers rescinded, but that didn't mitigate my concern. My fear was that the majority of my peers were offended the exam was so easy they didn't need the full time to complete it. The guy I'd seen in the bathroom then returned to the classroom.

"Five minutes," said Rupert. "Please ensure you save up a version so we don't have any issues." I didn't want to save up a version. I wanted to hurl my computer out the window, have it career off the Westminster bridge, sink to the bottom of the Thames, then have Rupert rely on the honor system when I told him my balance sheet balanced.

From the corner of my eye, I spotted Vikram flipping double birds to his computer monitor and shaking his head wearing a scowl. I felt a level of solidarity with him—almost made me smile.

A few moments passed. More computer keys were tapped.

"Yes!" said Vikram, louder than he should have. I whipped my head around and caught him as the birds were no longer flipped, and he was mid fist-pump. He rose, tilted a Coke up to his face, emitted a satisfied exhale, then made a show of gathering his belongings and leaving the room. I tried tripping him as he passed me, but my foot didn't reach far enough. So much for solidarity.

I scanned to the historical financials tab in the spreadsheet and checked that I input all the original data correctly. I did. Then I checked that my growth assumptions were in line with the information Rupert had provided. They were. But it was too late to go through all the troubleshooting steps I'd outlined on the one-page cheat sheet we were permitted to use.

"One hundred seconds," said Rupert.

I stared at that fucked-up row in my Excel spreadsheet. Part of me wanted to type "OK" in all the cells—and I would have, except the template Rupert had given us was configured in such that any hard codes (when a figure is typed directly in the cell) appeared in a bright blue font, while all cells containing functions (like the "IF" formula) appeared in black. So much for that honor system I'd imagined.

=IF(AE225=AE248,"OK",AE225-AE248). Logical test, I thought. How could I make it illogical? Fuck logic. There was nothing in the world I wanted more at that moment than to see the word "OK" five times. But the equation was false—AE225≠AE248. Then some neurons in my cerebral cortex decided to engage, the same devious neurons that fired when I tried to pick up a girl at a coffee shop. What if I inverted the scenarios? Then the display would read "OK" in the false scenario, and the equation would look almost the same: =IF(AE225=AE248,AE225-AE248,"OK").

"Fifteen seconds," said Rupert as he rose from his chair.

This was it. I quickly rearranged the formula in the far-left cell then dragged it over so it would automatically reconfigure the formulas in the four cells to the right, which aligned with the rest of the forecasted years. I hit enter and row 230 now read:

OK	OK	OK	OK	OK

I saved the document. Then saved it again…and a third time.

"Time!" said Rupert. He exited the room, and I heard him call for the class to reconvene. My fellow associates reentered the room, finishing up conversations they'd started over an hour ago in some cases.

"Please have your spreadsheets open, full screen, with your balance sheets showing," said Rupert as he picked a clipboard off his desk and removed a pen from the inside pocket of his suit jacket. He began in the front row, leaning over each person, inspecting row 230 of the spreadsheet. It was far from the cursory glance I was hoping he'd perform. I counted twelve "Mississippis" for the first person and thirteen for the second.

"Do we balance?" he said far too giddily before he began each inspection.

"We balance!" he then exclaimed, as he found the person's name on the sheet fastened to his clipboard and marked a check next to the name. Fist-bumps were exchanged between members of the Wharton crew as they rose from their front-row seats. Rupert made his way to the second row of seats, my row.

I looked to my left down the row of students. I had about sixty "Mississippis" left. The way his finger tapped the computer screen of each person gave me less and less hope that my inversion plan would work. Even worse, I began to wonder how I would explain to him what I'd done if he identified my ruse. For a second, I thought about switching the formula back, but then I heard it again—

"We balance!" he exclaimed to another associate. I didn't need a miracle, but I did need some fortuitous intervention. I looked up to the heavens: *Remember that time a couple weeks ago when I saw that pregnant woman on the Tube and gave her my seat? I know, technically, I didn't actually get up, but I thought really hard about how good it would feel to give it to her, and isn't it the thought that counts?*

"Mister Keenan, do we balance?" said Rupert. He leaned over my shoulder. I could smell the mix of Acqua di Gio cologne and his morning coffee on his breath. "Would you mind increasing the brightness of your screen?" he said. I had dimmed it to one-fif-teenth prior to his arrival and slowly increased the brightness to four-fifteenths. "One more notch up, please." I went to one-third—that was as far as I would go. Rupert muttered to himself as he eyed my spreadsheet. I held my breath.

"Let's see," said Rupert. He leaned in closer over my left shoulder. I could hear him breathing now. "Mister Keenan, make sure in the future, you format such that all negative figures are in parens…can you please hit F2 on cell—"

An eruption of laughter from the class—this time, not at my expense. In the doorway stood my divine intervention.

"Diyor, glad you could join us," said Rupert.

"I had personal issue this morning," said Diyor, wearing the same suit he had worn the previous day and the same facial expres-sion he'd had since the first day I met him. Diyor walked to his seat. "I can take the test now," he said.

"Yes, well…I suppose I can make an exception," said Rupert as he stood behind me watching Diyor power on his computer as if no other explanation was needed. This was my opening—I shut my laptop and began stacking papers on top of it. From the corner of my eye, I could see Rupert's attention drawn back to me.

"Feels good to balance," I said to the guy sitting in the seat next to me, just loud enough for Rupert to also hear me. I stood from my chair, the same way everyone prior to me had done after Rupert had informed them they had "balanced." I turned and faced Rupert.

"Right," said Rupert as he scanned the sheet on his clipboard, spotted my name, and marked a check next to it. The moment he walked to Diyor's desk, I reopened my laptop, closed the Excel spreadsheet, dragged it into the desktop trash, then emptied the trash, eliminating any trace of the final document.

* * *

The *Oxford English Dictionary* doesn't define "garbage goal," but my junior hockey coach defined it as "a horseshit goal that counts the same as an end-to-end rush, ya fucks." It's not pretty, but it gets the job done. It was this rationale that I carried with me as I bolted from the building after I'd finished the final exam.

Training was over. Later that night, I'd be on a plane to Sweden engaging in one of life's most notorious enterprises—trying to recapture something that no longer exists.

After grabbing a stale sandwich at one of the Pret a Manger restaurants that occupies every London street corner, I booked it down Westferry Road on my way home to pack. As I waited for traffic to pass, I spotted one of my fellow associates across the street—it was the guy I'd seen in the bathroom during the exam, the piss whisperer. He was one of the few people about to join full time who hadn't interned at the bank, so I'd only met him in London. Standing a little over six feet tall, he wore a well-tailored suit, and he always seemed overly concerned about his hair—in short, he was like me, which explains why I'd spent most of training avoiding him, fearing he might be a better version of me.

The universal force that ensures you're caught eyeing someone when you don't want to be caught was in full effect. I quickly turned my head, removed my phone, and scrolled through old texts. The group on the sidewalk surrounding me began trekking across the street, so I moved with them.

"How'd it go?" said a voice as I reached the sidewalk. I looked up. It was him.

"Hey," I said. "Jack, right?" He nodded. "Yeah, just glad it's over. You balance?" I said.

"Not that bullshit," said Jack. "The grundle trick. You try it?"

"Yeah, actually worked pretty well," I said. The sun poked through the buildings as we continued down the street, its warmth washing over my body.

"What'd you think of training?" I said.

"Glad it's over," he said. "Just hoping I proved myself enough to get the Fisher account." His comment lingered in the air.

"You're joining the Power and Utilities group, right?" I said.

"My passion." He flashed a smile. "Pretty limited options when you don't intern. I took what I could get."

The Fisher account—it was an *American Psycho* reference. Then it hit me: this was the guy who made the genius *The Price is Right* reference in the trivia game earlier that week.

"What you got on tap for dinner," Jack asked.

"Dorsia's," I said. A hint of a grin emerged on his face. He did his best to conceal it, but I knew I had earned his respect.

"Tough reservation to get," he said. "You start studying for these regulatory tests yet? I feel like I hear everyone talking about it like it's no big deal, but the books are like five-hundred pages long."

"I brought them with me—was gonna start studying on the flight home." I shook my head. "But I know what you mean—it's like everyone here is offended at how easy this stuff is."

"Don't get me started on those Wharton guys that sit in the front row," Jack said. "Where you from?"

"New York City."

"Manhattan?"

I nodded.

"You don't act like it." Maybe the best compliment I have ever received.

Jack stopped and looked at the street sign, then pointed at the Pret a Manger across the street. "Jesus, there's one of those on every corner." He turned around. "Did we bear right at that fork off West-ferry?" He looked at me.

"Not sure. Don't really recognize this street," I said. I had no clue. I usually followed a group of associates home each day, making sure I was at least a half-block behind them to avoid agonizing conversations about financial statements.

"Fuck," said Jack, removing his phone and opening up the Maps application. "I think we're lost."

8

The Morning Meeting

"May I speak with William Keenan, please?" asks the Indian-accented voice on the line, as I answer my first call as a full-time banker.

"This is him...he," I say.

"Good morning, Mister Keenan. This is Priyanka from your American Express corporate-card team. How are you doing this morning?"

"Good."

"Terrific, Mister Keenan. I'm calling because I noticed there are outstanding items on your American Express corporate card."

"I just started this job five minutes ago," I say. "You must have the wrong person."

"Am I speaking with Mister William Howard Keenan III?"

"Yeah, but I don't even think I've been issued a card yet." I look around my new cubicle—no evidence of anything resembling a credit card or packet containing one.

"Well, Mister Keenan, I do apologize for any inconvenience I've caused. We here at American Express do wish you a great rest of your day."

"Thanks," I say, then hang up.

It's official. I'm an investment banker in Deutsche Bank's Industrials group. I'm not entirely certain what "Industrials" are, but I know this: Andrew Carnegie has a hall named after him; Henry Ford has cars named after him; Cornelius Vanderbilt has a college named after him; and John Rockefeller has a center *and* a record label named after him. Historically, industrialists have a helluva track record. I wonder what they'll name after me.

"Let's go," says a fellow new associate in the group as he hustles down the hall. I grab a notebook and a black pen, sling on my suit jacket, cinch up my tie, and follow him into the main conference room on the forty-fourth floor.

Around the perimeter of the packed rectangular room are the analysts and associates, including all the new joiners, clearly identified, given we're all wearing full suit and tie.

Seated at the large table are senior bankers, a variety of individuals both thin and large, bald and well-coiffed, laughing and stern, mostly male and a few females.

"Thanks everyone for joining," says one of the most senior-looking bankers; he sits at the head of the table. "A lot of new faces. We'll do introductions at the end, but why don't we jump in and get started?"

A series of beeps chime from the spaceship-looking speakerphone device in the center of the table.

"Can you hear us-us-us-us? Chicago's on-on-on-on," says a disembodied voice on the speakerphone. It echoes, and the room fills with laughter—most forced, some genuine.

"Anyone know the moderator code?" says a senior banker as he disconnects the line and redials. Someone reels off a six-digit number. He dials again. "Chicago, you with us?"

"Chicago is on," someone says over the speakerphone, this time with no echo.

"You got Boston on the line," says another voice.

"London's on," says a British voice.

"Great—couple housekeeping items to start," resumes the banker at the table. "As most of you know, last week we had our Industrials-equity conference. A full slate of corporates were there across all our verticals. Got a lot of compliments—our building-products team did an event at Wrigley's rooftop one night, beautiful night, well attended, don't think the Cubs won, but that's neither here nor there. All in all, great conference. Make sure we extend thank-yous to clients. Great time to follow up." He looks around the room and nods at a few of the fellow seniors. "Might as well jump in. ECM, want to kick things off?"

A younger-looking MD with a slick-back straightens in his chair. "Sure. Look, the theme continues to be resiliency when we look at how the market's traded back half of this quarter. Despite a lot of the ancillary noise we've had between the UK elections and the Comey testimony, the major benchmarks reestablished all-time highs. Investors continue to be receptive to the asset class. One of the interesting trends—a blinking light on everyone's screens—is the crowded-out technology trade. Tech stocks are up about eighteen, eighteen-and-a-half percent this year. We saw them get hit last week and a pretty strong rotation into financials, energy, and materials names. This should provide some tailwinds that'll help us in the industrials space."

My right wrist cramps as I flip the page in my notebook. The girl to my right, a new analyst, appears to have written everything down in perfect print using a purple pen. The girl to my left, a senior analyst, stands with arms folded, no notebook on her person.

"Relatively light week in new-issuance front—eleven deals for about five billion. Couple of these bigger names are over their skis. But we do expect more names to issue through the summer, and we're already up about forty percent on a volume basis and sixty percent on a proceeds-raised basis. One big theme we've seen in the market is early lock-up releases—"

Early lock-up releases? I write in my notebook.

"A lot of guys have been getting waived from lock-ups early. We want to be cognizant of who controls the lock-up. Sometimes it's one party, sometimes it's two or three, so that's a conversation we should be having, and how we strategically approach that. Also the equity-linked theme and being creative around that—"

Equity-linked, I write with a heavy underline.

"We've had some great discussions around this with sponsors who historically would do your bread-and-butter sell-downs over time but are now looking to hedge their positions with collars, selling call-options on the position to help provide some near-term monetization if they still see some longer run in the stock before they want to sell. To that point, we did a really nice trade last week for Tesla—one-hundred-and-forty-five-million-dollar convert for equity exchange. So any conversations around the capital structure, bring us in and let's see what creative solutions we can provide."

Convert to, I write, but I forget the rest of it. I peer again to my right. I'm going to need to photocopy this girl's notes. I don't know how she does it.

The speaker leans back, seemingly finished.

"Should we flip to DCM?" says the banker at the head of the table.

"The story remains the same: what's the FED going to do with rates? Indications are dovish for the near term."

I know this one, I think. Dovish—doves fly south for the winter, so dovish is south, that's down, that means lower interest rates. Wait. Do doves fly together? Ducks definitely fly together. Quack, quack, quack, Mr. Ducksworth. I abandon thinking and return to note taking.

My notes on the debt capital markets spiel:

—*Spreads at pre-financial crisis levels.*
—*Eight percent return, 5 percent vol, depending on which metric used.*

—Toll trade priced fifteen bps wide of talk.
—Fixed to floating—rising rates.
—Industry headwind could be tailwind for company.
—Lotta left-leads.
—Headline leverage seven times—CRM receptive if good cash-flow characteristics.
—Legal issue.
—Continue pushing big clients, but nichey transactions to drive league-tables.

I shake my right hand and look up from my notes. No full-time analyst or associate looks halfway engaged. They look numb.

"…So I know a lot of this work is getting churned out from those on the perimeter of the room, so much appreciated." I scan the full-time junior bankers he's referencing. None smile or in any way acknowledge him. "Also want to flag, we'll be holding our twenty-fifth annual leveraged finance conference in Scottsdale. Great event. We're going to circulate a list of accounts who've accepted and those we need to follow up with. Need to get the logistics figured out so accommodations are settled. Great excuse to get on the phone with some of our accounts. And oh, by the way, got some pretty good guest speakers—Michael Milken, Sallie Krawcheck, George W. Bush. So that's a marketing spin we should be sending to clients." He taps the desk then leans back in his chair.

"Excellent, thanks. Investment grade? Who's here from IG?" says the moderator. A small woman with a bob raises her hand. "Lillian, great. Take it away," he says.

"*Echo themes…two year tights…triple Bs…tranche du jour…tail risk…dollar/Euro cross-currency swap…from a market perspective…LIBOR-based borrowers…from an issuer perspective… third-rate hike priced in…eleven year maturity duration paper…two spot one five,*" read my notes until I finally give in. I listen to Lillian, who uses zero intonation as she informs us about the current state of the investment-grade markets, which I semi-confidently conclude as being "pretty good," though I keep that assessment in the confines of my own head.

FX goes next. Then interest rates. Then CBC.

Who the fuck are all these people?

"Thanks all—our Industrials franchise continues to grow, and that's a testament to everyone in this room, so I want to thank you guys and gals for the hard work and for the work to come," says the senior guy. "I think we're through—"

"Um," says an African-American woman raising her hand.

"Compliance, right. Apologies. Take it away."

The speakerphone beeps once, then again, then a third time—people dropping from the line.

"A couple announcements from Compliance. The first pertains mainly to new joiners, but everyone should listen," she says as senior bankers all slide their BlackBerries out of their pockets and put on their glasses. She says something about FINRA questionnaires, conflict clearing, log-in credentials, prison time, and some other stuff, but no one seems to pay attention. "I trust you all have been following the Litvak case," she says, referring to the former MBS trader at Jefferies who was embroiled in a securities-fraud scheme. "Each week, there's a new story about someone getting Litvak'ed.[1] His name has become a verb. You don't want that." She tries to make eye contact around the room but fails to realize that the real reason no one is paying attention is that Jesse Litvak and all these guys getting indicted work in sales and trading, not the corporate finance division.

"Another friendly reminder that you *must* accompany the client if providing event tickets that exceed one hundred dollars. Absolutely no exceptions on this," says the compliance woman as she scans the room, though she's unable to meet the eyes of any of the apparent culprits. "Also, I want to remind everyone that political contributions must be pre-cleared," she continues.

---

[1] The charges against Jesse Litvak were ultimately dropped.

A senior banker perks up. "So for everyone planning on going to the Bernie Sanders rally this Saturday...." The room erupts in laughter, first from the senior bankers, followed shortly thereafter by some juniors. The compliance officer looks annoyed and leaves the room.

Once the political side-conversations subside, each new joiner introduces himself and herself—name, university, and hometown: Bill Keenan, Columbia Business School, New York. I don't fuck up. One new analyst does, fumbling between a slew of hometowns—born here, grew up there until age three, then moved to who-gives-a-hoot. No one cares.

"Go Blue Devils!" says a female senior-banker after a new analyst announces her undergrad as Duke.

The meeting adjourns.

How much of that meeting was I supposed to understand? I want to ask one of my fellow new joiners, but after my interactions with them in London, I fear they'll smell blood.

While I'm familiar with the obstacles to learning a foreign language, what happened in that conference room was scarier, since the words were in English.

My Excel proficiency is already suspect. And I only opened PowerPoint once during business school, and that was by mistake—the icon was right next to my Internet Explorer icon.

I drop my notebook at my desk and dash to the bathroom, where a junior banker with freshly wet, matted-down hair and a side-part is brushing his teeth. "Client meeting," he says mid-brush.

I walk into an empty stall as he starts to floss. I want to cry. Especially when my senses are exposed to the massacre occurring in the stall next to me.

9

Staffed

Here's how it works: you sit in your cubicle, your swivel chair positioned at such a height that the top of your head is visible to anyone walking by, but not so high that you can make eye contact. One of your monitors displays an Excel spreadsheet filled with numbers, a PowerPoint slide filled with colorful charts, a Word document with ¶ symbols all over the place, or a black-and-white company filing. The second monitor, the one that is less visible to passersby, you use to browse the Web, but it's slim pickings, since all social-networking sites—LinkedIn, Facebook, Grindr—are blocked, as are Gmail and really any other website that provides entertaining content. The key is layers—seasoned junior bankers will have six or seven "work" documents open with the left thumb and middle fingers poised. A quick tap of the Alt key, followed by the Tab key, allows you to toggle quickly between documents—Larry David's disgruntled mug becomes a free cash-flow output page in nanoseconds.

Girls typically shop online or check out the menus of the newest restaurants in the Meatpacking District, while guys check out pictures of expensive watches or browse non-prohibited sports websites to keep tabs on the players on their fantasy-football teams. Analysts and associates who've been around a couple years and have earned some respect in the group might stream a show on Netflix or Amazon, though even then, that window will be tiny and strategically placed in the lower portion of the less-visible monitor. But it's tough to focus on any plotlines with the anticipation of the inevitable….

The email hits your inbox—first thing you see is the subject: "Staffing," followed by the project name. On occasion, the assault comes verbally, a senior banker materializing at your desk and explaining what he needs and how he needed it yesterday. Once staffed, the only thing for certain is there will be agonizing, endless nights in the office and a slew of questions for which you'll never find answers. How long this pain lasts, you won't know until you open the email and read further details on the project—could be an afternoon, a week, a month, or it could be indefinite. That feeling you get in high school or college right before a final exam, where you need to do well but you know you didn't study enough—that's the feeling each staffing gives you every day for its entire duration.

But I don't know any of this yet.

MDs work the phones with clients, ultimately drumming up work for junior bankers. The MD then emails the staffer, usually a VP in the group, and outlines what he needs. Each staffing typically has four people: a managing director (MD), a vice president (VP), an associate, and an analyst—a fact that underscores how flat the culture is they advertise during recruiting. It is up to the staffer to determine who has capacity to take on a given project. After spending my first two days working through mandatory compliance protocols and getting my computer set up with the help of a slew of IT professionals in Chennai, I'm ready to work and have 100 percent capacity.

Our staffer in the Industrials group explains to us that in the first couple months, all staffings will comprise five people and include the typical four-person team (MD, VP, associate, analyst) plus one new joiner (either a new analyst or associate). As a first-year associate, my job is to contribute to each project, while also paying close attention to the veteran associate on the team.

"Staffing: Weston M&A" reads the subject of my first staffing email as a full-time investment banking associate at Deutsche Bank. My stomach doesn't churn. Instead, I'm excited.

"Fuck my life," says Ted, a senior associate who occupies the cubicle adjacent to mine. I'd met him briefly during the internship, but either he doesn't remember or doesn't care. He has short blonde hair, fair skin, and the ruddy complexion of a true Irish Catholic. I lean back in my swivel chair past the small partition that divides us and catch a glimpse of his left computer monitor, which displays the same staffing email.

"Bad?" I ask, giving him a minute to scan the details of the email.

"Could be worse…just a pitch," he says. Junior bankers' work can be categorized into one of three categories: live deals, which is how the bank generates revenue; pitches, in which the junior bankers put together a deck, which the MD presents to a company's CEO or CFO; and finally, miscellaneous internal work, which can vary widely in content but is invariably the least interesting.

I give Ted another minute to digest the email. "But Monday meeting," he says, as he turns to face me. "Brutal."

"Why?"

"Means we're turning comments all weekend and printing Sunday night," he says.

"Any chance we can get it finished Friday and print before the weekend?"

Ted smiles, then laughs as he returns his attention to his computer. I guess I'm funny again.

"Know what type of pitch this is? Like any idea what type of stuff we'll present?" I ask.

Ted finishes an email, then spins in his chair to face me. "Just like all other pitches—we'll jam every number ever created in a deck and ask the client if any of those numbers excites him."

"Ready, gents?" says a distinctly British voice behind me. Gareth, the VP on the staffing, holds a leather binder in one hand and a fountain pen in the other. He's impeccably dressed. While most bankers opt not to wear a tie, let alone a suit jacket, around the office, Gareth is the exception. His initials are displayed on the gold cuff links of his blue Oxford button-down. His dark gray suit fits snugly, with the top button on his jacket secured around his thin midsection. Though thinning, his dark hair is neatly combed to one side. Behind him, standing almost a foot taller than Gareth and about seventy-five pounds heavier, and seemingly less concerned about his appearance, is Joel, a former college-football player and the analyst on the project. Despite his imposing physique, Joel looks like a kid who just finished an oatmeal cookie.

I grab a spiral-bound notebook and pen and follow the group into the corner office occupied by Ethan, a relatively young-looking MD.

Ethan spots us through the floor-to-ceiling glass wall that separates his office from the rest of the floor. He waves us in, holding up an index finger as we enter. The sleeves of his dress shirt are rolled up and he fidgets in his chair as his attention darts from his phone to his computer monitor to us. His metallic-black hair is just long enough that he can apply gel to it.

"Let's sort this shit out mid-next-week. I'll be in Denver Tuesday, Dallas Wednesday morning, back in New York that night," says Ethan in the direction of his phone.

"Sounds good," says the voice on the other line. "I'll tal—" Ethan hits a button on his phone, ending the conversation. Through the window to his right, towering cranes stand in the distance, an indicator of low interest-rates—one of the few tidbits I picked up in business school. Through the window behind him, I spot the Statue of Liberty and a number of massive barges moving imperceptibly through New York Harbor. But this isn't a time for sightseeing. Gareth and Ted sit in the stiff, wooden chairs across from Ethan. Joel remains standing, looks at me, and extends his hand toward the third and only remaining chair in the office. I thank him with a nod and take a seat.

I met Ethan briefly during the internship, and by "met," I mean he tapped the top of the cube I was sitting in one day as he walked by.

"Look at this," says Ethan, extending his arms wide with his palms face-up. "Got my grade-A crew." I suspect he says this to every junior team.

"Pretty solid showing from the 'Skins last weekend," says Ted.

"Three hundred sixty-four passing yards, three TDs. Yeah, just pre-season, but if the O-line can keep Cousins healthy, it's a cake-walk through the NFC East."

"Not so fast," says Joel with a big grin on his face as he taps his dark blue tie that features a large New York Giants logo. "G-men have solid pass defense, and Eli is prime—" Joel raises his hands to his face, covering a sneeze.

"You sick?" asks Ethan.

"Allergies," says Joel.

"Do me a favor," says Ethan, eyeing Joel with one eyebrow raised. "Dial in from your desk. I'm going to DC for the game this weekend and can't take any chances." Ethan's attention darts to his computer to check an email. Joel glances at Gareth to get confirmation—*Is Ethan serious?* With a flick of his head, Gareth confirms what we all suspect—Ethan is serious.

"Don't touch the door handle," says Ethan as Joel walks out of the office, using his tie as a barrier between his hand and the handle. Thirty seconds later, Joel is on speakerphone, and it's go time.

"Alright, Weston," says Ethan as I poise the pen in my right hand and flip open to the first blank page in my notebook. "These guys are gonna do something, probably something fuckin' stupid. Spoke to their CFO last week. He opened the kimono. Their margins are for shit and their stock hasn't moved in three quarters. They got cash and need to make a move, so this book should be simple—section one, normal market-update bullshit from ECM. Section two, normal chems outlook pages, make sure that consolidation page is in there. Section three, actionable opportunities—check book we just did for FMC and use same format with the accretion/dilution stuff, same targets. Check old books to see if we've shown any other private companies and add them. Make sure the SOTP pages are updated for new research. Use same multiples…actually, take specialty ingredients for Ashland up a turn, half a turn maybe, see what makes sense. Then broker outlook page. Also get that firepower page. Need M&A creds page up front too, and make sure we get Vantage cred in there—don't show multiple though, deal hasn't closed yet. Should be a modular book."

Ethan scans our faces—I lower my head and stare at my notes, which ignites further panic, since the speed at which Ethan talks far exceeds my speed as a manual stenographer. From the corner of my eye, I see Ted make a mark in his notebook. Gareth looks unfazed. I even catch a glimpse of a smile from him.

"Let's also throw their financials in appendix. Normal EBITDA and revenue progressions," says Ethan. "Might as well do free cashflow too. Make sure to footnote this shit. I don't give a fuck how you calculate it, just make it clear in the footnote."

Ethan then grabs a few blank pieces of printer paper from a bottom drawer and rehashes the outline of the deck at breakneck speed in barely audible tones as he makes illegible marks on the pages in front of him. "Market outlook, chems bullshit pages, actionable ops, broker, firepower, creds. Easy." He clicks the top of his pen twice and leans back in his chair.

"And team page—need one up front. Throw in our APAC Industrials M&A guys. Need to show we got a strong team, specifically in China."

"Just looked into this for another deck I was staffed on. Believe we only have TMT M&A guys in China," says Ted. "The broader APAC M&A group covers—"

"So go in the DB database, find some Asian guys who work in the bank, and throw their headshots and names on the page, and call it APAC Industrials M&A. Just need it to look fulsome. Throw in all of capital markets too."

"Will do," says Ted as he makes a note.

"Here's markup." Ethan pushes the pages in front of me, which I tuck it into my notebook. "Let's not boil the goddamn ocean here. Should be a simple book—twenty-five, thirty pages max."

"Sounds reasonable enough," says Gareth.

"I got an eleven o'clock," says Ethan. "Get me a draft sometime Wednesday."

Joel is already outside waiting for Gareth, Ted, and me as we exit Ethan's office and convene to debrief.

I open my notebook and scan my notes, which read: *CFO meeting. Do something stupid. Section one nor…ECM…outlook… simple consol…simple shit FMC book…up a turn? maybe half… progression??*

Then I pull out Ethan's markup.

"Have you got it all, Bill?" says Gareth. "I think Ethan was fairly clear in his asks."

"Think so," I say. "I can—section one…." Two large hands apply pressure on my shoulders. I turn around. "He's kidding," says a beaming Joel.

"Give me fifteen minutes and I'll provide a markup with a little more clarity," says Gareth. "In the meantime, would you email the chaps in ECM and get—"

"On it," says Joel.

"And can you scan the markup and send around?" Ted says to Joel. Joel nods as I hand him the markup. "I'll start churning on the shell," says Ted. With that, we all return to our respective desks.

Every cubicle has a story. Much like stalls in hockey locker-rooms, remnants of past occupants shed light on the most recent chapter of that stall's story. While Ted, Gareth, and Joel get to work on the project, I busy myself by exploring my new cube. The three small drawers on the right of my desk are relatively empty, save for a few stray ballpoint pens, some pushpins, a box of binder clips, Post-its, a hair tie, an empty bottle of extra-strength Advil, and one of those compressed-air keyboard dust sprayers. In the two large drawers to my left are more substantial findings, including a slew of old Deutsche Bank pitch books held together by a rubber band, a couple confidential information memoranda (CIMs), and a few management presentations (MPs).

Affixed by pushpins to the walls of the cube are an assortment of papers and Post-its, most of which contain phone numbers and contact information for various help desks/resources or papers displaying Excel shortcuts and templates of PowerPoint charts.

"Yo," says Ted as he leans back in his chair and tilts his head in my direction, making brief eye contact with me. "Shell's gonna take me another fifteen minutes. Could you put the PIB together, then email BIS and ask them to pull growth rates for specialty silicas, engineered plastics, and high-pressure laminates? I'll also send you an email with any other pages I think you can work on."

Founded in 1919, the Press Information Bureau (PIB) is a nodal agency of the Indian government that disseminates information in various forms on government plans, policies, initiatives, and achievements. My first Google search for "PIB," while riveting, is misguided. However, my second search for "PIB finance" is more helpful, informing me that a public information book is an internal resource for investment bankers to glean historical and transactional information on a given company, and typically is comprised of the latest public filings and investor presentations, some equity research reports, and any other relevant news—probably something I should've learned during the internship.

After three unsuccessful Google searches for information on "BIS," a piece of paper pinned to the wall of my cube catches my eye: "Support Function Services" reads the title. Below are a number of rows, the second of which is entitled "Business Information Services (BIS)—Company and Market Research." I skim it, find the contact information, and draft an email requesting the growth rates for each of the items Ted had outlined—which I had luckily jotted down.

An email from Joel hits my inbox—it's the scanned version of Ethan's markup. Although Ethan had originally handed it to me, I'd never really leafed through it until now. I retrieve my notebook and cross-reference my notes with the pages Ethan put together, trying to make sense of them.

"Gents," says Gareth. Ted and I spin around in our chairs simultaneously. "Here's my markup. I've layered in a few more items I'm sure he'll eventually want us to add." He hands Ted a stack of pages held together by a large paper clip binder. On the front are Gareth's initials circled and the date. "Tried to fill in some of the gaps that Ethan left in his pages."

And boy, does Gareth fill those gaps with aplomb. Let's take page thirteen as a case study:

Ethan's markup

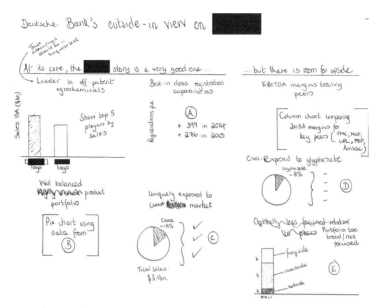

Gareth's markup

A box pops up on one of my monitors, displaying a new message on the internal office-communicator messaging system—AIM for work.

> **Chetandra Pratap Singh Chauhan:** Hello, William Keenan

While the name is unfamiliar, I feel like it's someone who can help me.

> **William Keenan:** Hi

> **Chetandra Pratap Singh Chauhan:** My name is Chetandra Pratap Singh Chauhan. I am contacting you in reference to your recent inquiry to Global BIS, job P17DHL3490.

William Keenan: Hey. Thanks for getting in touch. What's going on?

Chetandra Pratap Singh Chauhan: With respect to your query, could you please provide the geographic regions for which you would like the data?

"Hey, Ted," I say. "Just got a message from BIS. For those growth rates—"

"Get 'em all," he says, still typing away at his computer, his gaze fixed on his monitor. "If they're asking which geographies, we want global, US, North America, South America, Australia, EMEA, E-EMEA, MENA—the works." I relay the message to Chetan... Chauhan via messenger.

"Alright, shell's pretty much done," says Ted. Using his heels, he rolls his chair back and positions himself behind me. "If you click on the g-drive, you'll see I saved all the shit down in the latest Weston folder." Ted is patient as I click and mis-click a couple times, then finally open the correct folder. "So we'll typically have five or six folders in there—discussion materials, backup Excel for charts and shit, the model if there is one, then reference for the PIB, then other stuff we send to Presentations, BIS, or MAKS."[1] I nod my head slowly as I navigate the various folders with Ted looking on behind me. "Yeah, so I think me and Joel are gonna try to get cranking on the heavy lifting now and hopefully get it out of the way by early tonight, so why don't you just get familiar with the drive and take a look at the shell and backups and stuff."

"Early tonight" soon becomes 10:00 p.m. Through most of the afternoon and evening, aside from becoming far too familiar with everyone's bathroom frequency and duration due to the proximity of my cube to both male and female restrooms, I sit and listen

---

[1] According to their website, Moody's Analytics Knowledge Services (MAKS) is a "leading provider of high-value research, analytics and business intelligence to the financial services sector." In practice, they are a service based in India that many banks use to outsource work and thus are treated as one rung below analysts. Like the other services that DB outsources, MAKS is paid a yearly flat fee.

to Ted speaking with Joel on his headset as they methodically go through Gareth's markup, updating some pages and creating others. At 10:17 p.m., Chetan…Chauhan from BIS emails me with the market growth rates I had requested. Ted has me comb through the source documents and spread the growth rates in a new Excel document—in total, there are five geographic regions for each of the three markets, meaning a total of fifteen numbers to spread.

"What's the average rate for engineered plastics if you take all the regions?" says Ted.

"Three-point-five percent," I say.

"How 'bout if you take out any of the regions in Africa," he asks.

"Three-point-eight percent," I say, running the average formula, this time excluding the growth rate for the MENA region.

"Fuck that. Do a weighted average of the top four regions—sixty percent for the one with the highest rate, twenty percent for the second highest, and ten percent each for third and fourth. What's that get us?"

"Okay," I say, typing in the various percentages next to the appropriate regions. "Wow, now we're at seven-point-six percent."

"Perfect," says Ted. "Do the same for the other markets so they come out between six and eight percent."

"How do we know about those percentages though?" I ask.

"We don't—all about optics though. Just footnote the fuck out of it and chalk it up to 'DB estimates.'" Ted pokes his head behind the partition wearing a wry smile. "That's investment banking."

> **John Bukowski:** Do you add restricted cash to cash balance in cap table?

> **William Keenan:** think so

> **John Bukowski:** you have no clue

> **William Keenan:** don't ask me then. Just footnote it

Jack, my buddy from training who now works in the Power and Utilities group, is also on the forty-fourth floor.

"I also couldn't find that page Ethan wants from the M&A target section. He said it was in a prior PolyOne deck. I searched—"

"Check the June 1892 CFO meeting deck?" says Ted.

"June 1892?" I say.

"Joking," says Ted. "But that page Ethan wants doesn't exist," he continues. "MDs'll say they saw some page in a deck and we should re-purpose it, but nine times out of ten, the page doesn't exist. They just have no fuckin' clue what they want, and since they know we can't question them, they'll just say it exists and we'll have to come up with something."

"That blows," I say.

"Unless we can quickly *Inception* into the head of the Weston CFO and see what he dreams about, we'll have to come up with our own shit."

"I think the comps page is done too," I say, pulling up the chart that shows the trading multiples over the last five years of Weston and its set of eight comparable companies.

"Is that Calibri? So help me God!" he says with a smile. "We can worry about the font later. More importantly, see this?" Ted taps my screen where the line of one of the companies plummets before quickly returning to the cluster of the other companies. "If that was Weston's multiple, we'd have to dig in and figure out exactly what happened—maybe something weird with broker estimates, or a piece of bad news was released. The client is going to know exactly what happened there, so we would need to tell Ethan what the deal was. Good news, though, is that it's just one of the comps, so the Weston guys probably won't know." Ted pauses as I nod slowly, trying to register the rationale. "Having said that, what do you think—maybe a plant shutdown or soft-earnings release," says Ted.

"Are you asking me?" I say.

"You choose," he says. "My recommendation is we say they had shitty earnings due to a delayed product launch from a manufacturing issue. Sounds specific and believable."

I smile and make a note.

"Honestly, the key with these books is knowing what's important. I've been to a bunch of these meetings, and they're all the same—first, the banker and the corporate guy measure dicks, talk about vacations, kids, that type of stuff. Then they do some shitty self-deprecating stuff. Then, if and when they finally open the pitch book, the conversation revolves around one page, usually just one number on one page—a growth rate, a margin, a trading multiple. The important thing for us is to make sure we at least have an answer for where every number came from and identify the key ones. This multiple thing," says Ted tapping my screen again, "isn't that important since it was like two years ago and is of a comp."

"You ever see companies follow through on stuff bankers have pitched them?" I ask.

"Occasionally, but the utility of the meeting for MDs is to just get information from companies. Then, when they meet with one of that company's competitors a few weeks later, the banker has some good information to pass along. Most of these big companies know what deals they're gonna do, at least the big ones. Getting tidbits of info to spread around is how these MDs stay relevant. Once the company decides to do a deal, they just choose the bankers they like, usually the ones who gave them the best info, to lead the deal and get the fee."

"You tug me off, I'll tug you," I say.

"Bingo," says Ted.

"How are we looking?" says Gareth as he walks up to my cube.

"In good shape," says Ted as he stands. I stand too and nod.

"Splendid," says Gareth. "Ted, why don't you take a crack at page eight—punchy bullets. I can provide further color on the next turn. And I know Ethan asked to see the deck sometime Wednesday, but let's get him a draft by tomorrow, first thing. You know how he can be with his turns." Gareth exchanges a knowing glance with Ted. "I'll be on my BlackBerry until midnight or so. Feel free to ping me with any questions. Have an early flight tomorrow, so will be out of pocket until 'round about noontime." Gareth looks at me then at Ted. "Sound good?"

"All good," says Ted.

"And Ted, for Project Mercury, can you rerun the model with L+325 on the TLB? Decrease in twenty-five bp increments until pay down is roughly fifty-eight percent on credit case. And do a quick sanity check to ensure those figures align. Then send a bilateral note with updated figures, including lev fin and the senior team. They should provide a little more color around assumptions. If not, please chase the folks in DCM." Gareth takes a sip of the cardboard box of water he's holding, "Boxed Water Is Better—Sustainability" in large black font on it. Then he tosses it and returns to his cube.

"What's Project Mercury?" I ask Ted.

"We're doing the refinancing of one of the biggest plastic manufacturers in the world. We ambulance-chase these guys a bunch."

"What do you mean?"

"We advised on an acquisition they did a few years back. The company went to shit, then we did their restructuring. Then took 'em public about a year ago, now doing their debt."

Ted and I watch as Gareth puts on a dark-blue quilted vest in his cube across the floor.

"He knows his shit, huh?" I say to Ted.

"Early promote to associate, early promote to VP. Probably early promote to director," says Ted. "Which means he'll most likely be gone the year he becomes a director."

"Why?"

"As a VP, he still works for the MDs. He tags along to meetings and stuff and is on accounts, but he's not bringing in clients. When he's a director, he'll be competing with the other MDs, like Ethan, for business. Once he's a threat to take Ethan's clients, Ethan will make sure he's gone. Saw it happen with this other VP we had who was really good a couple years back."

"What'll happen to him?"

"Probably end up at some other bank where they need a new young MD to cover industrial companies. It's revolving doors with these guys."

"Make sense, I guess. Use 'em till they're a threat, then kick 'em to the curb."

"Check this out," says Ted tapping my arm. Gareth slips of out his immaculately polished, black dress shoes and into a different pair. "His casual shoes are Ferragamos." Within seconds, Gareth disappears down the hallway.

"Joel should be able to take care of the rest of the stuff. We'll send to Ethan tonight and probably go over tomorrow at some point with him," says Ted. Ten minutes later, he slips out of his beat-up brown loafers. "See you tomorrow, man," he says as he leaves in a pair of New Balance 407s.

10

Getting My Harvey Ball Bearings

A spot in the bullpen is earned, not given. As you may recall, MDs occupy the windowed offices, which lie on the perimeter of the square floor. On the interior are the cubicles, where everyone from directors to analysts sit, save for one group—senior analysts, comprised of second- and third-year analysts. This group sits in the bullpen, a rectangular, windowless enclave situated directly in the middle of the floor, ten steps from my cube.

I tread carefully into the bullpen around 11:00 p.m.—might as well be 11:00 a.m. in here. Without a hint of natural light, there's a casino quality to the space. An assortment of sounds, both human and computerized, churns incessantly. Rational behavior is a long-lost thought.

Joel's broad shoulders and large head block most of what's on his dimmed dual monitors. With his cube situated so that his back is facing the bullpen entrance and thus visible to all passersby, Joel is clearly one of the newcomers to the senior analyst crew.

"Billy boy, what's up?" he says. I'm still at least five steps from him as I enter, and he's facing directly away from me at his desk.

"You got eyes in the back of your head?" I ask. Joel reaches out his right arm and taps an adjustable mirror he's set up on one of the walls of his cube.

"Associates in mirror are closer than they appear," he says before doing a 180-degree spin in his chair and greeting me with a wide grin. "Put this baby up the day I moved in. Gimme two minutes—just gotta finish something quick and send to an MD."

Of the twelve cubes in the bullpen, all but two are occupied. Most of the ten occupants wear large headphones and are in work mode. I'm completely ignored as I slowly circle the 'pen, and that's fine by me.

The walls of the bullpen are covered in an array of items—from old *New York Times* and *Wall Street Journal* clippings, slightly browned by age and lack of sunlight, to photoshopped pictures of analysts' (both past and present) heads on characters from *The Wolf of Wall Street* to *Pokémon*, to old emails with highlighted sections (e.g. "WTF??? makes no sense. Figure it out. Need ASAP"). On the wall next to one analyst hangs a sign, "Ø hours without an Excel issue," with the "Ø" written in black permanent marker on a Post-it. Above another analyst's cube is an official looking sheet titled, "The Ten Commandments of Excel." Across the back wall of the bullpen, separated by a flat-screen television that perpetually broadcasts CNBC on mute, hang two banners—one is a dark blue "Deutsche Bank PGA Tour Championship 10th Anniversary" banner, the likes of which you'd find in a college dorm room. The other is a large white sign with massive handwritten block letters—"NOT MUCH HAS CHANGED. JUST A LOT MORE WORK." Below the banners on the back wall is a mantle with countless discarded deal-toys, many of which, upon closer inspection, have been collecting dust since the '90s.

In the middle of the bullpen is a large island counter. Filing cabinets line each side, and on top are two large printers and a donut box with one donut remaining. On one side of the printers is a small Christmas tree, and on the other side is a menorah. Both the lights on the tree and the menorah are lit, which for some reason, even though it's early September, doesn't feel odd here.

Many cubes in the bullpen proudly display a pennant of their current occupant's alma mater, as well as some pictures of siblings and parents. These knickknacks provide reassurance that a world outside the bullpen exists, even if these senior analysts are no longer part of it.

There's a corner of one wall with pictures of former analysts.

"He was a beast," says Ted as he approaches and taps a picture of an Asian kid in a trench coat, under which someone has written "The Assassin." "Never saw him take that coat off in the two years he was here. Barely ever heard him talk, but the shit he could do in Excel and PowerPoint...." Ted shakes his head in awe.

"How 'bout this guy?" I ask, pointing to a picture of another Asian kid with acne, under which someone has written "The False Prophet."

"Had all the makings of a good analyst but couldn't cut it," says Ted.

"Yo," says Joel, poking his head above his cube and summoning me toward him. It's then that I notice the slew of shirtsleeves (from the elbow to the cuff) pinned to the wall, high above everything else. Two full rows of shirtsleeves in a variety of colors and patterns line the entire interior of the bullpen wall.

"What's the story with the sleeves?" I ask, approaching Joel's desk as I roll an extra chair alongside me and situate myself behind Joel.

"Eventually happens after a while. I have three sleeves up there." Joel tilts his head up and points to the right. "That blue-and-white striped one, the light pink one, and the yellow."

"Kinda like a rite of passage thing," I say wondering how a company stays in business manufacturing dress shirts the color of Grey Poupon.

"I guess, yeah. My mom tried to sew in little pieces of fabric to reinforce the elbows."

"This her?" I say pointing to a picture of Joel in his football gear with his arms draped around a small lady he dwarfs.

Joel smiles. "That's her."

"Your house? Pretty unreal," I say now looking at the picture of a majestic mansion you'd see on the cover of a Sotheby's catalog.

"Don't have any of those in Bayonne, Jersey," he says. "That's the house I'm going to buy her though."

"Nice. You were a lineman I assume?"

"Right tackle."

"So not the blindside?"

"Actually, yeah. Our QB was a lefty."

"Can't imagine playing a sport in college and doing all the banking, recruiting, and internship shit junior year. Was hard enough for me in business school, and I didn't even play a sport anymore."

"I had it all planned out when I was a kid—was gonna play in the NFL, be a lawyer during the off-season, then retire as the President of the United States. Fall back plan was banking, so had to make it work."

Joel opens one of his drawers and hands me a laminated sheet of paper titled, "Does Athletic Participation Impact Academic Performance? Senior Economics Thesis of Joel Janowski."

"This is just the summary page," he says.

I look in amazement at the page, formatted as meticulously as the banking books I've seen, and peppered with colorful pie charts, regression analyses, binomial theorems, and other formulas containing symbols like ß and the other weird looking "y" that's Greek. "I could email you the whole presentation if you want," he says.

"I'd like that," I say. "So is there anything I can do to help out with the book? Ted said you guys had made some good headway."

"Let's see," says Joel, scanning the PowerPoint pages of the latest draft of the Weston pitch book. "How 'bout you put in the Harvey balls[1] on page three, then maybe give the sum-of-the-parts page a try. Those two pages are good to help you practice formatting stuff in PPT, creating waterfall charts, and also doing SOTP analysis. I'll send you an old book to show you how the SOTP page should look— each segment has a different multiple. You can find the segment EBITDAs in the company presentations. Show the build up to TEV, then subtract net debt to get to implied-equity value."

I return to my desk with my marching orders. It takes me forty-five minutes to get the two rows of Harvey balls formatted properly, both in alignment and size.

John Bukowski: Yo, you still here?

William Keenan: Yeah, you?

John Bukowski: Obviously, idiot. How would I have just messaged you?

William Keenan: Coulda used that Ras thing and logged in from home

John Bukowski: If I hear someone use the word "jammin" again, I'm gonna quit

William Keenan: J

William Keenan: A

William Keenan: M

John Bukowski: Swing by my desk

William Keenan: M

William Keenan: I

William Keenan: N

---

[1] ●●◐○

"Jammin', I wanna jam it with you. We're jammin', jammin'," I sing as I approach Jack's cube on the other side of the floor.

"Any clue what the difference between FY+1 and NTM is?" Jack asks. I shake my head. He exhales then leans back in his chair. "You have any idea what you're doing?" A stream of panic flashes across his eyes.

"Like thirty percent understanding."

"What they have you staffed on?"

"M&A pitch. You?"

"Financing for a utility. We had a sit-down earlier today for an hour," says Jack.

"How'd it go?"

"Barely understood a word. Only thing that was obvious is that someone has a shit-ton of work to do, and it's probably me," he says. "What's the company you're pitching do?"

"Think they do like five hundred million in revenue a year," I say. "Ten percent EBITDA margins."

"I mean what do they actually *do*?" he says.

"End markets are in specialty silicas, laminates, and engineered plastics, which have pretty high market-growth rates, if you apply random percentages to specific regions." I say.

"You don't know what they do," he says.

"Has something to do with why tires are black."

"Man, I'm glad I have you around—makes me feel so much better about myself. You're dismissed," says Jack.

"What was that?" I say, looking at the ceiling.

"A/C must shut down at midnight."

"No wonder I'm so hungry."

I order dinner from Hwa Yuan Szechuan since I'll be looking for hope everywhere tonight, including inside a fortune cookie.

* * *

"What in the hell is this?" says Ethan, holding up the sheet of paper like it's a baggie of dog shit. With Gareth away at a client meeting and Ted informing us this morning that he'll be out for the next week with a family emergency, Joel and I sit alone across from Ethan in his office.

"Latest draft of the Weston book," says Joel, who emailed the deck the night before, around 1:00 a.m. Ethan eyes it with skepticism. "Why's there shit on both sides of the page?"

"Sorry," I say. "Think the default setting on my printer is set to double-sided."

"Go print another copy—single-sided, in color."

Four minutes later, I return with a new baggie of dog shit.

"Alright," says Ethan grabbing a red pen and leaning forward to inspect the deck. "Fine," he says flipping through the first couple pages. "Generally okay with this." He holds the pen in his right hand, centimeters from the paper, seemingly eager to make his marks. "Kill this shit," he says striking a large red line across one of the "market outlook" pages. "Broadly okay with that." He flips back to the first page of the section. "You know what, just kill the whole fuckin' section." He flips to the next section, where most of the new-page creates are. "Okay," he says, his right hand now bouncing slightly so the tip of the pen barely touches the page before recoiling into a ready position. Then he makes a huge circle. "Why are we using '16 multiples? It's September. Use '17...Ecolab EBITDA growth looks too low—make sure it's pro forma for that ingredients acquisition they just did...add a key message here," he says before mumbling something inaudible and scribbling something illegible.

"Got it," says Joel, making a note in his notebook as he cranes his neck trying to catch a glimpse of Ethan's page.

"Just listen, Joel," says Ethan. "I'm writing the shit down for you. Focus on listening."

"Sorry," says Joel.

Ethan flips to the SOTP page, the one page in the deck I did. He stares at it for a few seconds but doesn't make any marks. Instead, he looks up, first at Joel, then me. "Who did this page?" Before I can say anything, he's off. "Because I want to know how the fuck does it make sense to pitch divesting the life-sciences division when we're saying they trade two turns higher than the other three segments?" Ethan shakes his head, sporting a menacing smile. "Let's start with some logic. Last time I checked, companies sell their dog-shit assets that weigh down their multiple. But this page," he continues, tapping it with his pen, "tells me the dog shit is trading at eleven times, and if they sell it, the RemainCo will trade at a discount to its current multiple." He leans back, spinning the silver wedding band on his finger. "Hey, maybe I'm fuckin' wrong, right? I don't know everything. Maybe I'm the one who doesn't know what the fuck I'm doing. You tell me."

The room falls silent.

"Who did this page? You can tell me. Blame it on Ted—he's not here."

My mouth is dry, but the back of my undershirt is soaked with sweat. I exhale slowly, summoning the courage to admit it's my work.

"I made the page," says Joel.

Ethan smiles. "You've been here two years, Joel. I know you love futzing with the goddamn colors, but you ever consider thinking shit through when you're done making the bars different shades of magenta?"

"My mistake, Ethan. Won't happen again," says Joel.

"I'm not going through the rest of the book. I leave Friday for DC. Won't be looking at shit until after the 'Skins game Sunday, so I don't care when you email me a new draft, but make sure the numbers are right and shit makes sense." An electronic ding from his computer gets his attention. "I gotta get on a call."

Joel and I stand. Ethan flicks the few pages he marked up across the table, and Joel slides them into his notebook. "Ethan, as far as work streams, I'm still working on the CRM for Ingredion. Between this deck and that memo, do you have a preference which I should prioritize?" asks Joel.

"Both," says Ethan as he dials his phone.

"Will do. Open or shut?" says Joel as we leave the office.

"Closed."

Joel and I walk back to the bullpen. "You didn't have to take the—" I begin.

"I should've done a better job checking," says the twenty-three-year-old analyst. "You'll have the chance to pay it forward down the road."

"Thanks," I say trying to find any other words to convey how grateful I am but coming up empty.

"Let's just hope Redskins win," says Joel. "For now, why don't you work in the master and take Ethan's comments for the market outlook pages, and I'll open a rider and look into the SOTP page."

Seconds after returning to my desk, Phuc, the diminutive Vietnamese associate in my class, appears and rests his elbows on the top of my cube. "Jammin' on anything live?" he asks.

"M&A pitch," I say as I pull up the latest PowerPoint.

"Dang. That sucks. Pitches are pretty easy, but still," says Phuc.

Trying to decipher Ethan's latest comments without Gareth proves impossible.

"I got staffed on a sell-side today. Should start ramping up soon," continues Phuc. "Think you'll get anything live?"

"No idea," I say as I rotate one of Ethan's pages slowly, trying to figure out what he's written.

"No need to get all mad about it."

My phone rings. I shoo Phuc away as I slap on my headset.

"Hello?" I say, eyeing the caller ID number I don't recognize.

"Am I speaking with Mister William Keenan?"

"You are. Who's this?"

"Hi Mister Keenan. My name is Philip, and I'm contacting you on behalf of your dedicated American Express corporate-card team. How are you doing today?"

"Fine," I say.

"Glad to hear. I see in your records there's an outstanding balance on your card, and I'd like to help you resolve it to avoid any further late fees."

"Yeah, I got a call about this not long ago. I literally just got my AmEx card the other day and haven't used it once. I think you have the wrong person," I say.

"Mister Keenan, I do apologize. Let me contact my supervisor and see if we can resolve it on our end. Can I ask you one final question?"

"Sure."

"Can I request that you wear a big smile for the rest of the day, Mister Keenan?"

* * *

"That brings up fourth and long with twelve seconds remaining in this seesaw game here at FedEx Field. Redskins need twenty-two yards to get into field goal range to give Dustin Hopkins a chance to kick a game-winner. Once again, their fate is in the hands of franchise quarterback Kirk Cousins, who's had a career day despite a below-average showing from his supporting cast." I turn the volume up on my television, lean forward in my couch, and clasp my hands together as the Redskins break from their huddle and line up in a shotgun formation with five receivers.

"Cousins drops back...." says the announcer.

"What the fuck are the receivers doing?" I yell at the television. "Why would you run into double coverage?"

"Since when did you give a fuck about football?" asks my roommate as he emerges from his bedroom after a lengthy session of *Call of Duty* on campaign mode.

"Starting last week," I say, now standing a few feet from the television with my hands clasped behind my neck. "Fuckin' get rid of it. Heave the thing down field, idiot!"

"...Cousins...sacked again...for the sixth time!" says the announcer. "This Redskins offensive line with a dreadful ending to an already awful afternoon they've had defending a faster, more powerful Philadelphia Eagles rush defense. The Redskins turn the ball over on downs and that should do it. Week one in the books here in Landover, Maryland."

I lean back, sinking into the couch.

"A bunch of guys are meeting at some bullshit bar in the Village. You wanna come?" asks my roommate.

My BlackBerry dings. "Expect comments," reads the subject of an email from Ethan. Nothing in the body of the email.

"Think I gotta stick around here for a while, but I'll text you if I can meet up later," I say.

At 10:37 p.m., just over three hours after Kirk Cousins was sacked for the sixth and final time that day, my BlackBerry buzzes as I sit on the same couch, having barely moved. I open up the email from Ethan: "Error 317: message download failed—content too large."

I'm on the forty-fourth floor fifteen minutes later. The lights in all the MD offices are off, and while the rest of the floor is relatively quiet, the bullpen is jumping.

After printing out two copies of Ethan's comments (seven pages, double-sided, single-spaced), I pull up a chair behind Joel, who's scarfing down a chicken-parm sub.

"Here." Joel, a large red Gatorade stain above his top lip, turns and hands me a plastic bag with another steaming hot chicken-parm sub. "Delivery guy at Potbelly is my boy—always gives me an extra on Sundays." I accept the sub as I hand him Ethan's latest comments.

"Almost seems like he changed around the entire book," I say. "That normal? Changing a ton of shit the night before a meeting?"

"Yeah," says Joel. He opens up the Excel backup and latest draft of the PowerPoint presentation. "Oh! 11:11," he says pointing at the date and time in the lower right corner of his right computer monitor. "Make a wish."

He already answered mine.

* * *

The first final version (WestonDM_vF) has a formatting bust we detect when scrolling through the PDF. The next final version

(WestonDM_vFF) has a P/E multiple on page six that doesn't tie with the multiple on page twenty-four. The actual final version (WestonDM_vFFF) of the book is sent to print at DB's in-house reprographics team at 2:35 a.m.

"Is it usually this bad just for a pitch?" I ask.

"Just be thankful the meeting is in Midtown," says Joel.

"Why's that?"

"It can get a lot worse if the MD has to fly or take a train to the meeting. Gives him time to go through the book. Can take heavy fire via email or on the phone if that's the case."

"But even after the deck is printed...day of the meeting?"

"One time I had an MD tell me to change an assumption for a firepower page like twenty minutes before his meeting. I emailed him the updated page, and he printed it at the client's office."

A new email pops into Joel's inbox. Industrials isn't the only banking group scrambling to turn comments and print books this Sunday. Repro informs us the wait will be about two hours. Joel ensures me he can stay up, flip the books once printed to be certain there are no other issues, then courier them to Ethan's house on the Upper West Side.

Fuckin' Redskins.

When I stumble into the office Monday morning just after 9:30 a.m., the first thing I hear as I walk down the hall to my cube is Joel's laugh from the bullpen.

11

Popping My F1 Key

"Cash and Big Macs," my sister said after brief consideration.
"I can't tell if you're fucking with me or not," I responded.

"Tell me the right answer then, asshole," she said.

"The two types of capital a company, like McDonald's in this case, can raise are debt and equity. You can only eat Big Macs." I enjoyed my weekly conversations with my sister during my two years at business school. While my fellow classmates, many of whom had worked in finance for a handful of years before business school, were insulted by the pace of our corporate finance class, I was learning new things every day and relished the opportunity to impart my newly acquired wisdom to my older sister in a manner equal parts informative and condescending.

A significant function of bulge-bracket banks, which have their own balance sheets,[1] is to help companies raise debt and equity to

---

[1] Bulge-bracket investment banks (Bank of America, JP Morgan, Deutsche Bank, and so forth) have a balance sheet, which allows them to lend to borrowers. Boutique investment banks (Lazard, Moelis, Evercore, and others) only provide advisory services.

help finance things like working capital, acquisitions, and other growth opportunities. The cost of debt is typically lower than the cost of equity, meaning that companies will prefer to seek debt financing rather than equity financing. Likewise, the premise behind leveraged buyouts, made famous by private equity companies, is to find businesses that generate steady cash flow from their operations, and use the cash to service debt (make interest payments). Using a significant amount of leverage (and little equity), the PE firm purchases the business, makes some sort of operational improvement, thus increasing margins, then sells the business in three to five years. The business can sustain the leverage, since it generates enough cash to make the interest payments on its debt. Additionally, if all goes to plan, the high leverage amplifies the equity returns that the private equity firm realizes after five years. Bored yet?

At its founding in 1870 in Berlin, Deutsche Bank's statute laid out that its primary objective was to serve as a specialist bank, facilitating trade relations among Germany, other European countries, and overseas markets. Like any other corporation that survived both World Wars (including ties to Hitler) and depressions, Deutsche Bank's role and credo evolved over the next century. The bank's acquisition of UK-based Morgan, Grenfell & Co. in 1989 was its first major step toward building a global capital markets operation. Ten years later, Deutsche Bank purchased Bankers Trust (which itself had just acquired Alex. Brown & Sons to broaden its own investment banking platform) for $10 billion, the largest foreign takeover of an American bank, catapulting Deutsche Bank ahead of UBS and Citigroup as the world's biggest bank by assets. With increasing competition in its European investment banking operations, Deutsche Bank had long been considering a transformational acquisition to firmly root itself in the United States. Bankers Trust had been a leader in underwriting high-yield junk bonds through the 1980s and 1990s, which fueled the leveraged-buyout boom. It was through these acquisitions that Deutsche Bank built its reputation as a "debt house" with expertise in debt financing, and thus the current nightmare model that will be igniting waves of panic through every fiber of my being.

* * *

"If you are the leader, please enter the required security passw—" says the automated voice into my headset before I cut it off by typing in the seven-digit code. I open the line three minutes before the conference call is scheduled to begin and catch up on the seven new emails in my inbox that arrived while I was refilling my water bottle on the other side of the floor. Then I revisit the staffing email I received a couple hours prior that outlines this new project.

Beep.

"Hi, who just joined?" I say.

"This is Arthur," says an MD from the leveraged finance (lev fin) group.

"Hi, Arthur, it's Bill from Industrials. You're first to join."

Beep.

"Hi, who just joined?" I say.

"You got Mason," says a VP from lev fin.

"Hey Mase. You got Arthur on. No one from Industrials on the line yet," says Arthur.

Beep.

"Who just joined?" I say.

"Brett's on," says a voice. I search the invite list for the call to identify Brett—a director in the financials sponsors group.

"You got Arthur and Mason on the line, Brett. No one from Industrials yet," says Arthur.

A minute passes. On the line, I hear the light tapping of keyboards.

"Hey, Phil, can you resend the dial-in," says Arthur.

"Will do," I say, as I copy all the info from the previous dial-in into a new email and send it to the group.

Beep.

Beep.

Beep.

"Hi, who just—" I say.

"Ethan's on."

"You got Brad."

"Boris is on."

"Hey guys. Got Arthur here. Ethan, you're only one on from Industrials, but think we have a quorum on our end, so why don't we get started?"

"Thanks Arthur," says Ethan. "Just got an inbound from TTZ—looking for commitments ASAP. Target is Ariavo, big distributor in specialty chems space. Look, this is a good business, okay. Mid-teens margins through the cycle, good management. Schulman is the comp here. Should be able to get aggressive with the leverage."

While a few of the junior lev-fin guys jump in to corroborate Ethan's assessment, I scroll back through the staffing email, but it sheds little to no light on what exactly the project is.

"We've seen trades in the five to five-and-a-half range for distributors," says Arthur.

"This is a six-times business—churns out cash flow, good contracts with some of the biggest players in the industry—nice little business. This is a six- to six-and-a-half times business," says Ethan. "We can sit here and debate this and that, but the reality is, this trade is happening at six, six-and-a-half times, whether we're in it or not."

"Alright," says Arthur. "What juniors from lev fin are on?"

"Boris is on," says an associate from lev fin who's in my class.

"Team needs to put on our thinking caps. Boris, let's pull together the cap comps. Take a look through all distribution folders, not just chems, and see what sort of leverage we got to historically. We can discuss specifics offline. Regardless, we need to sharpen our pencils here and will have to get creative to get this through internally above five-and-a-quarter."

"Will do," says Boris.

"We'll need to get this to cap com in next thirty-six hours. Who's holding pen on the model?" says Arthur.

The line falls silent.

"Industrials can take model," says Ethan. "Got a little math to do today." My throat constricts as my mouth suddenly dries up.

"Great. Phil, touch base with Boris if you need anything," says Arthur.

"Will do," I say.

"Let's run this up the flagpole and jump on the phone tomorrow first thing to see how we're looking," says Ethan. "I can do seven-thirty. Have another call at eight."

"Let's do seven-fifteen," says Arthur. "I have a breakfast in Midtown at seven-forty-five."

"Let's just do seven o'clock," says Ethan. "Someone send out a planner."

"On it," says Boris. Seconds later, an invite pops up in my inbox for a 7:00 a.m. phone call.

"Let's chop some wood here," says Ethan.

"Thanks, guys," says Arthur, followed by a series of beeps as people hang up.

William Keenan: Yo

Boris Popov: What up, Phil haha

William Keenan: Hysterical, this is an LBO, right?

Boris Popov: holy s**t. U serious?

William Keenan: dead serious

Boris Popov: yeah, LBO. Do you understand how private equity firms work?

William Keenan: are you able to help with the model? I've never done one of these and not sure what to do

> **Boris Popov:** dude this project is 7th on my priority list. Have your analyst figure it out

> **William Keenan:** he's MIA

> **Boris Popov:** that sucks, I'll send you template, but don't have time to help

"What they got you cranking on?" says a voice, as a head, then an upper body, slowly emerge from behind the cubicle divider diagonally from me. Bart, another senior associate in the group, raises a DB coffee mug to his mouth and takes a sip. He's thin in an unhealthy way and has a face that tells the story of countless sleepless nights on the forty-fourth floor.

"LBO for chems distributor," I say, now rifling through files in the chemicals drive and trying to find something, anything, that will provide some guidance on how to do this model.

"Lev fin punting all the work to Industrials?" he says, running his hand through his thinning dark-brown hair, accented by specs of gray on the sides.

"All the hard shit," I say.

Bart pushes his glasses up so they rest on his forehead. I can feel his eyes on me as I scroll through the endless folders, searching for something, but I'm not even certain what. He reaches down onto his desk, then extends his arm across the cube divider, a bottle of tropical-fruit-flavored Tums in his hand. He shakes the bottle. "Yellow is my favorite," he says. Three tablets fall into my right hand.

"Thanks," I say as I stand up. On Bart's desk, I spot a few unmarked prescription bottles.

A towering MD slams a nearby printer with his meaty hand, then walks to Bart's desk, holding out a black stapler. "Reload this," he says to Bart. "And throw this out." He hands Bart the stapler and a crumpled piece of paper. Bart does as he's told before returning the stapler to the MD, who walks back to the printer.

"Call IT," barks the MD to Bart. "This goddamn printer doesn't work."

Bart walks to the printer before following the power plug from the back of the large device to the ground, where it has been partially unplugged. Bart plugs the power cord back in. "Should work now," says Bart.

"Smells like a sulfur deposit over here," says the MD as he scrunches his face.

"Put your shoes back on, Bart," says Ted.

The MD retrieves his freshly printed stack of papers from the printer and returns to his office.

"So who's your analyst on this deal?" Bart says to me as he pops two Tums tablets in his own mouth.

"Leighton," I say. Bart smirks then sits down in his cube.

"Good luck," he says. As I return to my chair, I notice the steam rising from the humidifier in Bart's cube.

"Any idea where Leighton is?" I ask.

"Probably the gym," says Bart. "Believe he does legs and back on Wednesdays. I'm sure he'll tell you all about it."

"The key to working with Leighton," says Ted as he removes an earbud from his right ear and spins his chair in my direction, "is to pose your problem not as a question, but rather as an academic issue. He'll go cross-eyed and talk himself into a coma."

Bart pushes out his lower lip and nods as if in sudden recognition of the validity of Ted's point.

"Bottom line is that fuckin' kid eats, sleeps, breathes, and shits finance—has to be one of the best third-year analysts on the Street. There's a reason he comes and goes when he pleases."

"Show Keenan the backups," says Bart to Ted, who then slides back up to his keyboard and begins typing.

"Check out the folder I just sent you," says Ted. "Go into the Excel backup—get in there, snoop around."

I open the file, slowly scanning each of the sheets. There's a ton of data on the company, though the flow of the document is difficult to follow: financials are spread between multiple sheets; the discounted cash-flow model has references flowing from other files; in the input tab, the data on comparable companies is littered with various font styles, colors, and sizes.

"That file was created in an era I like to term 'B.L.'" says Ted. "Before Leighton. Now please go ahead and check out the Excel backup—same company, mind you—but created for a project done about a year after that, in the 'A.L.' era." Ted types away and sends through another email with a link to a new file.

"Good God," I say, opening the file. The uniformity, organization, and detail of each sheet in the Excel document are astounding. It's like being in a museum—I almost don't want to click around for fear of disturbing the integrity of the file. The input tab is formatted with meticulous care, and each comp has its own color (all of which are on the DB palette). The financial information is contained in a single sheet, and each of the three financial statements is laid out and labeled clearly, with dates italicized, all items in bold, and numerical figures in normal font.

"He reconfigured the template we use in all backups now," says Ted. "And no one ever staffed him on this. First weekend on the job, he was distraught because he didn't get to build any models yet, so he came in Saturday morning and redid the backup for a book he was working on. Then he created some macro, or some bullshit, that made it so the file was easily transferable to all subsequent books."

"You meet him during your internship?" says Bart.

"Think I saw him briefly once…was talking about a recapitalization or something," I say.

"He foams at the mouth talking about dividend recaps and mezzanine financing," says Ted.

"And don't get him started on the implications of Trump's economic reforms on companies' cash-flow statements," adds Bart.

"Any idea when he'll show up?" I say.

Ted taps his iPhone. "Probably'll see him power walk in here by dusk."

* * *

"If you read the literature, the training theory with the most scientific merit for building mass is hypertrophy-specific training. Empirical research has unequivocally demonstrated that overloading a single muscle group with sufficient stimulus will ensure protein synthesis occurs in said muscle group, and hormone levels will return to normal states within forty-eight hours. Now, does much of this depend on the central nervous systems of a given body and the rate at which an individual's endocrine system can produce hormones? Absolutely. I'm simply speaking in general terms." Leighton stands above me as I sit in my cube. A blood-red tie with a wide knot hangs from his neck against a skin-tight, white Oxford shirt with a spread collar. His dark-blue suit looks like it was tailored for him about fifteen chest-and-legs days ago. His headphones, now hooked behind his ears, are wired through the back of his shirt as if he's in the secret service. "So to answer your question," he continues, "I would never work out legs and back in a single session—that's asinine. The fallacy of the push-day, pull-day concept gained traction through unsubstantiated case studies. Today, I hit my quadriceps, hamstrings, and gluteus, both maximus and medius."

"Got it," I say. "So just to circle back to the Ariavo model...do you—"

"Let me drop my galoshes and bag at my desk. Pull up the model lev fin sent you. Be back in three minutes." Leighton disappears into the bullpen, where, as the most senior analyst in the group, he occupies the most enviable spot—opposite Joel. Leighton's computer monitor isn't visible to passersby, and it's almost impossible to even see if Leighton is at his desk, given that the seat is tucked into the front corner cube.

Three minutes pass. Then five. Then ten. I get up and stride into the bullpen, where I hear him before I see him. "...My point, Joel, is that if you look at the fundamentals behind the two, investor sentiment is essentially the same thing as the market-risk premium." Leighton sits in his chair with his back to his own desk and faces Joel's desk, which is only a few feet away. Meanwhile, Joel's working at his computer, his back to Leighton. Undeterred, Leighton continues. "What are the components of the market-risk premium? Namely, the capital-asset pricing model, which describes the relationship between systematic risk and expected return for assets. Investor sentiment directly correlates to this idea, given that systematic risk is, in essence, the inherent day-to-day fluctuation—"

"You *love* CAPM, Leighton. If you could, you would marry it and have the beta of the S&P be your best man," says Joel, still not looking at Leighton.

"And you know who wouldn't be invited to my wedding?" says Leighton.

"Can I ask you a question?" asks Joel.

"No," responds Leighton.

"I'm looking at the ten-day forecast on Weather.com, and there is zero percent precipitation across the board. How do you explain the galoshes?" says Joel.

Leighton shakes his head, then spots me in the bullpen.

"Joel, get the hell out of the Kraton backup," yells a voice from a nearby cube.

"Joel's the king of sitting in backups," says Leighton.

"I am a king, and you're my queen," says Joel.

"I have to go do some actual work, Joel, and help the bank generate revenue," says Leighton as he follows me to my desk where the Excel model is already maximized on my right monitor.

"You drive," says Leighton as he motions for me to sit in my chair, while he props himself up on the desk just to the right of my computer monitors.

"I updated the financials since last process—" I begin.

"Why are your gridlines on?" says Leighton.

"What?" I say.

"Gridlines in Excel. Why are they on?"

"Just how the spreadsheet was when I received it."

"Alt W V G," says Leighton. I fumble to execute the shortcut, turning off the gridlines.

"From what I understood—" I continue.

"Why are the historical financials and projected numbers on the same sheet?" he asks.

"I updated the projected financials with new equity research, but wasn't sure—"

"Okay, that's fine for now, but we're going to want a single sheet with strictly historical figures, no projections," he says.

"Okay, I can change that later."

"Are auto colors on?" he asks. "So you can see which cells are hardcoded, formulas, references." In the cube next to me, I hear a quiet chuckle from Ted. Then Bart stands up from his chair and shoots me a quick smile as he walks to the small kitchen on the floor to refill the water in his humidifier.

"Auto colors? Not sure. Don't think so though," I say.

"Ctrl Alt E," Leighton says. "And both rows showing margins should be italicized, with percent sign, and best practice is to not take it out to a decimal. Shift, space bar, Ctrl I, Alt Shift %, Ctrl +, Ctrl C, arrow down to the other row showing margins, then Alt H V S T."

This is a catastrophe—I highlight the row in bright pink, turn the figures into date format, then finish off by completely deleting the entire row. I then put my right hand on the mouse. Leighton looks at me like I committed an act of mass genocide. Moments later, he gathers himself.

"May I?" he asks.

"Please," I say.

Still propped on my desk, using only his right hand, Leighton quickly restores the deleted row. Then, in a split second—using a series of keyboard shortcuts—he formats the rows as he verbally outlined before. Watching his fingers dance across the keys is like watching a concert pianist perform a Liszt étude.

He then uses the Alt and Tab keys to quickly scan through the open documents on my computer. "You're using Internet Explorer?" he says with an air of astonishment as he comes across an Internet-browser window that is displaying the LBO page on Investopedia.

"Yeah. Is that bad?" I say.

"Download Vivaldi browser tonight," he instructs. "Where'd you get this keyboard?"

I lift the keyboard up and inspect it. "Was just the one that was here when I started. Think it's same as everyone."

"Yeah, the Genuine HP KU-0316," says Leighton. "I'm not saying it's a bad keyboard. What I recommend, however, is that if your intention is to utilize this keyboard going forward, you should pop out your F1 key. Now if you want to upgrade to a keyboard with quicker response time and better functionality, that's a different story. For me, keyboard integrity is paramount and I have a board that fits my style of modeling, formatting, and so on. But if your plan is to use this one, you should pop out your F1 key."

I slowly put my left index finger on the F1 key, but don't press it.

"F1 has no utility," says Leighton. "Go to cell D 44." He points to the cell on my monitor. "Show me the formula." I hit the F2 key to show cell formulas. "Now quickly go across and show me formulas of every cell in that row. There'll be times when formulas aren't dragged over properly, and you need to check all cells."

You have to hit the ESC key each time after hitting the F2 key to move to the next cell. As I speed up my process of checking the row, my left index finger accidentally hits the one key separating the ESC and F2 keys—the F1 key, which when tapped brings up a help window, throwing a wrench into the rhythm of my checking and forcing me to use the mouse to close the window.

"Allow me," says Leighton. He retrieves a set of keys from his inside jacket pocket, picks one and lowers it to the right side of the F1 key, and in a quick motion, pops F1 off the keyboard. It somersaults six inches above the board, falling somewhere on the floor.

"V up." Leighton says.

This one I know—periodically, you should save up a version of the file you're working in whether it's Excel, PowerPoint, or Word. So if you're working in FileName_v3, you'll "save up" to FileName_v4. Prior versions are then filed away in an archive folder so should anything happen to the current file, you have access to all prior ones.

"Alt F A," I say, just loud enough to ensure Leighton hears. Before I contort my left index finger to hit the Alt button—

"F12," says Leighton. "It's quicker." The distinct ding of a new email gets Leighton's attention before he can become any more annoyed with me. He reaches into his pants pocket, pulls out his BlackBerry, and reads the message. "You have to be fuckin' kidding me," he says, slowly scrolling through the email.

"Everything okay?" I ask as I finish saving the new version of the model.

"My sell-side blew up. Client just sent new financials with different segments...Fuck!"

"Should we circle back up on this model in a little?" I say.

"Gonna be a fire drill on this." Leighton stands, glances at his phone, then back at me. "I'm going to need you to run point on the model." He taps my shoulder lightly, but hard enough that it makes me want to crumble and disappear. As he beelines it into the bullpen, I see Leighton insert both earbuds into his ears and enter his own world.

"Yo," says Ted, as he wheels his chair into my cube. "First time running a model on live process?"

I nod slowly, still looking at the Excel model, which somehow is now completely "reffed out," meaning that nearly every cell in the sheet displays the #REF error instead of a numerical figure. "What the fuck happened here?" I say. Ted leans over and quickly restores the model with a few taps on my keyboard.

"The key is to stay calm," says Ted. "There's a ton of noise in these things, but only a few important inputs. The tabs with inputs—like control tab, sensitivities tab, shit like that—are your home bases—only mess with the cells in blue, the hard codes. The template, if it's running properly, should have all the formulas flowing through to the output. And when in doubt about what's driving shit, go to the output cell and hit control, shift, left bracket. That'll trace all precedent cells so you can see what inputs are driving that output."

"Alright," I say, exhaling slowly and focusing on my breathing—the same tactic I used prior to hockey games when the nerves kicked in. "Only the cells in blue...control, shift, left bracket," I repeat.

"Sorry about leaving you and Joel out to dry on that Weston book," says Ted. "Had some stuff come up with my fiancée's parents—had to go up to Albany."

"No problem—it was fine. Joel was a big help," I say.

"I know it was probably a nightmare—fuck, speak of the devil," says Ted.

Ethan emerges from his corner office, flying down the hall as he throws his suit jacket over his shoulder. "Kirk Cousins, baby," says a grinning Ethan in our direction as he makes a few football-throwing pumps with his right arm. "If we can get the receivers to run a post pattern correctly, I like their odds this Sunday. Panthers are for shit."

"How'd that meeting go?" says Ted as Ethan approaches our cubes.

"I've had six meetings in the last four days. Need to be more specific," says Ethan.

"Weston meeting last Monday—the one me, Joel, and Bill were on," says Ted. Ethan pauses, resting his arms over my cube divider, and flicks a head nod at me.

"It was the first pitch I got staffed on," I say as if Ethan cares.

"Weston, yeah. That got cancelled Sunday. CFO is a real dick," says Ethan sliding his jacket on as he disappears down the hall.

12

Busting in Models

There are sixteen sheets in the Excel model template: LBO model, control, sensitivities, company, S&U, FCF, comp, DCF, beta, de-risking, football field, multiple progression, sell-side, DB credit, downside, and financials. Within each sheet, there are hundreds of cells, some of which are hidden. When I hit the small "+" sign next to the condensed hidden rows and columns, more numbers and data pour into the sheet.

Each cell can be identified by its row and column. Rows are sorted numerically, while columns are sorted alphabetically—thus, cell A 1 is the topmost left cell, cell B 1 is to its right, and cell A 2 is below it. There is data in cell QER 389 in the "multiple progression" tab. If the models I worked on in business school were at a high school JV level, and the model I "completed" in London training was Division III college level, what I'm looking at now is Olympic, like final-heat level—at least to me.

In the distance, I see the bright red EXIT sign next to the stairway. Part of me—the vast majority—wants to hightail it down the forty-four flights of stairs to freedom. Then I see Phuc, his BlackBerry in hand, looking like Ari Gold from *Entourage*.

As I contemplate my escape, Joel's smiling face and behemoth body come into view. Passing by my cube on his way to the bathroom, he sticks out his right fist. I reciprocate, giving him a fist-bump. "My man," he says, mid-stride, before disappearing into the bathroom.

With restored hope, I retrieve my headphones from my top drawer, queue up some country music, and methodically go through each sheet of the model, recalling Ted's advice to focus primarily on the blue cells, the inputs, which will drive the outputs.

My first task is to separate the historical financials from the projected figures to avoid giving Leighton an aneurysm next time he looks at it. Then a new email pops up in my inbox from Arthur, the MD in lev fin, to the whole deal team: "Pls run 2 cases: 1) 6x—unfunded RCF, $1445 TLB, $360 bonds; 2) 6.5x—fund $150 of RCF (L+175); $1355 TLB, $450 bonds. LIBOR floor 1%, TLB OID 99.5, notes pricing 6.5%. 50% CF sweep. Tx."

Before I can process the instructions, Arthur sends a follow up: "And try scenario 2 w/o RCF funded, 50 percent of TLB issued in Euro. Same floor, E+165. Tx."

Slowly switching from sheet to sheet in the model, I stumble upon the sheet labeled "control," which contains a series of headings containing the word "assumptions" along with columns of blue numbers. "Capital structure assumptions" reads cell D 43—this is the one. I celebrate the small victory by mouthing the words to the refrain of Kenny Chesney's "Keg in the Closet," which blares through my headphones.

Ten columns to the right are the interest rate assumptions and OID assumptions. Having no understanding of what OID actually means isn't an issue. What matters is that the assumptions Arthur gives me are input into the model correctly.

After double-checking I input everything correctly, I scan up in the control sheet and toggle through the two cases. After setting the capital structure, operating assumptions, interest rate, OID, and cash-flow sweep all to "Case 1," I hit the F12 key to refresh the spreadsheet. Unfortunately, F12 brings up the "Save As" box. I hit ESC and then hit F9, the key that refreshes the spreadsheet.

A few seconds pass. My screen dims slightly and my cursor disappears, a surefire sign Excel is freezing. "What in the shit?" I say, removing my headphones.

"Freeze?" I hear Ted say from his cube.

"All I did was toggle through the first case," I plead. "I wasn't—"

"Give it a second—should be fine. Go to options, formulas, then make sure 'automatic except for data tables' is selected."

Seconds later, the screen brightens. I follow Ted's instructions, deselecting "automatic" and selecting "automatic except for data tables." I then toggle to case two, and the spreadsheet quickly updates without a hitch.

"That work?" he asks.

"How'd you know that was the issue?"

"When you toggle through cases and refresh the spreadsheet, *everything* gets refreshed. In models with a bunch of data tables, it takes forever to process, so best to just update data tables manually."

Over the next three hours, I go through each of the sixteen sheets, carefully updating relevant cells in each sheet and tweaking formatting so output pages are consistent with the financials and data provided by the company. After updating the data for the comparable companies and precedent transactions, I check the football-field sheet.[1] It looks reasonable, visually, and that's what's paramount. All ranges are relatively in line, with the management DCF showing the highest range and the precedent transactions next highest. The LBO, public comparables, and DB credit-case valuations are clustered around the same range, while the downside DCF shows the lowest valuation range.

---

[1] A summary output of all valuation methods used. The name is derived from the fact the output resembles a football field—or at least what bankers think a football field looks like. I don't see it.

John Bukowski: Any idea what LCAF is?

William Keenan: no, why?

John Bukowski: apparently I'm supposed to lead an LCAF call tmw

William Keenan: send me dial-in. will have popcorn ready

John Bukowski: you still lost in that model you're working on

William Keenan: pretty much

John Bukowski: k good.

John Bukowski: also, pls take me off as "Jack DB" on your phone contacts

William Keenan: only if you offer to captain the banking kickball team

At 11:17 p.m., Arthur sends an email: "Where are we on model? How do numbers look???" It's then that it occurs to me I'm not even certain what the ultimate goal is for this exercise. I spend the next hour compiling a set of pages, trying to summarize the data including valuation metrics and outputs, a comparison of the various assumptions used for each case, and a summary of the sources and uses and the pro-forma capitalization table.

I open up a new email response to Arthur just as the humming of the floor's air conditioner shuts off. Attached to the email is a comprehensive six-page deck with every possible number I can think could be important. Within seconds, Arthur sends a response: "Don't need all this. Just send paydown for both scenarios."

My Ctrl-F search for "paydown" hits on the eighth sheet, the free cash-flow projections output page. After toggling through scenarios one and two, I copy the paydown figures (both 47 percent)

and paste them into a new email to Arthur and the team. His email response comes within sixty seconds: "Must be bust in model. Not good enough. Do better."

The bullpen smells like a mall food court when I walk in around 12:30 a.m. The first cube I pass emanates the distinct scent of low tide. On the desk, a brochure for Pad Thai pokes out of a greasy, ripped-open brown paper bag. The analyst who occupies the cube wears large headphones and periodically twists his plastic fork into the container of food, shoveling brown noodles into his mouth without taking his eyes off the monitor, which is teeming with colorful column-charts. On the counter in the middle of the bullpen is a pizza box with two slices of pepperoni pizza and an empty tray of bite-size Baked by Melissa cupcakes that threw the group into a frenzy when they were delivered earlier in the day.

"So how is the deferred tax-asset created?" asks Leighton in Joel's direction.

"The difference in accounting methods," says Joel before he spots me, and spins his chair in my direction. A paper napkin with blotches of vodka sauce splattered all over it is tucked into the collar of his shirt. "Wild Bill, I got an extra meatball if you want it. They're delicious." Joel picks up the plastic container and offers it up to me.

"Difference in accounting methods? Be more specific, Joel," says Leighton. "Joel, are you listening to me?"

"No," says Joel. "Seriously, Bill. These are like homemade meat-balls, and this sauce is incredible, so creamy."

"Then why did you ask me?" says Leighton.

"I didn't. You overhead me talking on the phone to someone about it and then butted in," says Joel.

Leighton shakes his head then turns back around in his chair. He's the only person I've seen on the entire floor who only has one computer monitor, though it's the size of two combined. I'm afraid to ask the rationale, but I don't even need to. "People waste too much time twisting their head from monitor to monitor," says Leighton as I approach his cube.

"Makes sense," I say.

"Already eat?" I ask.

"I consume my daily caloric intake by 6:30 p.m. Only liquids thereafter." With that, he pops open a tangerine-flavored LaCroix sparkling water, one of six on his desk. "Used to drink Poland Spring, but this has less carbonation and limits number of bathroom breaks." Leighton then removes the black compression-sleeve from his right arm.

"What happened to your arm? From lifting?" I ask.

"He developed golfer's elbow from modeling too hard," says Joel from his cube.

"Something you know nothing about, since you can't even tell me the basic components of a balance sheet," says Leighton.

"You should get Tommy Modeling surgery," adds Joel.

"Know you're cranking on your sell-side, so not sure if you've been able to keep up with the email traffic," I say. "Didn't find any busts in the model." Leighton scans through the most recent emails from Arthur, quietly mumbling to himself. His souped-up keyboard emits a distinct clicking sound with each tapped key.

When he arrives at my most recent email with the paydown figures, he shakes his head, "Yeah, that doesn't work."

"I'm not quite sure what Arthur means when he writes, 'Do better,'" I say.

"What we care about is the percent of total debt paydown after year seven," says Leighton. "This essentially determines whether it's feasible for DB to underwrite the deal and market it to investors. We need DB credit case to be above fifty-three percent after year seven—that's the key number. Thus, 'do better' means get to fifty-three percent."

"Any idea how?" I ask.

Leighton looks at me as he unhooks the earbuds behind his ears and places them in his ears. "Any way you can."

At my desk, I recheck every formula in the free cash-flow output sheet. Then I go back through the financials, both historical and projections, to ensure all the numbers are correct. Everything in the control tab, including debt assumptions, are exactly as Arthur instructed. Then Ted's advice from earlier that evening hits me—work backward from the issue. He mentioned an Excel shortcut that quickly traces all precedents. I scan the list of shortcuts pinned in my cube by the last occupant—"Trace precedents: control, shift, left bracket," reads one of the items near the bottom of the sheet. The paydown percent figure in year seven—Cell R 89—is my issue. I trace the precedent cells once, twice, three times, until finally I find the blue hardcoded figures that are the root numbers driving the cell's output. Ultimately, the LTM EBITDA figure and the interest expense on the debt, which, combined, largely determine the free cash flow produced each year, can be used to pay down outstanding debt.

While Arthur's email states the rate on the bonds, there is one variable that can be flexed—LIBOR. Interest rates on term loans are typically quoted at LIBOR plus an additional rate (L+175 bps). Hundreds of cells down in the control sheet of the model are the LIBOR rates. In the top right corner of the first LIBOR cell is a small red triangle, indicating a note. I hit Shift F2 and read the note that explains the LIBOR curve was last updated over six months ago—*Aha!* I refresh the FactSet code of the cell, which in turn updates the entire LIBOR curve. Except this doesn't solve my problem. It worsens it. With interest rates rising over the past couple months, the LIBOR figure jumps twenty bps. This consequently lowers the paydown in both scenarios. I check the time in the bottom right corner of the monitor: 1:10 a.m.

"So answer this, Joel," says Leighton as I pass by the bullpen to get water. "Is an NOL a tax credit or a tax deduction? And what are the key differences?"

"What is, 'Who cares?'" I hear Joel say.

By 2:00 a.m., aside from the clattering of keyboards in the bullpen and some ambient light flooding out of its opening, the rest of the floor is dark and quiet.

In my cube, I stare at the LIBOR curve, for which there is a given rate for each duration, including overnight, one week, one month, two months, three months, six months, and one year. The LIBOR figure driving the rate in this model is the six-month rate. As the duration decreases, so too does the rate, which makes sense, since long-duration debt instruments typically command higher rates than shorter-dated ones due to greater interest-rate risk. What if the driver is the three-month LIBOR? I try it out—the paydown increases to 50 percent in both cases. The left side of my mouth curls into a half-grin. How about one-month LIBOR? Fifty-seven percent in both cases. The jump seems too big to justify. I settle on the three-month LIBOR[2] then turn my attention to the LTM EBITDA figure.

The note (which I wrote) in the cell references the LTM EBITDA figure. It comes from the company's latest confidential information memorandum. There's no changing that figure, which is presented by the company. But in the company's folder, I notice a recent management presentation I had only glossed through earlier. In the appendix on that presentation, there's an EBITDA reconciliation with a series of adjustments, which are the same as the ones found in the CIM, excluding one. The omission of the one adjustment means the LTM EBITDA in the MP is $6 million higher than the figure shown in the CIM.

Replacing the LTM EBITDA from the CIM with the figure from the MP[3] gets the paydown to 53 percent in both cases. At 2:48 a.m., I email Arthur and the team the updated paydown figures and then head home.

I arrive back at the office just over four hours later to dial into the previously scheduled 7:00 a.m. call, but it gets cancelled at 6:57 a.m. The corner offices are nearly all occupied at this time as MDs work the phones with their office doors closed, generating more work for those of us sitting vulnerable in the cubes. The floor itself

[2] And footnote the fuck out of it.
[3] Footnoted this fucker too.

is quiet, since junior bankers typically trickle in from 9:30 a.m. to 10:00 a.m.

Despite the call being cancelled, I sit at my desk from 7:00 a.m. till noon and field a maelstrom of emails from Arthur, instructing me to fund, defund, then refund the credit facility, increase the notes, decrease the term loan, and add a mezzanine piece. It's virtually a one-on-one exchange between Arthur and me, with the rest of the team cc'd on the emails. My response time to update the model and resend the outputs decreases each time a new request comes from Arthur.

"Look at you, balls-deep in that model," Ted says as he walks behind me at one point. I barely hear him as I send Arthur the most updated paydown figures.

13

Compliance King

"Pencils down," reads the email Arthur sends the team just before 1:00 p.m.

> **John Bukowski:** lunch time. Swing by my desk

> **William Keenan:** where you wanna go?

> **John Bukowski:** sandwich place on water and pine st

> **William Keenan:** that place blows

> **John Bukowski:** how bout new Mexican place on maiden lane. Couple laughs, couple cervezas

> **William Keenan:** I do banking and I do just fine for myself

> **John Bukowski:** we do the new Mexican place and that's what we do

William Keenan: it has a B rating

John Bukowski: who cares, get your affairs in order then swing by my desk

William Keenan: you swing by mine

John Bukowski: na, you swing

William Keenan: you swing

"Another head fake from TTZ," says Ethan, who materializes at my desk. He shifts his weight from side to side as he rolls up the sleeves of his light pink button-down shirt. "They'll pull this shit every once in a while, but we'll be in good spot when they pull the trigger. Lotta dry powder, but they weren't gonna write an equity check this size."

"Seemed aggressive, but I thought they've cut checks this size in the past," I say. It's like someone else is speaking through my mouth. I'm not even sure what I said makes sense.

"Paydown looked good to me, but you never know what these PE guys are up to. Sometimes it's a chess match with other guys—who's interested in what assets, bidding up price tags," says Ethan as he shakes his head, still shifting now front to back. "Hey, you mind if I get some juice for my phone?"

"BlackBerry or iPhone?" I reach down for the two chargers that I've plugged into my power strip under my desk.

"Berry." Ethan hands me the phone which I plug in. "What the hell's this?" he says, his eyes fixed to my computer monitor as I resurface from below my desk.

"Another deck I'm working on—regression analysis," I say.

"We do that shit?" Ethan shakes his head then walks away.

John Bukowski: starving. Swing

William Keenan: u swing

John Bukowski: swing with purpose and precision

William Keenan: swing with fervor and fury

"Watch your head, dude," says Ted as he sits, slowly wheeling his chair toward my cube. In his right hand is a markup of a pitch book, rolled up like a swatter. "Don't move…just landed on your shoulder." I freeze as he cocks his right arm and whacks my left shoulder. Then he slowly retracts the pitch book.

"Get it?" I ask.

"Yep," he says. "Fucker's been buzzing my tower all morning."

"Mosquito?"

"Na, they don't bite or anything. Just annoy the shit out of me. Pretty sure bullpen has the infestation with the goddamn leftover food in there all the time."

John Bukowski: swing

William Keenan: swing

John Bukowski: swing or I take you off my premium spotify family plan

William Keenan: be there in 2 mins

As I retrieve my wallet from my drawer, my desk phone rings.

"Hello?" I say.

"Am I speaking with Mister William Keenan?" says the voice on the other line.

"This is Bill."

"Good afternoon, Mister Keenan. My name is Jed, and I'm contacting you today in regard to the outstanding balance on your American Express card."

"Can you give me a minute, please?"

"Of course, Mister Keenan."

Rhonda, the administrator I've been assigned to, sits two rows of cubes away. I walk to her desk where she's mid-conversation, holding the phone receiver to her ear with her left hand and cupping her right hand over her mouth, though it does nothing to diminish the clarity of her words. "Don't give her that moment," she says in a hushed tone before spotting me. "I gotta go," she says before hanging up. Rhonda's cube tells the tale of someone whose tenure at the bank predates many of the senior MDs. A scripture labeled "Habakkuk 2:3" is pinned to the left of her monitor. To the right is a "serenity prayer," under which is a small piece of paper with bold, black letters reading, "Doesn't matter the method as long as you get the result."

"Hi, Rhonda," I say. "I've gotten a couple calls from American Express telling me I have an outstanding balance on my corporate card—"

She shakes her head in a knowing way and removes a notepad from her desk. In the same fancy font you'd see on monogrammed stationery, the words "Shit List" are embossed at the top of the sheet. "AmEx," she scrawls on the list while audibly exhaling. Above it, I recognize two other items on her list: "Delta" and "Ethan."

"You have any idea how to resolve it?" I say. "They said they're gonna charge some fee because I have an outstanding balance, but I haven't even used the card yet."

"They should waiver the fee," she says. "This happens sometimes. I'll try to get it sorted out, but if they call again, tell them they should know to waiver the fee."

"Thanks."

I return to my cube and put my headset back on. "You still there, Jed?"

"Yes, Mister Keenan."

"I was told to tell you that the fee should be waived. I was told I had an outstanding balance even before the card was given to me, so clearly there was a mistake on your end, not you personally, but AmEx messed up."

"Thank you for that clarification, Mister Keenan. I do see in your file that you have previously been contacted—"

"Yeah, a few times. Can you just please waive the fee and stop calling? This is getting ridiculous that you can't resolve it on your end. So please waive the fee, since I've been told you've done that in the past with DB AmEx corporate cards."

"May I place you a brief hold while I look into this?"

"No."

He puts me on hold. Instead of hanging up right away, I stumble upon an idea: instead of playing brutal elevator music while on hold, why not tell the person a story or a joke? Entertain me. I conjure up the mechanics of a licensing deal with a publishing house or Amazon for companies that rely on customer service. It's at about this point in one's banking experience that these start-up ideas generate at a torrid pace. They're then discussed over beers on Saturday nights with friend(s) and quickly forgotten by Sunday morning. Just another fantasy coping mechanism to help get through the week. After making a note of this genius idea on a Post-it, I'm about to hang up when—

"Mister Keenan, I do apologize for putting you on hold. We've sorted out the problem and fixed it. We here at American Express value you as a loyal customer."

"Great. I gotta go."

"Have a wonderful day, Mister Keenan."

> **John Bukowski:** de-activating your Spotify privileges in 3

> **John Bukowski:** 2

> **John Bukowski:** 1.5

> **John Bukowski:** 1

> **William Keenan:** coming

"Shitty sandwich place or Mexican?" asks Jack as we exit the building on the Wall Street side to a blustery September day. We pause outside the building as a gust of breeze funnels down the street from west to east.

"Too windy on Water Street," I say. "My hair's on point today—can't take any chances. How about the brutal buffet place on Exchange Place?"

"Line is always crazy long," says Jack.

"But ramen is decent."

"Fine."

"So what the hell did you do?" asks Jack. "You're the talk of the forty-fourth floor. That analyst who looks like a drill sergeant—"

"Leighton," I say.

"Yeah, he was talking to one of the VPs in your group who sits near me and singing your praises. Then I hear some other guy in your group asking about the new MBA associate who ran the model."

The sun peeks through the towering skyscrapers in the Financial District and shines on my face. "I guess you could say I'm glowing," I say. We enter the jammed buffet place, lower our heads, stick out our elbows, and make a straight line to the ramen-noodle station.

"I wish they could've seen you in training," says Jack. "You didn't know the difference between Word and Excel."

"You guys have flies on your side of the floor?" I ask after ordering a chicken ramen bowl.

"Seen a bunch in the bullpen but nothing near me really."

After receiving our bowls from the sweaty guy in an apron, Jack and I stand in the mass of people, which could serve as a business school case study on how to create a bottleneck.

"What're you staffed on?" I ask as we finally emerge onto the Wall Street sidewalk.

"I spent four-and-half hours this morning scouring the Internet for pictures and bios of board members for three private companies."

"You email BIS to see if they could find anything?"

"Obviously."

"You ever get calls from American Express about overdue charges?" I ask.

"No, but this guy from Northwestern Mutual calls me twice a week at 4:05 p.m. 'cause he thinks I work until the market closes or something. It's like my aunt who thinks I trade stocks for a living."

The ding of my BlackBerry is followed by some vibrating. I remove it from my pocket. "Fuck me," I say.

"Staffed?"

"Worse—gonna get a red flag if I don't complete those compliance bullshits by 5:00 p.m. today."

"The hell is a red flag?"

"No clue. Maybe three red flags and you get a stern talking to."

They hit your inbox once a week on average and are largely ignored, until one day an email with subject line: "URGENT— ACTION REQUIRED" pops up, accompanied by threats of flags in an assortment of colors. Today's task is completing the "Anti-Money Laundering" module. This is primarily an exercise in clicking your mouse[1] as quickly as possible. In previous modules, the "next" or "→" buttons were located in the bottom right of each slide. Since these modules were estimated to take thirty minutes to complete but were ultimately completed in two minutes, the format was changed. Not only do the "next" and "→" buttons pop up in random locations on each slide, but modules now end in a ten-question quiz. Plus, they incorporate these devastatingly slow transitions between slides.

As I return to my cube on the forty-fourth floor, Ted waits patiently for the competition to begin.

"Alright," says Ted as he pokes his head behind the partition and glances at my monitor. "Ready...set...comply!"

---

[1] One of the few times a junior banker can use his mouse without being lambasted by his peers.

We hit the "Begin Module" button simultaneously, and the race is on. The mouse clicks are rapid-fire. I rifle through the first three slides but lose ground on the fourth slide when the "→" button is camouflaged in the top right corner of the screen.

"Quiz time," says Ted, moments before I get to the ten-question quiz.

"Already on question three," I lie.

The first few questions are straightforward, along the lines of:

A potential client, who has no prior affiliation to Deutsche Bank Securities Inc. or any of its subsidiaries, calls and asks if you could help finance the acquisition of assets located in North Korea. He refuses to disclose any further information on the nature of the transaction. You should:

  A) Give him Deutsche Bank's most competitive financing rate and begin the CRM process.

  B) Ask for his name, and if it sounds normal, provide preliminary financing rates.

  C) Shoot the breeze with him and see if he sounds like a good guy. If so, offer to help.

  D) IMMEDIATELY CALL COMPLIANCE AND ALERT THEM TO SUSPICIOUS ACTIVITY.

But they get progressively more difficult. The required score to pass is 70 percent. Basic strategy says you sabotage the first attempt at the quiz. Since the module alerts you of the correct answer after each question, you can jot down the answer and ace it on the second attempt.

"C...A...A...D," I hear Ted mumble in his cube.

"Mother fu...nbags," I say as I narrowly miss passing the test on the first try. I'm redirected back to question one after the 60-percent score.

"Done!" says Ted. "And new PR: three minutes, thirteen seconds." He marks it on the sheet pinned to the inside of his cube. "Here's the thing, you develop instincts over time. As a senior associate, there are some things I just can't teach you, and one of them is knowing where to click on compliance-training modules. That said, I think you're looking at two guys who are fully compliant." He stretches out a reversed right hand, palm up, and I slap him five just as I'm notified of my 70 percent passing score.

* * *

"BlackBerry or iPhone?" I ask.

"iPhone," says Ethan. "Fuckin' battery is dog shit. I charged it an hour ago." I retrieve the charger hooked on my middle drawer handle and plug in his phone. As Ethan disappears into the bathroom, Joel jogs out of the bullpen, stops, and surveys the floor. He looks like a kid who just saw Mickey Mouse for the first time, though the stubble on his face ages him slightly. "Guys," he says with little success in garnering anyone's attention. "Guys!" he says louder this time, puffing his chest out and adjusting his tie, which features enormous footballs. Bart spins around in his chair. Ted continues to ignore him. I look up from my cube, as do Gareth and a few others who sit in the cubes one row over.

"Have you ever seen a term loan with grid pricing of a low single-B company trade at a discount?" Joel scans the faces of his audience. Gareth puts on his headset while Bart spins back around to face his computer.

"Sit down, Joel," says Leighton from the bullpen. "And yes, I've seen plenty." The bickering between Joel and Leighton subsides as my attention turns to the computer screen a row across from me, which determines my fate on a minute-to-minute basis.

"Uh-oh," says Ted.

"Yep," I say. "Not good."

One row of cubes over from Ted and me sits the group's staffer, a VP responsible for determining who has capacity to get staffed. He determines all workflow for junior bankers, and thus serves as the group's puppet master. His decisions determine the fate of weekend trips, friendships, relationships, and even marriages.

Raising the height of my chair slightly so I can peer over the cubicle divider, below is what I see on the staffer's left monitor:

It's the gray—unstaffed projects—that's terrifying. And let me tell you something, after the 1:00 p.m. "pencils down" from Arthur, I'm as vulnerable as it gets.

The staffer's phone rings. He picks up the receiver. "Hi…yes…I'm sorting it out now…I understand, working as quickly as possible… okay…understood." He returns his attention to the staffing log. The anticipation is all-consuming—I can barely focus on the episode of *Curb Your Enthusiasm* I have streaming in the lower right-hand corner of my left monitor.

John Bukowski: something's abrewing in industrials. Sounds bad

William Keenan: details pls

John Bukowski: just heard industrials MD in office behind me barking orders to get something staffed immediately (with fist pound)

William Keenan: pray for me

John Bukowski: na

It's like spotting an enemy sniper loading his rifle. The staffer cranes his neck from left to right. Then he types into one of the rows of gray cells, and although I'm too far to see names, someone's in for it. The next step is drafting an email to the targets.

"Christ," whispers Ted. "Lengthy fuckin' email—never good... ever."

I'm forced to pause the episode of *Curb* during the denouement, of all places.

"Already on fourth paragraph," I say to Ted.

"Fifth," he says. "If I had to guess, which I will, I'd say we're looking at a financing for a new client—full KYC, CRM from scratch with no prior model, Industrials doing everything, lev fin doing jack shit...looking at two fucked weekends, possibly three."

The staffer retracts his hands from the keyboard, then rereads the email before putting his hand on the mouse.

"Here it comes," I say.

But then the staffer stands, walks over to another VP, and they have a short exchange in hushed tones.

"Pure agony," says Ted. "Just toying with us."

After concluding their conversation with successive head nods, the staffer returns to his seat, puts his hand on the mouse, and clicks "SEND." The message disappears from his monitor, and I instinctively hold my breath.

One, one thousand.

Two, one thousand.

Three, one thousand.

Four, one tho—

"You gotta be kidding me," says a voice in the cube across from me. Bart slowly rises beside the constant stream of steam produced by his humidifier.

"Was I right—new client, financing?" asks Ted.

"Spot-on," says Bart. "At least I don't have to go to the in-laws this weekend in Poughkeepsie." Bart shrugs, pops a couple pills from an unmarked prescription bottle, then washes them down with black coffee from his DB mug.

"Who's the analyst?" ask Ted.

"Barty boy!" says Joel as he struts out of the bullpen. "Looks like a nice, juicy term loan." Joel rubs his hands together as he approaches Bart's desk.

I fight off a smile as I lower my seat and nestle down in my trench. Joel and Bart's conversation, sorting out who's doing what, fades as I put my earbuds in and resume the episode of *Curb*.

14

Dentist Appointments

"Everyone have a handout?" asks Tom McNamara, the building's chief of safety, who I recognize from the first day of the internship. He's met with some nods and a few verbal affirmations from the group of junior bankers on the forty-fourth floor.

"Good. I'll make this quick. I know you guys got paperwork and whatnot to get to." He runs his finger up the page in his hand and squints through the glasses that sit on the bridge of his nose. "What we have here is an infestation of Indian meal moths. These suckers can lay up to five hundred eggs in their lifecycle so...let's see," he says scanning down the page, using his finger as a guide. "Green hues, cracks and crevices, prevention...look, old containers of food, pizza boxes, empty soda cans—these items need to be thrown into a receptacle—can't be left around on counters anymore. We had the same issue on forty-five last year." Tom points up with his right hand. "Winter's almost here—cooler weather will help eliminate these suckers, but won't kill 'em all. My guys are coming in Saturday night to fumigate. Real important to keep it spick-and-span as best you can from here on out, especially once they're done extermi-nating." He looks up from the piece of paper and surveys the room. "Any questions?" he asks. Most everyone's head is buried in his BlackBerry. "Going once...twice...all right, thanks."

"BK," says Joel as the meeting adjourns. "Wanna go over the markup?"

"Let's do it." I grab a pen from my desk and meet Joel at the middle counter in the bullpen, where he's waiting with two printed copies of the markup for a recent automotive M&A pitch we got staffed on.

"Notice anything new?" asks Joel, flashing a big grin, like a kid trying to show off losing a tooth.

"New tie?"

"No! Up there," says a beaming Joel, pointing to the wall. "New torn sleeve—fourth one."

"Nice...how's the deck looking?" I say, tapping the markup we received earlier in the day.

"I got this page," says Joel as he flips the first page. "Got this, and this too." He flips a couple more pages. "Section two...alright." He flips through the next five pages. "I'll send this to MAKS."

"The whole section?" I ask.

Joel keeps flipping through the pages. "Yeah, and section three too."

"Works for me."

Joel continues flipping through the deck. "Section four...can have MAKS do this too. I'll send this one page to Presentations—they can make it look fancy."

"Or you could actually do some work instead of outsourcing everything," Leighton says from his cube.

"I'm helping global GDP when I send those requests. It creates jobs and drives the economy," retorts Joel. The two rarely have an exchange facing one another.

Joel reaches the end of the markup. "I can shoot those emails to MAKS and Presentations now, and then put together those first couple pages—pretty sure I saw them in a book someone was working on last week."

"Great."

"And just so you know—I have a dentist appointment this afternoon, so I'll be off the desk for a couple hours, but will have my BlackBerry on me."

"Sounds good."

"Yeah, just routine cleaning."

"Anything I can do to help on the deck?"

Joel shrugs, and says in a louder voice: "You could explain equity-method accounting to Leighton, since he has no clue—"

Leighton spins in his chair at this jab, and I dart out of the bullpen and back to my desk before getting caught in the crossfire.

> **John Bukowski:** the admin who sits near me has a swear jar. She just nabbed me for 50 cents for saying "damn"

> **William Keenan:** if she sat next to ethan, she could retire by EOD

> **John Bukowski:** how'd you do on last compliance module?

> **William Keenan:** 4 minutes 17 seconds. You?

> **William Keenan:** ???

> **John Bukowski:** 4 mins 16 sec

"You pay for that thing?" asks Ted, pointing to the power strip by my feet.

"Yeah, why?"

"Could probably get it expensed," he says. A BlackBerry and an iPhone are plugged into the chargers attached to my power strip. I make a face as I remove my phones from my pants pocket. "Ethan," says Ted.

"You ever work with Betty?" I ask.

"You staffed with her?"

I nod.

"Lucky you," he says.

"Second-year analyst?"

"Third. She went home last year for Chinese New Year and had visa issues getting back to the US. The entire Industrials group literally ground to a halt without her. She's a beast," says Ted. "There's a reason this group has set new records in revenues at the bank the past three years. And she's almost entirely responsible for this one director getting promoted early to MD."

I open the email from the VP who's working on the project with me and Betty to sort out what needs to be done. After a couple hours of compiling relevant old spreadsheets and presentations, and downloading the company's financials, I open the Excel backup I found that seems most applicable to the project.

Phuc materializes at my desk. "You jammin'?" he asks. His tie is securely tied, but instead of hanging down the center of his shirt, it is flung over his right shoulder, a tactic employed by several MDs when they take a leak at the urinal. Phuc has misinterpreted it as a sign of seniority.

"Yeah, what's up?" I ask.

"Thinking of dressing up for Halloween this year. I heard all first-years are supposed to. You got any ideas for costumes?"

"Yeah, analyst promote," I say.

"How you gonna—"

"You need something, Phuc? Trying to do some work here." I fumble through some more files in search of anything useful I can do before touching base with Betty.

"Live deal?"

"Another pitch," I say as I open up a PowerPoint of a prior deck for the company Betty and I are working with on this project.

Phuc shakes his head, then mindlessly pulls out the pushpins that hold up my sheet of Excel shortcuts. He then pushes them back in without looking, rendering the sheet crooked.

"You got the life, man," he says. "I got two live projects—been here past 3:00 a.m. last four nights." I refrain from engaging in this game, but I remember passing Phuc's cube the other night around 10:00 p.m. and he was long gone—I heard his analyst complaining to someone about it.

"Wouldn't say I have 'the life,'" I say as my PowerPoint suddenly freezes.

"You don't have anything live—" he begins.

"It's a live pitch, okay Phuc?" I make eye contact with him and then remove his hand from the pushpin he's fiddling with. "Now I got shit to do. If your live deals are so brutal, maybe you go back to work." Phuc makes a face and walks away.

Fired up from my daily dose of Phuc, and fortified with some confidence generated over my first few months of banking, I zip around the spreadsheet using the Ctrl key, which acts like a turbo booster to jump from cell to cell. Within seconds, I'm in cell XFD 1048576—the Siberia of the spreadsheet. And I'm not talking Omsk; I'm talking Кемеровская область. I reach for my mouse and scroll up desperately, then back to the arrow pad, striking the ↑ key repeatedly, but I am still light-years from home—cell A 1.

"Fuckin' A," I say. "How in the hell do I—"

> **Yu Yan (Betty) Liang:** Hi Bill!

> **William Keenan:** hey, what's going on?

> **Yu Yan (Betty) Liang:** I saw you created a new folder for our project. Thanks so much!

> **William Keenan:** No problem

> **Yu Yan (Betty) Liang:** Can you please get out of the master Excel and PPT files and I will start work on it?

> **William Keenan:** sure

> **Yu Yan (Betty) Liang:** Thanks! :)

Only one person can edit a given file at a time. I don't even bother hitting "save" on the two files before closing them.

"All good?" asks Ted.

"Check this out," I say. Ted scoots over and reads my office-communicator exchange with Betty.

"Did you feel it?" he asks.

"What?"

"The bitch-slap she unleashed on you," he says, squinting at my screen from behind my left shoulder. "Here's what you do: open up a 'read-only' of the backup and get some reps in while Betty does the heavy lifting. Can't do any damage in a 'read-only.'"

Three hours and two "read-only" copies later, I take a break to stretch my legs and walk a lap around the office before returning to my cube.

"You hear from Ethan today? He said he was gonna send some comments through this morning," I say to Ted.

"He's probably at his country club sipping Mojitos," says Ted.

"Would be nice if he showed a pulse," I say.

"That would imply he was human."

> **John Bukowski:** incominggggggggggggg

> **William Keenan:** who?

> **John Bukowski:** huge analyst in your group who looks like he should be holding a cherry popsicle

> **William Keenan:** joel

John Bukowski: strutting in with all sorts of confidence. Like winking and tapping top of people's cubes as he walks by 'em

John Bukowski: rounding corner in 4

John Bukowski: 3

John Bukowski: 2

John Bukowski: s**t. he just stopped to talk to admin

John Bukowski: okay...rounding in 2

John Bukowski: 1

John Bukowski: now!

William Keenan: got him

I tilt my head up and catch Joel as he emerges from the the far side of the floor, grinning ear-to-ear as he finger-guns someone.

"Where the hell has he been?" asks Ted from his cube.

"Dentist appointment," I say.

"Welp, he's gone," says Ted.

"Gone where?"

"Private equity, maybe hedge fund."

"After a dentist visit?"

"What'd he say it was for?"

"Routine cleaning."

Ted wheels around into my cube. "Then ask him where his little goody bag is, the one you always get after a teeth cleaning...and when's the last time you saw him clean-shaven?"

"Any cavities?" I ask Joel as I enter the bullpen.

"All clear." Joel runs the tip of his tongue over his top row of teeth. "MAKS said they can get us those pages by tomorrow morning and Presentations will send over their stuff by 6:00 p.m."

"Nice. They give you any floss at the dentist's? Got prosciutto or something stuck in my teeth from lunch and can't get it out," I say.

"Hate when that happens." Joel reaches into his jacket pockets then his pants pockets. "Shit, must've tossed the baggie they gave me. Let me check though..." Joel opens one of his desk drawers. "Think I have some somewhere in here."

* * *

Her cube is more furnished than my apartment. Below her desk is a mini fridge, fully stocked with Tazo Organic Iced Green Teas and a leftover salad from the night before. Next to the fridge is a pair of sneakers poking out of a duffel bag. In the large drawer to her left is a change of clothes, an umbrella, plastic cutlery, a full set of Tupperware, and a forensic-accounting textbook. To the right of her monitors on her desk is a Sperti Vitamin D lamp; to the left is a bamboo plant. Surrounding the plant is a collection of deal toys—a formidable collection for even a senior VP, let alone an analyst. Pinned to the side of her cube is a picture of five pint-sized girls in caps and gowns following college graduation. But that's not the most prominent picture in her cube.

"What's his name?" I ask.

"*Her* name," she says. "It's Gummi—she's a Shiba Inu." Betty smiles at the pictures, then at me, an eager smile that belies the puffy eyes from frequent all-nighters. Her jet-black hair is cut straight across in the back just above her shoulders, and her bangs cut a straight line just above her eyebrows. There's a hollow sink to her drained, yet hopeful, eyes, which feature dark crescents underneath them.

Betty picks up her iPhone, swipes and taps it, then angles it toward me. On the screen is a live feed of Gummi, sprawled on a kitchen floor, enclosed in a large exercise pen. "Tap this button," she says pointing to a little yellow graphic in the shape of a doggie bone. I do as I'm told, and up jumps Gummi, scampering to gather the treat that darts out of some device.

"Wow," I say as I ready my finger to tap the button again.

Betty retracts her phone. "Only one. Can't spoil her."

"Makes sense."

"Do you want to go through the deck?" she offers, referring to the deck she completed by herself.

"Sure." I pull up one of the stray swivel chairs in the bullpen and roll up behind her. Her fingers dance across her keyboard as spreadsheets and PowerPoint files dart from one monitor to another. The screen is a blur of web pages, PDFs of company filings and research reports, Excel files, PPT presentations, and utter chaos—to me, not to Betty.

Seconds later, the left monitor displays the PPT presentation titled "Discussion Materials" while the other monitor shows the Excel backup.

"Okie dokie," says Betty. "Let's start from the beginning."

"Project Diamondback: URGENT client request" reads the subject of a new email notification that appears in her bottom right monitor.

"I can come back later if you need to deal with that," I say.

"They can wait," she says.

Over the next three hours, twenty-three emails of increasing urgency for Projects Sox, Vector, and Crest hit Betty's inbox, none of which she acknowledges. Instead, she walks me through our entire deck, sensing the questions posed by my facial expressions. She slowly explains where each number came from, how she created each chart, and the rationale for setting up certain things in such a way to create a more dynamic spreadsheet to expedite future changes when comments inevitably come from the senior bankers. Armed with ten pages of notes that are worthy of lamination and a Tazo Organic Iced Green Tea that Betty wouldn't permit me not to take, I return to my desk around 5:15 p.m.

How I, as an associate, get paid twice as much as her makes no sense.

* * *

There's a dead period each day in the early evening. MDs, at least the ones who show up to the office, typically trickle home between 5:00 and 7:00 p.m. Accordingly, once turning the latest set of comments from their MDs in the evening, juniors often enjoy a reliable hour or two of respite before the night shift commences. While not as reliable as true clockwork, it's as close to a predictable daily occurrence as it gets for a junior banker. Some juniors hit one of the two gyms located on Wall Street, and others meet up with their significant others—who are usually bankers in the same bank, if not the same group. There's an outside chance it's a banker from another firm, a relationship facilitated by a Merrill DataSite party.

A couple juniors undoubtedly will take the elevator down ten flights and catch a quick nap in one of the few beds located next to the nurse's room. Betty usually uses this time to dart home and take Gummi to the South Street Seaport dog park, after which she'll return to the office in sweats and sneakers. A tad casual, you may say?

"If you could do what Betty does, feel free to wear assless chaps and a cowboy hat," Ted notes. While the majority of junior bankers use this lull in work to reacquaint themselves with the outside world, there's always a group who uses this period to catch up on emails or rework a model to make it more dynamic. Today I'm in the group that remains planted in their seats as I comb through the Excel and PPT files prepared by Betty, performing small fist pumps as I successfully work to recreate certain charts and reconcile the countless numbers. For the first time in months on the job, I sense progress.

Around 7:00 p.m., a stream of analysts with flushed cheeks, wet hair, and DB gym bags slung over their shoulders return to the floor as do a few other juniors with wrinkled shirts and slightly less hollow-looking eyes than they had an hour prior.

John Bukowski: I'm swinging by you with clarity and consensuality

William Keenan: no. I'm working

John Bukowski: gotta use bathroom

William Keenan: 1 or 2?

John Bukowski: 3. Get timer ready pls

Jack rounds the corner seconds later. "I hate when you do that furrowed brow look like you're cranking on work," he says as he approaches my desk.

"I hate when you say 'cranking,'" I say before raising my hands to the ceiling, arching my back slightly, and stretching upwards.

"You could at least look presentable," he says. "You got stopwatch ready?" He lines up just in front of the bathroom entrance, one foot slightly in front of the other.

"I'm as presentable as it gets," I say, before tapping the timer app of my iPhone.

"Not with that torn-up shirt, bitch." Jack pushes open the bathroom door as I twist my arm and eye the tear in the elbow of my shirtsleeve with a smile.

15

[TBU]

"Pine Street or Wall Street?" I ask into the phone.

"YES!" screams the muffled voice on the other line.

"Sorry, so you're on Pine—"

"YES!" says the voice.

"You have to go to Wall Street side. Pine Street closes at si—"

"YES! ON STREET NOW!"

"Fuck it," I say as I hang up the receiver, grab my wallet from the drawer, and head to the lobby. Once there, I walk to the roped-off area blocking the Pine Street exit, which closes at 6:30 p.m. No sign of the delivery guy.

Walking through the elevator bank to the Wall Street side, I pass two fellow associates from other groups. We exchange head nods as one mutters something about "getting *crushed*," but I don't catch it all, because I'm busy not caring. I hear another utter, "Forty-seven days," a reference to how long until we get our bonuses. Whatever gets you through the day.

Once through the revolving doors, a flurry of snowflakes greets me, as does a biting wind that immediately makes me regret my decision to leave my jacket upstairs.

The line of delivery guys, half on foot and half on bikes, is no fewer than ten across and two deep. Across from them are a group of six or so bankers, who are cautiously approaching.

"Roast!" yells one delivery guy. He's met with a series of head-shakes, before a small Asian girl in an enormous jacket scurries toward him and takes a big brown bag.

"Chopt!" yells another guy. More shaking heads, before a guy who's far too young to be bald walks up to grab his food.

"Neapolitan Pizza!" Another guy's hand shoots up before he scampers up to retrieve his food. It's Seamless bingo.

"China Fun!"

"Harry's Italian!"

"Luke's Lobster!"

"Oaxaca Taqueria!"

The snowflakes accumulate quickly on my head, and blowing hot air into my cupped hands isn't doing shit. I pace quickly up and down the row of delivery guys as they announce their employer, most in heavy accents, and simultaneously show me the receipts for clarification.

I check my phone—7:17 p.m.—five minutes since I was told the guy was on the street. I retreat inside, hurry through the long elevator bank, and check the Pine Street side again—nothing.

I return across the way and wait just inside the revolving doors on the Wall Street side. A few more minutes pass until I see a figure emerge, pedaling his bike in the distance, approaching the mass of delivery guys. I recognize him—my guy. I time my exit just as he engages his hand brake.

"Barbalu!" he yells as he hits the kick stand on his bike.

"Yep!" I yell as I run out to meet him. "Jumped the gun a little on the call," I say, not entirely expecting him to hear or understand.

"I was on street!" he says.

"I literally just saw you bike up."

"Johnson?" he says, displaying one of the receipts stapled to a large paper bag.

"Keenan," I say. He rummages through a couple more bags, then shows me another receipt.

"Keenan, Williams!" he says eyeing another receipt.

"Yep, here." I grab the bag from his hand. As I turn around, water dripping from my eyelashes and snowflakes covering my head and body, I hear him behind me.

"Barbalu! Johnson! Barbalu!"

Opening the brown paper bag at my desk is always an event rife with anticipation. After five months of ordering dinner every weeknight to work, I know the items on the receipt rarely resemble the items in the bag—no utensils or bread today, which wouldn't piss me off aside from the fact that I specifically asked for "extra bread" and received none.

"Joel!" I yell from my cube.

"Ketchup?" he yells back from the bullpen.

"Utensils and bread!" I say.

"Got 'em!"

I walk into the bullpen. On Joel's desk is a set of wrapped plastic utensils, a couple pieces of bread wrapped in tin foil, and a small plastic container of olive oil.

"Bread's from yesterday, so should be fine," says Joel nabbing my arrival in his rear-view mirror. As I swipe the items off his desk, he spins around in his chair. "Wait. You fill out your size yet? Ordering tomorrow." He retrieves two sheets of paper from his desk and hands them to me. "Got final designs back yesterday. Went with the zipper pockets—pretty money, huh?"

"You said they run a little large, right?" I say, looking at the graphic of a gray vest with black trim and "Deutsche Bank Industrials Banking Group" embroidered on the left breast. There is no chance I will ever wear this thing.

"A smidge in the mid-section," says Joel. I find my name on the list and check off "large" under size and "one" under quantity before handing the papers back to Joel.

"Ted," shouts Joel. Across the bullpen, Ted is propped on the desk of another analyst going over a markup.

"You fill this out yet? For the vests," says Joel.

"You've asked me five times. Filled it out already," says Ted. He returns to his discussion with the analyst he's working with before lifting his head back up. "Hey Joel. Was mulling this over and think you should go in a different direction with the gear: forget the vest; how about *just* sleeves?"

"I like that idea," says an analyst who pops his head up from his cube.

"Me too," says another analyst in the bullpen.

"It's settled. Your vest idea sucks. We just want sleeves," says Ted.

"You're *so* funny, Ted. The funniest managing associate on the Street," says Joel.

"Watch yourself or I'll get you staffed to the gills so you won't know which direction is up," says Ted. "How much are these vests anyway?"

"Fifty bucks plus tax," says Joel.

"Pretty steep. You getting your beak wet on this deal?" says Ted.

In the back of the bullpen, Betty sits, her head silhouetted against the two bright monitors in front of her. I've yet to properly thank her for helping me with our project a few weeks prior. As I approach, her phone rings.

"我不想要酱汁!" Betty yells into the phone. "你不会阅读笔记!" I inch nearer, but silently, so as not to draw attention to myself. Betty opens Yelp and drafts a scathing review of "#1 Chinese Restaurant."

* * *

They take the training wheels off at the six-month mark. The days of getting staffed alongside senior associates are over, as is the safety net of getting senior analysts on all staffings. And if we truly learn more from our failures than our successes, I should be a financial whiz by now. I'm not.

Of more concern, the quantity of work gradually inflates from just a couple projects at a given time to having to juggle four to six staffings. While projects vary widely in workload, they're like ticking bombs, exploding your weekend when you least expect it.

After mumbling some obscenities targeted at Barbalu's executive and sous chefs, given the portion size and lukewarm temperature of my pasta Bolognese, I eye the Post-it affixed to the bottom of my right computer monitor outlining my to-do items for the rest of the night.

Up first is turning comments for an equity pitch for a shipping company. I review the latest set of comments from both the VP and the MD. More often than not, comments from the VP and MD on the same project will directly contradict one another. The VP wants page seven to say X, while the MD wants it to say Y. Ultimately, the final page will say Y, or actually Z when it changes at midnight the night of printing. Regardless, juniors have to somehow incorporate both X and Y in prior turns of the deck to appease both the VP and MD, after which we will be berated. But in an incredible six-sigma event, I cross-reference the VP's latest comments with the MD's comments, and they match.

But of greater importance is the type of comments. I mark each page of the deck after reading the corresponding comments. Like *Barstool*, often the comments are the most entertaining part of the whole thing. A smile grows with each page I turn. If done properly, I can outsource nearly every page of this deck to the various resources we have at our disposal.

I draft up four new emails to the following resources—presentations services, MAKS analytics, FactSet, and BIS. Within seconds, they all respond with customary auto replies explaining they're working over capacity and will get to my request ASAP. "I hope this is fine," end most of these emails. It's not fine; quite frankly, it's BS.

I grab my headset and get to work.

"Thank you for calling presentations services, this is Michelle, how may I help you?" says the voice on the line.

"Hi, yeah, can I get connected to the person working on my request I just put in—it's number three, nine, four, five, nine, eight."

"Just a moment," she says.

"This is Suvarna from presentations services. How may I help, Mister Keenan?"

"Following up on the request I sent over a couple minutes ago."

"Yes."

"Want to make sure it's clear. Those logos on the page need to be sized exactly the same size and left-aligned. And the colors, especially the green and orange on that page, need to be DB color palette—looks a little off now. On the second page, the fonts need to be conformed, and can you just make the page look prettier? It's all jumbled, spacing's fucked up. Third page, just leave the boxes blank, but can you make sure the charts are same size in all four quadrants? That stacked bar chart in bottom left looks stretched. They're not pasted as images, so you should be able to make that change. If not, I can send the Excel backup."

"Yes, Mister Keenan. I've got it. I will be in touch should any questions come up."

"Great, thanks."

Click.

I spiral some spaghetti on my plastic fork as I type "[TBU—from prez]"[1] in a text box on the top left of the page in the shell of the pitch book. Then I look up the MAKS phone number on the page pinned to my cube.

"Hello and thank you for contacting MAKS analytics," says the voice.

"Parin?" I say.

---

[1] You put [TBU] (to be updated) text boxes on pages so others working on the deck know which pages are incomplete. These can be tricky, though. You can put [TBU] on a page, meaning it's someone else's problem, and five hours later, that someone is you.

"This is Ashu. Parin is not yet in the office."

"Hey Ashu. What's up, it's Bill Keenan from Industrials."

"Hello, William. How may I help you?"

"Just a couple follow ups on that request I sent for the shipping companies. I was spot-checking some of the comps and saw, for example, that you previously used latest 10-K for the ASC financials. They released an 8-K a couple weeks ago and pretty sure they filed a 424b3 within the last month. Both those files should have more updated financials. Can you just go back through all the comps and make sure you check all public filings for latest financials?"

"I do apologize for this, William. I will ensure all financial figures for comparable companies reflect most updated filings," says Ashu.

"No problem. Would be great to have updated stuff by tomorrow morning around 9:00 a.m., my time," I say.

"Of course."

"Thanks."

Click. [TBU—from MAKS].

Next: FactSet.

"Thank you for calling FactSet. If you know your serial number, please ent—" says the automated voice. I enter the seven-digit code.

"This is Julie. Am I speaking with William Keenan?"

"Hey, yeah. Was hoping I could send over a list of companies and have you guys make a stock-price chart and some multiples charts."

"Sure, William. Can you provide a little more detail on the charts you'd like?"

"I just sent over an email like ten minutes ago but can send it to you individually."

"That would be terrific," she says. I send her the email outlining the exact parameters of the four charts I need her to make.

"Basically need standard five-year and LTM stock-price charts with target company, its comps, and S&P. Then a TEV/NTM multiple progression chart," I say.

"Just received it," she says. "Okay, this shouldn't be a problem. I can either create these as active graphs or static—"

"Honestly, don't give a shit. Just need them in next couple hours."

"Not a problem. Thanks for choosing FactSet. Have a good rest of your night."

"What're you up to this weekend?"

"Sorry?"

Click. [TBU—from FactSet (Julie S.—sounds cute, follow up)].

More spaghetti twirling and more Bolognese sauce splattered over my shirt—should've gone with penne.

> **Srinivasulu Laxminarayana:** Hello, William Keenan

> **William Keenan:** I'm gonna call. What's your number

> **Srinivasulu Laxminarayana:** My name is Srinivasulu Laxminarayana. I am contacting you in reference to your recent inquiry to Global BIS, job P17DGL2876.

> **William Keenan:** phone # pls

> **Srinivasulu Laxminarayana:** +91 11 63230132 ext. 895938365

> **William Keenan:** Christ almighty

> **Srinivasulu Laxminarayana:** I look forward to speaking with you.

"Hello. This is Srinivasulu Lax—"

"Hey, it's Bill Keenan. Just was messaging with you," I say into my headset. "For that request I sent, please use all available resources to get rates for the markets. Every and all regions you can find. Also, please pull average annual historical prices, last twenty years I'd say, for those four products I put in the email. Need this by tonight."

"I will surely complete this as soon as possible and look forward to your valuable feedback, William."

"Thanks."

Click. [TBU—from BIS].

Now, an argument could be made that I could complete the above tasks myself quicker than it takes to explain to four different people around the world how to do it. But I don't have Leighton's facility and expertise with Excel and PPT, or his financial acumen. Thus, that argument is void and can kiss my tuchus. Plus, I have other shit to do.

Next on the to-do list is fixing a page for a client whose LBO we're leading. The page consists of an overview (half historical, half projected) of data for various commodity prices. I originally created the page a month ago, after which we received a "pencils down" on the project. A few weeks later, pencils were back up on the project, so our MD now wants the page from a month ago to be updated. Take a gander at this chart:

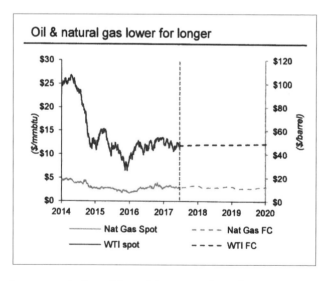

That vertical, dotted line delineates where historical info ends and projected numbers start. So what we're talking about is updating a month of historical information, which will have the effect of pushing that vertical line micro-millimeters to the right, while also turning a miniscule amount of the horizontal dark and light lines from dotted to solid, because previously projected numbers will now be historical. I have three options:

1. Don't update anything since the changes are so miniscule. Seems safe at first glance. However, when the VP compares the updated page versus the old page in PDF format, he'll be able to quickly determine if any change was made. Thus, I need to show a change.

2. Revisit the Excel backup notes and find updated pricing information for the last month—not to mention projected figures—though those shouldn't change much. The issue here is that the page consists of eight of these charts, meaning eight different commodities to analyze. On top of that, most of the charts show the prices of that commodity in different regions. You want to find prices of heavy naphtha in southeast Asia for the last month? I'm looking at a combination of battling the Bloomberg Terminal, scouring the IHS database, combing through equity and industry research reports, and so forth. Inevitably, all the data will be in different units, so then there's converting yuan per ton, or God knows what, to some standard USD metric. BIS could help pull some of these numbers, but even Bart doesn't have enough prescription medicine to deal with the headache that would create.

3. Nowhere in The DB Way, a three-hundred-plus page document distributed to all new hires outlining best practices, will you find an endorsement for using the Paint tool. Now, I never read The DB Way, but I did Ctrl F and search "paint," and it ain't there. Would Leighton go into cardiac arrest if he knew what I was considering? Absolutely. But I'm eyeing an early exit for the first night in months, and this goddamn page isn't going to stop me, not tonight. Paint tool it is.

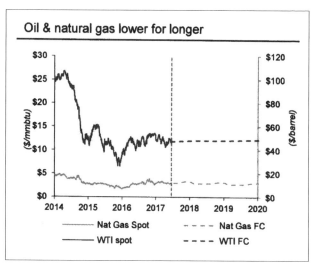

Old Deck

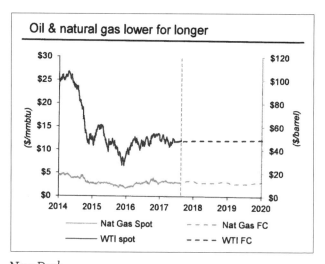

New Deck

There's a difference in the charts, and the VP will see it when he toggles between the two PDF versions to ensure it's been updated. How do I know he'll toggle and check? 'Cause that's what VPs do.

After a lightning-quick Google search to ensure nothing crazy happened in the last month to materially impact the prices of the various commodities, I reason that a bullshit commodity-outlook page in a deck that the company's management (let alone the PE firm) will probbaly not even look at is not going to stop the transaction from happening.

This is all to say that the key to successful investment banking is working backward. You don't draw conclusions based on the the data in front of you. You draw conclusions based on what clients want (or on what you, as a banker, want clients to want), and then you cherry-pick data and figures to justify the conclusion to avoid MDs blowing up at you.

Speaking of explosions, the model an analyst just sent me to "check" is riddled with landmines—hidden rows, sticky-ifs, self-referencing formulas, nested statements, macros running up the wazoo, not to mention the plethora of circularity switches—it's the North Korean side of the DMZ.

What does this all mean? One wrong tap of the keyboard, and this model containing thirty-three sheets and thousands of unique numbers (many of which are dependent on formulas that run three lines long) will turn into an endless sea of cells displaying "#REF." I arrow over to one cell in blue font indicating a hard code and highlighted yellow indicating double trouble. "Shift F2" opens the note—"as per client call." I close the comment box and continue exploring the model. It's only a matter of time before there's bloodshed. My pinkie slips, hitting ENTER on the wrong cell, and the model "REFS" out.

"What's up?" says my analyst, answering on the first ring.

"Hey, man. I sent this model to the guys in lev fin 'cause they wanted to make a change on the financing stuff. They just sent it back to me, and of course it's reffed out," I say.

"Again?" says my analyst. "Those guys are killin' us."

"Asinine, I know. Can you take a look and see if you can fix it? I'm working through some stuff on another deck. Everything else looked good, so once you get it fixed, just send it back to lev fin."

"Sure."

Crisis averted.

I dip the final piece of bread into the container of olive oil and scarf it down as I admire my handiwork. Then I throw my suit jacket over my right forearm.

As I'm about to leave, a new email from an MD pops up—subject line: "What are covenants on secured debt, breakage costs etc," while the body of the email is empty. These "one-off" requests are a staple of MDs. At least this guy fires off a question which has an answer I can find. The beauty of deals is the number of motivated individuals at the law firms. And the beauty of business school is that while it doesn't teach you to become smart, it does teach you how to identify those individuals who are smart: lawyers.[2] I copy the text from the subject line of the MD's email into the body of a new email, then add a greeting and sign-off. Then it's a quick consultation of the deal's WGL (working group list), where I copy the email of every lawyer whose title is associate and paste them into the "To" line of the email. I get four breathtakingly comprehensive responses (100 percent conversion) within five minutes. The text of the most comprehensive response is then copied and pasted in a response to my MD's original email. And presto, I investment banked.

Suit jacket back on my right forearm, and off I go.

You get dirty looks from other juniors any time you leave before 10:00 p.m., so instead of looping around the floor to the elevator bank where I'm exposed, I lower my head and dart for the emergency stairwell a few steps from my cube to walk down a flight of stairs, then take the elevator from the forty-third floor to the lobby.

"Must be nice," says Joel as I open the stairwell door at 9:38 p.m.

"It is," I say just before the door slams.

It's a six-and-a-half-minute walk home. I make it in five tonight. Alone in the one-bedroom flex walk-up I share with one

---

[2] Plus, the hottest girl I know is a lawyer (hope she sees this and sends me nudes).

of my college roommates, I take inventory of my life. Since banking started six months ago, I've lost touch with most of my friends. My desire to go out on free weekends has diminished. The last time I went out to dinner on a Saturday I was so preoccupied with the poor formatting of the menu and the fact the text describing the entrees and appetizers wasn't left-aligned that my friends threatened to cut ties with me. I know I'm learning stuff at work; I'm just not sure if it's anything I *want* to be learning. There are times when I wonder what my motivation is for doing this job, the real motivation—not the one I tell people or myself—but the deep-rooted one. Then there are times like this, when I look out the fourth-story window of our 550-square-foot apartment. In the dark room, I step over my bed, which sits on a box spring on the floor, moving toward my one window to the beat of the unrelenting hammer of my radiator. Taking in the view of the empty parking lot vandalized by tons of graffiti and the homeless person urinating on the side of a dumpster, I think to myself, *Not bad for a kid from the Upper East Side.*

16

Running with the Process

In college, my roommates and I would return to our dorm from hockey practice around 7:00 p.m., at which point we would order buffalo-chicken calzones, briefly consider opening a textbook, then power on our Xbox 360 and play *Call of Duty 2*, where I'd serve my country proudly for the next five hours. The night would typically conclude with a two-on-two team death-match in Vossenack. You could arm me with the bowie knife, that bullshit pistol, no 'nades, and spawn me in the crosshairs of my opponent's scoped Kar89k rifle, and I'd still finish the game with the most kills. I say this not to be a blowhard. My point is that after five hours of *COD* each night, you start seeing red dots in your sleep, a result of using the scope feature on many of the guns in the game. The frequency of red dot appearances in my dreams subsided once I graduated and henceforth focused my attention on *NHL 10*.

But it's back.

Despite its modest dimensions, the work BlackBerry determines not only the fate of my weekends, but every move I make—in short, my hopes and dreams. More specifically, it's the red blinking dot in the top right corner of my BlackBerry—illuminating at the arrival of a new email—that haunts my sleep these days. There are two types of emails you get as a junior banker: the bullshit emails and the horrific ones. The bullshit emails cast a wide net—anything from DB propaganda pushing corporate responsibility or an exciting opportunity to volunteer painting murals at P.S. 17 (at noon on a weekday??) to the daily EIA coal pricing updates that I signed up for during my internship in a misguided attempt to make it look like I really cared. The only thing sadder than the person reading those emails is the person who writes them.

The bullshit emails are also comprised of auto-replies from my brethren at MAKS analytics, BIS, Presentation services, and FactSet, as well as email blasts from fellow junior bankers in desperate need of some page their MD claims was already created in another deck. Spoiler alert: it was probably never created. Seeing one of these bullshit emails in my BlackBerry inbox over the weekend results in a sigh of relief and is subsequently ignored.

But then there are the horrific ones—the ones you can't ignore. These are sent by your MD or VP. If you're lucky they'll tell you to "change this," "do that," or "fix them." That's best-case scenario, when the demands are relatively clear. Of greater concern are the emails with comments like "makes no sense," "WTF?," or my personal favorite: "???????" While the level of guidance and method of conveying disapproval varies, the message is always the same— get to the office and turn these comments immediately, or the world will end.

So when the morning sun floods into my room on a frosty Sunday and wakes me from my Saturday-night stupor, my first instinct is to eye the square black device on my nightstand. As expected, the red dot blinks, just as it did in my sleep, but the question remains—bullshit or horrific? I type in my password with bated breath and check the inbox. The verdict is in: this Sunday will not be a day of rest.

The weekend gear at the office makes spending the day confined to the forty-fourth floor worth it. For guys, it's a potpourri of unstructured ball caps, Patagonia vests, three-quarter zip pullovers with the logo of where they (or a friend) are a junior summer-member, snug khakis, boat shoes, and pastel Polos. For girls, it's Lululemon tights, puffy vests, Tory Burch sneakers, and contrived "messy" ponytails.

I reread the email from my VP on my BlackBerry as I swipe my ID card to gain entrance to the forty-fourth floor. "Bill—Have last minute client meeting in Indy on Monday. Need you to run with this process and lead credit call tmw. Tx." I would've preferred ten pages of comments to this two-sentence knife in the chest that ultimately transfers full responsibility of this deal from the VP to me.

The internal credit committee at DB is the team that determines whether and how much the bank can lend to a client. To make money, investment bankers need to lend when the client wants to issue debt. There was some noise in 2008 about lending standards being too lenient resulting in some credit issue, though I don't remember the details fully. It's up to the investment bankers to convince the internal credit committee that we should provide the financing our clients want. The credit committee's duty is to ensure the bank is prudent in lending reliably to companies so they won't default. The clash in incentives is clear. The credit team is on the brink of being smart enough to know that bankers are typically lying to them about the company they're trying to get financing for.

In this case, Marx Industries has asked DB to enter into the company's revolving credit facility. An RCF is essentially a company's credit card that is used to fund day-to-day operations. Entering a bank's RCF is one of the least—if not the least—risky types of debt to provide. After all, it's only a commitment to lend, since companies rarely fully draw their revolver. None of this is important, and I'm not even sure I'm explaining it correctly. What matters is the following: this isn't a risky deal. In fact, banks typically lose money on this type of transaction. Why do it then? It's a show of good faith—and by being in the company's RCF, it puts DB in a good position to lead future profitable transactions like an IPO, acquisition financing, or a sale. And while RCFs are usually painless, this process is made more complicated since this is a new client of the bank. Had it been a company we lent to in the past, there's more familiarity internally. But we haven't, so more explanation is needed to convince the credit committee that this should happen.

My original plan was to play the standard role of associate on this type of process—have the VP do all the high-level work, communicating the merits of the business to the credit committee and providing all the model assumptions to the analyst. Then I'd have the analyst put together the majority of the memo and run the model while I performed "industry research." Once the analyst finished the first draft of the memo, I'd "review" it while watching the season finale of *Curb* I started during my "industry research." I'd then give some broad comments with little substance to the analyst, forcing him to revisit all sections due to the vague nature of my comments. He'd spend another few hours on it; then it would be ready to send to the VP.

But with the VP away, I'm in deep shit. Especially with a first-year analyst. Extra especially since my prior roles on credit calls were of the nonspeaking nature.

I smell her first, the pungent aroma of the newest Chanel fragrance. Then I hear her.

"You should've just hooked up with his best friend," Ophelia proclaims with the conviction of someone who's employed this strategy.

As I round the corner, I see her sitting perched on a desk, talking with the only other female first-year analyst in the group, a cute Southern girl. I considered asking her out once, but there's something about a girl who knows her way around a debt schedule that doesn't do it for me.

Ophelia spots me walking down the hall, and I hear her say with her head lowered, "To be continued," to the girl whose cube she's commandeered. She then slides off the desk, returns to her feet, and walks toward me.

"Lovely email to receive on a Sunday morning," she says as we meet halfway down the hall.

"Exactly what I was hoping for," I say.

Ophelia's nothing spectacular, but she checks all the boxes to be the focal point for all guys on the forty-fourth floor—former college athlete, from Manhasset, hair the color of the toilet water at Brother Jimmy's on Saturday night—you know the type. A couple weeks ago, I saw her enter the bathroom with her hair down, only to reappear at her cube twenty minutes later with her hair in a bun. Henceforth, in my head, she'd always be referred to as "dumps." She needed to be knocked down a peg after her confidence skyrocketed in the first month—she was competing for attention with the Bloomberg Terminal.

"So I pretty much have most of the memo filled out—leveraged a bunch of old stuff from the memos of the comps we're using. Still tweaking the model, but should be able to send you something in the next hour or so."

"Great." She returns to her cube as I walk to mine.

I pass by one analyst whose head is buried in a CFA level-three study guide, another who's got a timer propped on his desk and a GMAT book open, and a third who's rifling through a stapled document titled "Vault Guide for Private Equity Interviews."

"Thought you had a protected weekend," I say as I see the steam rising from the humidifier in Bart's cube.

He pops his head up—a few strands of hair poke out around his forehead through his backward snapback hat. "Yeah. In-laws in town though. Can stream the game here—not missing the wildcard game to hear about my mother-in-law's new watercolor paintings. What you cranking on?"

"Gotta run with this CRM process. Just a revolver, but new name and no VP on credit call."

Bart stands, coffee mug in hand, and gives me a hard look. "Better get smart on the business and industry. They can be real sticklers with new names, especially if we're gonna be losing money in their credit facilities."

It's the type of thing fellow junior-banker peers say to one another for some reason, as if there isn't enough stress already from those above us.

"Yeah," I say as I comb through the industry research reports saved in the drive, trying to figure out a plan.

"And," Bart continues as he leans over the partition dividing our cubes. "You really gotta be able to justify the add-backs." He taps the cube divider with the tip of his middle finger as if to emphasize the point. "That's crucial. They're gonna grill you on that. Justifying those EBITDA add-backs will make or break this process—definitely the difference maker between getting through credit."

His advice is useful and appreciated, but his delivery makes me want to crack his coffee mug on his head.

"Sounds good. Thanks, Bart." I make eye contact with him as I put on my headphones, though the wire dangles by my feet.

Though the bullpen is relatively quiet this Sunday, the cubes of most of the familiar-looking first-year analysts are occupied. As I trudge through the research reports on my computer, taking notes on both the business and industry—notes I hope will help me sound relatively competent on tomorrow's call—I'm periodically distracted by two first-year analysts who stand in the hallway a few feet from me, tossing a Nerf football just close enough to one another so as not to expose the fact that neither knows the proper way to throw a football.

"Dude, that's savage. Pure savagery," says one with an unstructured Polo ball cap propped up on his head, revealing a tuft of blonde hair on his forehead. He looks like it's "Take Your Son to Work Day" and he got lost in the office. On his left wrist is one of those Swatch watches that works three hundred meters below water, in case he wants to take a quick midday dive in the Mariana Trench.

"What choice did I have?" says the other with a smug grin as he catapults the mini-Nerf football to his partner like it's a shot put. I feel bad for this guy. Rumor has it, his go-to move on Saturday nights is to take girls to the forty-fourth-floor corner conference room and dazzle them with the view of New York Harbor and a bottle of Pinot Noir. No word on which was more expensive—the wine or the "date."

"But hardcoding your WACC in a board deck?" says the guy as he catches it and shakes his head. Then he tucks the ball under his arm and removes his BlackBerry from the pocket of his corduroys. "Fuckin' A," he says as he scrolls through an email that most likely will end this game of catch. Then the small scrolling-ball in his BlackBerry pops out of his phone.

"Dude, you need to download the BlackBerry Work app on your iPhone. Life's much better with one phone," says his partner.

"No way. Gotta separate church and state," he says, now on his hands and knees searching for the little ball.

A few rows of cubes away, another first-year analyst standing with a baseball bat in his right hand, the barrel resting on his shoulder, fields questions from a seated analyst. While I can't hear the question, I see the confidence grow on the batter's face. The content of the conversation is lost due to the distance between us, but the cadence carries. As he prepares to answer a question, he lowers the bat, letting it slightly swing from his left hand, before taking a batting stance. Then, as his mouth starts moving, he brings the bat up in a cocked position, his hands a good three inches apart, and takes a haphazard cut that nearly wipes out the deal toys perched on all adjacent cubes.

"GDP still includes government spending—i.e., welfare checks, which don't really accurately reflect economic value-add," says one analyst to another as they exit the bathroom.

Down the hall, I catch a glimpse of another first-year analyst showing his parents around the floor.

These are the future bullpen tenants.

The ding of a new email from Ophelia returns my attention to my computer. The message contains the most recent version of the CRM memo.

CRM memos are usually around forty pages—comprehensive documents replete with text, charts, graphs, and other graphics with a very specific template. Beginning with the transaction overview, the memo then describes the company and industry, after which it presents historical financials with a discussion on relevant items and growth patterns. Then there is the presentation of all three model-cases: management, DB credit, and downside case, with detailed explanations on assumptions used. This is the section in which the all-important "paydown" is shown. After the three cases, there are a few pages on DCF valuation, then the football-field valuation comparing the different methods used. The appendix, sometimes even longer than the actual memo, details the comparable companies used, as well as any extra information deemed important by the bankers. Typically, the longer the appendix, the less likely the transaction is to get through credit.

Ophelia Green: Hey, just sent over memo

William Keenan: Thanks, will take a look now

It's always helpful when someone emails you, then moments later contacts you via a different medium to tell you she's emailed you.

The first few pages look fine as I scan the PDF of the document. While it needs to look presentable, most of this information will be relayed to the credit team during our phone call, so it's more important that my verbal explanation is on point, as opposed to what's on the page.

Then I get to the model. The management, or upside, case is usually driven by laughable assumptions. Growth vastly exceeds peers, and if you forecast the model another ten years, the company is usually big enough to take over the Milky Way.

As you likely don't recall, the goal is to have the paydown in year seven of the DB credit case be around 53 percent. This is more important when actual debt is being issued. With the revolver, tweaking the paydown shouldn't be too difficult. A flood of numbers peppers the model output pages. I quickly dart to the DB credit-case paydown row. Year seven paydown—(1,999%).

> **Ophelia Green:** FYI, I have no idea what I'm doing with the model haha

That is for damn certain.

> **William Keenan:** Can you get out of the master and I'll take a look

> **Ophelia Green:** lol sure. sry

I scan the page and the items that drive the cash available to pay down the debt—all dollar amounts in those rows look reasonable. Then my eyes track left, column by column, and I spot the likely culprit—the percentage paydown formula doesn't look to have been dragged all the way right, so I redo it. This fixes the issue partially with the paydown (now at 86 percent). Clearly, there are more issues, but I can futz with that later.

"What you jammin' on?" Phuc taps the top of my cube with his right hand. His Oakley sunglasses are upside down, hooked behind his head.

"Credit call tomorrow," I say. I spot the handle of a squash racket poking out of the duffel bag slung over his shoulder. I want to whack him with it.

"Live deal?" he says.

"Yeah, I guess," I say.

"Cool account?"

"It's fine."

"I pulled an all-nighter last night. This sell-side is taking over my life." While it might initially seem reasonable to sympathize with Phuc, I know there's a part of him, probably a big part, that doesn't mind and maybe even likes spending Saturday nights at the office. It's the most densely populated area on Earth containing individuals like him. I'm convinced there are even junior bankers who hang out on weekends at the office just because that's where they prefer to be.

"Term loan? Financing? Any mezz piece?" he says as he peers over my cube, trying to catch a peek of my monitor.

"Credit facility," I say.

"Jeez, that's easy, man."

"So you wanna do it for me?" I pick up the compressed air duster canister next to my monitor and spray it in Phuc's direction.

"Bro! Come on!" He backpedals a few steps. "You have any idea how bad that is for the environment?"

"Bad for the environment? All you ever talk about is that sell-side you worked on, advising a massive plastics manufacturer that produces polyoxybullshit, which is probably killing dolphins by the dozen and fuckin' with ozone layers."

Phuc checks the grip of his squash racket then looks back at me.

"Polyoxybenzylmethylenglycolanhydride," he mutters as he begins his trek down the row of cubes, eyeing his next victim.

Aside from the paydown, the next most important element in the CRM process is the "Structuring EBITDA" section. While usually only a page or two in the memo, this is where the credit committee focuses most of its attention. Since EBITDA drives the initial leverage at which the bank enters the credit (and thus whether it's a viable transaction from a regulatory standpoint), coming to a consensus on which EBITDA to use is a focal point of all calls with credit.

Earnings before ITDA—a proxy for a company's operating cash flow and an industry metric widely accepted as defining the cash flow a company generates from its operations, which excludes components like how the company finances itself. Though it's relatively straightforward to calculate EBITDA by looking at a company's financial statements,[1] the "adjusted EBITDA" number, a figure bankers obsess over, is a product of alchemy and deceptive artistry. While EBITDA isn't a GAAP metric and won't be found in financial statements, nearly every company provides an adjusted EBITDA figure in some sort of document, whether it be an earnings presentation, information memorandum, or something similar. The "Structuring EBITDA" section of the CRM memo reconciles the company's true EBITDA figure to the adjusted EBITDA number with a series of "add-backs," all of which must be justified in detailed explanations.

Add-backs are traditionally costs that companies determine are one-time events, and thus not indicative of the company's future ongoing operations. For example, if a black-swan hurricane forces a plant shutdown, a case could be made to have the cost incurred to return the plant to production added back. If a company has an unusual legal fee for a restructuring or some other atypical event, that cost could also be added back. Every add-back is scrutinized by the credit team to ensure it will not be an ongoing cost.

Ted stops by the office around noon to send a couple emails and charge his lunch to DB.

"How's the CRM going? Ready to lead your first credit call?" he says as he peruses Seamless.

"Nope. Any advice?" I say.

"Drop your voice a couple octaves when you talk to them. It'll make you sound smarter."

"I've given you all the data points I have," Bart says into his personal cell phone, his hand cupped over the receiver. "For the fifth time, I'm finishing up and should be done in thirty minutes." When I make eye contact with him, he puts his index finger to his temple, then pulls the trigger with his thumb. "Just get me something from wherever you order...I don't care...fine, we'll go out.

---

[1] Earnings before interest, tax, depreciation, and amortization (EBITDA) is calculated by taking the company's net-earnings figure found on the income statement, then adding back interest, tax, depreciation and amortization, which are found on the income statement and the cash-flow statement.

The quicker I get off the phone, the quicker I'll be done. Okay, hun. Bye." He hangs up then looks at me. "This never happened before I started banking."

I spend the evening fixing the model and staring at one particular add-back that will require some of my best stuff to justify.

* * *

"But isn't that tournament part of the FedEx Cup?" says the credit officer. I adjust my headset, then wipe the beads of sweat from my forehead. A new batch forms instantaneously.

"Technically, all PGA tournaments provide players with FedEx Cup points. But the event Marx sponsors isn't part of the FedEx Cup playoffs is what I mean."

After spending forty-five minutes having moderate success walking the credit officer through the Marx Industries CRM memo, we are back at the single issue that could determine whether this transaction occurs: an EBITDA add-back.

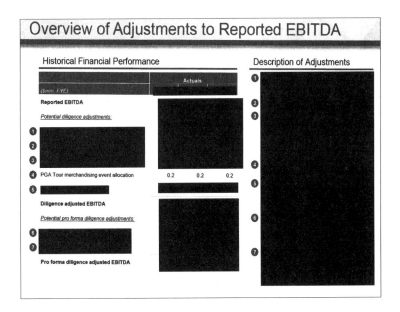

My issue is twofold—first, this isn't an add-back we can breeze through, given its unusual nature. The company is saying they have incurred costs to provide merchandise at a PGA Tour event it sponsors, and that the costs should be added back; second, it's hard to make a case for this cost being a one-time event, given that it's been the same cost the past three years. But it's only $0.2 million—who cares, right? Well, this accounts for 6 percent of the company's adjusted EBITDA, not an insignificant amount considering the leverage the company already has, which is high for a company in this industry, especially for one this small. Bottom line—I gotta figure this shit out and justify this to credit.

"So how is the FedEx Cup point relevant? And I don't quite see how Tiger's comeback relates," says the credit officer.

Both those points I brought up are in no way relevant, but it's the best I can think of.

"Look," continues the credit officer. "At almost five-and-a-half times leverage and an interest coverage ratio at under one, this company is already at risk of breaking covenants if you look at the term sheet in appendix two. Without this add-back, the numbers just don't work."

"If you look historically at the sponsorship contracts of PGA tour events, they're between two and three years. Marx's contract expires this year, its third year as the event's sponsor," I say, gaining momentum. "And it's almost certain they won't renew the contract to sponsor it."

"And why's that?" says the credit officer.

"The old chairman of the board," I say. "He was a big golfer—played in college and had a cup of tea on the Hooters Tour before he decided to join the corporate world. He was the driving force behind the sponsorship. But he's out as of last December. The new chairman has no ties to golf." I remember seeing the picture we cropped of him to put in the memo—he didn't look like a golfer. His face reminded me of my second-grade art teacher. "Not to mention the PGA has publicly stated they want to diversify the locations of their events, and the course where the Marx event is played is within twenty miles of four other PGA tournaments. Given it's the most recent addition to the circuit, they're most likely to scrap the event altogether."

"I see," says the credit officer.

I have him on the ropes. "Let's not forget that at its core, this is a good business," I say. "Hockey-stick growth in all end-markets, two product launches happening next quarter, iron-clad contracts with industry leaders. And they're not asking for an accordion for the facility—these guys know the cash they need for working capital." I pause. "That's prudent cash management." It's something I heard Leighton say a few days ago—sounded smart.

Ted leans back in his chair, just far enough that I can see his face. "Secret sauce," he whispers.

"What?" I respond, covering the microphone on my headset.

"Work 'secret sauce' into the explanation," he says.

"Their cash-flow characteristics do appear solid relative to peers when I look at page thirty-two of the memo," says the credit officer.

"It's sort of their secret sauce," I say. Ted flashes a thumbs-up.

"Okay. I think this works if we can give them credit for the $0.2 million PGA add-back, but I'll have to give it some more thought. Also, I'd prefer to see a bigger haircut to the downside case-growth assumptions, but we can table that for now. I'll be in touch later today with a decision."

"Terrific." I hang my headset on the cubicle divider and lean back in my chair. A few moments later, Ophelia, my analyst who's been listening to the call on mute, walks down the hall and flashes me a double thumbs-up before futzing with her infinity scarf.

"Tell me you made all that shit up," says Ted as pokes his head around the cube divider.

"Details—hallmark of any good lie."

"Starting to sound like a real investment banker. I like the bit about the chairman of the board—gonna try to work that into my next credit process."

John Bukowski: high time we get luncheon. Swing by my desk

William Keenan: swing

John Bukowski: swing

William Keenan: swing

John Bukowski: swing or I'll tell everyone you use Rogaine

William Keenan: don't care. swing

John Bukowski: swing and I'll get that HR chick I went to school with to answer your DMs

William Keenan: gimme 5. Gotta do system update or computer will explode

John Bukowski: 4:59

John Bukowski: 4:58

I click a series of "OK" buttons instructing me that Microsoft Office updates need to be installed. After the three-minute installation is complete, the computer restarts and greets me with an unfamiliar black screen peppered with words like "bitlocker" and "encryption," prompting me to input a ten-digit password.

Introducing the 7s.

While resources like BIS, MAKS, Presentations, and FactSet are resources DB provides to help with actual work content, the 7s are DB's "internal" IT team headquartered in Chennai, India. In my first week of work, I spent more time jawing with them on the phone than I did speaking with anyone on the forty-fourth floor. Their name is derived from the phone number you dial to reach them: you basically hit seven a bunch of times until someone with an Indian accent picks up.

I won't bore with you the conversation—below is the mandatory report they sent following our call.

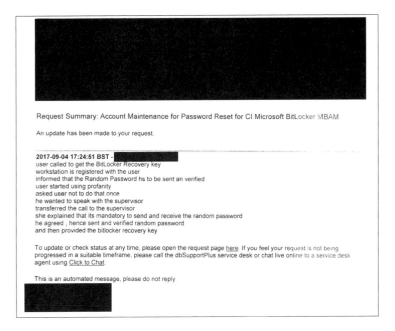

Request Summary: Account Maintenance for Password Reset for CI Microsoft BitLocker MBAM

An update has been made to your request.

2017-09-04 17:24:51 BST -
user called to get the BitLocker Recovery key
workstation is registered with the user
informed that the Random Password hs to be sent an verified
user started using profanity
asked user not to do that once
he wanted to speak with the supervisor
transferred the call to the supervisor
she explained that its mandatory to send and receive the random password
he agreed , hence sent and verified random password
and then provided the bitlocker recovery key

To update or check status at any time, please open the request page here. If you feel your request is not being progressed in a suitable timeframe, please call the dbSupportPlus service desk or chat live online to a service desk agent using Click to Chat.

This is an automated message, please do not reply

And this is one of the more painless interactions I've had with them.

John Bukowski: -8:53

John Bukowski: -8:54

John Bukowski: -8:55

William Keenan: swinging now

* * *

"Lotta dentist appointments recently for analysts in the bullpen," says Ted.

"Must be all the sugary treats in there rotting their teeth," I say. "When do they actually quit?"

"Couple weeks—right after we get bonuses," says Ted. "You hear back from credit?"

"Not yet." I eye my inbox, which is jammed with emails of increasing panic from the VP who entrusted me with handling the credit process; he's requesting updates.

"By the way, to capitalize operating leases, do you know—" I begin.

"Rule of seven," says Ted. "Multiply it by seven."

I nod, then lean back in my chair. "What do you think banking was like before PowerPoint, and Excel models, and BlackBerries?" I say.

"Better...or at least more useful, I'd imagine," says Ted. "No hundred-page pitch books, CIMs with ten thousand charts...just an old white dude at a bank doing arithmetic on his HP 12c and telling a CEO to buy something."

"I did it!" shouts Joel from the bullpen. He emerges from the bullpen, arms raised high, before strutting to Ted's cube. "The perfect order from Toloache."

"Bullshit!" says Ted. He jumps out of his seat and follows Joel into the bullpen. Another email from my VP pops into my inbox. I ignore it and trail Ted into the bullpen.

"Many have tried, all have failed. I have a lot of people to thank. It was not an individual effort by any means," says Joel as he slowly loops around the bullpen. "First and foremost, I need to thank my mom for giving me genes that ensured I'd be hungry around the clock. I also need to thank my fifth-grade teacher, Ms. Snodgrass, who said I could do anything I wanted to, if I channeled my energy properly." Joel fields a couple high-fives from other senior analysts before returning to his cube, where Ted is now seated and inspecting the Seamless order displayed on Joel's computer.

"What's the deal?" I ask.

"Ted has ordered dinner from Toloache hundreds of times and claimed it's impossible to place an order of exactly twenty-five dollars," says Joel, referencing the twenty-five-dollar limit the bank places on our dinner orders. "But lo and behold, the star Industrials senior managing analyst finds a bust in the menu and does the impossible."

Ted stands from Joel's chair. "Clearly a glitch with the pricing of the side of *pico de gallo* when you don't add chips. And what the hell is *huitlacoche*?"

"I went deep in the menu. Gotta celebrate their entire catalog," says Joel.

"This doesn't count," says Ted.

"Don't be jealous," says Joel.

"Joel," says Ted as he gently lifts Joel's bright blue New York Giants tie. "You make it impossible to be jealous of you."

"When are we getting our vests?" I ask.

"They had an issue in their facility where they manufacture them," says Joel.

"Sounds like a reasonable add-back to me," says an analyst's disembodied voice from across the bullpen.

"But should arrive in two weeks," finishes Joel.

"And my sleeves?" asks Ted.

"They're on back order," says Joel.

"Lovely. Keenan, you want to knock out those two compliance modules?" says Ted. We return to our cubes and open the email from compliance marked "URGENT" that we both received earlier in the day. This week's module: preventing discrimination and harassment in the workplace.

"Ready?" says Ted from his cube.

I open the module just as an email notification appears in the bottom right corner of my monitor. "Marx Industries CRM Decision: APPROVED" is the subject.

"Let's fuckin' do this," I say.

17

Page Eight

They say you're the sum or derivative of the five people you surround yourself with.

"See, I disagree. I would prefer to jump off a bridge, like the Brooklyn Bridge," says the first-year analyst as he eyes it outside the forty-fourth-floor window. "Drowning is better, since once you give up, it's not that bad."

Bart stands from his seat. "Have you ever talked to someone who's given up? That makes no sense."

"You'd die from a heart attack on the jump before you even hit the water," chimes in another analyst as he walks by.

"The way to die is getting shot in the back of the head," Bart says.

"I'm gonna shoot you all in the heads if you don't shut the hell up," says Ted.

"What the hell is that smell?" I ask.

"Put your shoes on Bart," says Ted.

"No," I say. "It's like an electrical type thing—"

"Ozone from the overhead lights burning out," says Bart. We all look up at the hazardous gas wafting in above us.

"Should we call someone about that?" I say.

"Who? MAKS?" says Ted.

"Maybe that'll be what kills us," says Bart.

Electrical fires be damned. There's work to do.

"Pg. 8—format bust," reads the highlighted comment in front of me. I leaf through the six pages of comments I printed earlier, double-checking that this is the only outstanding item.

"What the fuck is he talking about?" I say mostly to myself, but loud enough that everyone in neighboring cubes can hear.

"Just call him," says Bart from his cube.

"I tried—still on a plane," I say. VPs make a point of traveling only when you require their guidance.

"It's almost like he didn't want me to figure out the issue he has. Like he says there's a bust, but as punishment he won't explain what the hell it is," I say, hoping to elicit some sort of sympathy from my cube mates. They don't care.

"Just mark it as fixed—maybe he won't check," says Ted.

"It's Gareth," I say.

"Shit. Yeah, he'll definitely check," says Ted. "Lemme take another look." Ted wheels around his chair into my cube, his eyes darting from the sheet of comments to the PDF version of the deck on my computer.

"You sure that's DB blue, not primary blue?" He clicks the far-left column on the waterfall chart and checks the color code of the shade of blue. "Fifteen, forty-seven, one-eighty-one, yeah, guess that's right. Maybe the gray in the table…." Ted cross-checks the color codes of the table below the chart. "You sure those headings are all left-aligned?"

I maximize the PPT version of the deck and turn on the grid lines, answering his question.

"Welp, I gave it an effort," says Ted as he wheels back around in his cube.

"When's the meeting?" asks Bart.

"Original meeting was a month ago," I say.

"Follow-up deck?" he says.

Often after we pitch an idea to a company, they'll request we send follow-up materials: maybe a more in-depth look at a possible acquisition target, or a couple-page analysis of a potential reverse Morris-trust transaction, or really anything they mention on a whim at the tail end of the meeting. I can never tell if companies request these materials because they're really interested in seeing how the reverse Morris-trust math looks (never good) or just because they relish the opportunity to have bankers flail around and churn out material that will probably never be read.

This deck isn't a follow-up deck. As the folder in which it resides is labeled, it is rather: "Follow-up to follow-up to follow-up to follow-up to follow-up materials."

The early-evening buzz of the bullpen restores me with hope. After printing out a copy of page eight, I catch Joel, post-Seamless order, and have him take a look. After some consideration, he wrangles up a few more analysts from the bullpen, and within minutes, there's a symposium in the middle of the bullpen with talk of 95 percent transparency colors, heated debates on footnote-font size and spacing, and arguments over pasting charts as HTML format versus enhanced metafiles. I tune out while Joel moderates, but even after consulting prior decks, the problem remains unresolved.

A VP enters the bullpen, markup in hand, with designs on ruining Joel's night.

"Ready to go over this," says the VP as he taps the thick deck against the top of Joel's cube.

"Any chance we could push like forty-five minutes? I was gonna get a quick workout in."

"You can do push-ups on the floor here while I go through the deck."

No one laughs because he's not joking.

"Any luck?" asks Ted as I return to my desk.

"Nada," I say.

"Got one last idea—you're not gonna like it though," he says.

"Anything at this point."

"Right on cue," says Ted as he flicks his head toward the hallway behind me.

Leighton's 6:38 p.m. arrival to the office happens not a moment too soon.

"Just remember," says Ted lifting an index finger. "You got no shot if you tell him *you* have an issue and need help. Gotta make it some sort of academic exercise or challenge."

After letting Leighton get settled in his cube, I meander back into the bullpen with page eight in my right hand. With Joel preoccupied by his Mexican food and in no position to rile up Leighton, I make my move.

"Hey, man," I say. "Just had some free time and made this page for kicks to practice my charts. Purposely made one single-format bust. No one's found it. Want to give it a go?"

Leighton, his eyes fixed to his one enormous monitor, lifts his right hand with an open palm. I place page eight in it. His eyes move from his monitor to the sheet. He grunts, then removes a red ballpoint pen from the mug beside his monitor, uses his teeth to remove the cap, and draws a circle around the bust. It takes him all of five seconds to find it.

"That it?" he asks.

I'll give you a hint: you won't find it. (See next page.)

In what has become standard bimonthly practice, DB recently updated the nomenclature for its various divisions. Bottom left of the page—"Banking" to "Bank."

I make the change. My VP signs off on the deck around 11:00 p.m. that night, and the MD gives his sign off just after midnight, after which I send the deck to the client. Two days later, they revert: "Appreciate this, guys. Can we see analysis including all EMEA gas comps? Tx much."

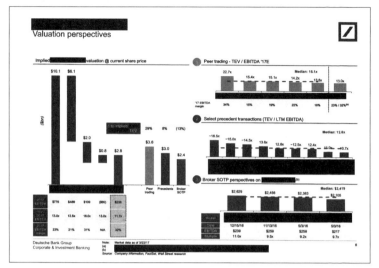

Old version

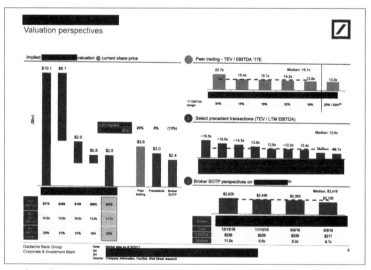

Updated version

Follow-up to follow-up to follow-up to follow-up to follow-up to fuck my life.

18

Bonus and Out

"We start in K-town, then work our way south," says a senior analyst to another in the bullpen as they stare at a map on one of their computers, their fingers tapping various parts of the screen. "I figure we'll be six beers deep by the time we get to Village Tavern if we do this right."

"We're off to see the Wizard, the wonderful Wizard of Oz," sings Joel quietly as he adjusts his tie and wipes lint off his blazer's lapel.

"What time you talking to him?" I ask Joel.

"Supposed to be one-thirty p.m. but think they're running behind."

"My buddy at BAML said low-end this year was $30k," says an analyst from his cube.

"My roommate—does TMT at Goldman—said their median was $85k," says another.

"Bullshit," retorts a third analyst. "What year?"

"Heard mean at Evercore for third-years was six figures," says another analyst.

For the first time since I started work, every analyst in the bullpen is in a suit and tie, with a clean-shaven face.

While the chatter in the bullpen revolves around bonus figures across Wall Street, Leighton sits in his cube, a miniature screwdriver in his right hand as he works on his keyboard like a high-end mechanic. Seemingly either immune or uninterested in the bonus-day buzz, Leighton carefully removes one of the SHIFT keys, partially revealing the underbelly of his supercharged keyboard. Then, with a heart surgeon's touch, he inserts the screwdriver and twists slowly.

"What's shaking, man?" I say.

"Just some maintenance work," says Leighton. "By the way, I'm impressed how you were making those pages the other day for practice. Those repetitions are what will separate your work product from peers."

"Thanks. Impressed you were able to find that bust I planted on the page," I say. "How's the keyboard looking these days?"

Leighton sighs. "N-key rollover obviously a plus, cascading keycap design decreases finger fatigue, and of course the blue switches are superior to red, but there are no doubt questions about durability. Marketing material claims fifty-million-key lifespan, but I don't buy it." Leighton looks over his shoulder at me. "And quite frankly, it's concerning. Durability is paramount." I nod as he pops open a passion-fruit-flavored LaCroix sparkling water. "Want one?" he asks, handing me a can.

"Thanks."

I watch as Leighton returns his attention to his keyboard. It reminds me of the care I took when preparing my hockey sticks prior to a game. It was about getting each detail exactly right: the overlap of each wrap of white tape on my blade; the number of loops, each perfectly in line, on the handle to create the butt end; the candy-cane tape job I did on the shaft because I saw my favorite player do it; sand-papering the shaft where my bottom hand held the stick. Leighton is one of the few people at the bank who seems to enjoy the process, rather than viewing the job as a means to an end.

"Goddammit, Joel!" shouts Leighton as a foam bullet ricochets off the back of his head. I turn around and see Joel smiling, an enormous Nerf gun in his right hand.

"I'll put the Nerf N-Strike Elite Strongman Blaster toe-to-toe against your keyboard any day of the week," says Joel. "You *love* blue-switch keyboards, Leighton." Leighton's mouth opens momentarily, but he restrains himself and instead puts on his headphones and returns to his screwdriver and keyboard.

Moments later, an analyst returns to the bullpen wearing one of those restrained smiles where you know he wants you to know he's excited but doesn't want to make a scene about it, though in so doing, he shines a light on how happy he is.

"How'd it go?" asks Joel, giving in to the bait.

"Uh, yeah. Not bad," says the analyst nodding his head. "Pretty go— …Not bad, I'd say. You're up, Joel," he says returning to his cube and loosening his tie in the process.

Joel stands and fidgets in his suit jacket before exhaling deeply. "Go time," he says. "I trust you'll keep things in order while I'm gone." He hands me the Nerf gun before exiting the bullpen.

The second- and third-year analysts and associates have their one-on-one meetings first. Then the first-year junior bankers have their bonus meetings. But there isn't much anticipation for us first-years—we receive stub bonuses, a standard practice across Wall Street, given we haven't worked a full year yet. My meeting lasts under five minutes. I sit across from a guy in his late forties who I've never met before; he calls me "William" a bunch of times, then he tells me the bank is invested in my personal development. Then I leave.

By early afternoon, a group of senior analysts heads to K-town to start their bonus-day celebration, which will most likely end in a long line somewhere in the Meatpacking District.

"Hey, Bill," says a lanky first year analyst as he passes my cube. "A bunch of us are heading over to O'Leary's—probably grab a couple IPAs and watch the Fed meeting on TV. You should come.

We got a pool going on whether they hike rates and by how many bps. Pretty decent-sized pot thus far."

"Gotta couple things to finish up," I say. "Maybe I'll swing by when I'm done."

"Sound pretty dovish on drinks, Chairman Keenan," says Ted after the analyst is out of earshot.

"Don't get paid enough for that," I say. "So what happens when Leighton quits?"

"One of two things," says Ted. "Either a glass case drops from the ceiling and his cube becomes an exhibit in the Wall Street hall of fame...or theory two is everything is packaged up—keyboard, monitor, computer, the whole shebang—and sent to a research facility in Switzerland."

"I mean to the group—what happens to the group when all these senior analysts quit?"

"Gonna be trouble for us until the first-years get up the curve. But that's the nature of the beast. They did their two, three years here," says Ted like it's some sort of prison sentence.

* * *

By the end of the day, three analysts from the bullpen inform the group they're quitting. Two weeks later, another two analysts quit, including Joel. All are off to jobs on the buy-side, either at private equity firms or hedge funds. Their legacy lives on in the sleeves they leave behind and the email snippets they posted on the bullpen wall. On their last days, they each place their BlackBerry and DB badge on their desks.

Juniors typically field personal phone calls in the vacant conference rooms at each corner of the floor. The soundproof glass windows prevent those of us on the floor from hearing what's being discussed on the calls, but you don't need to hear anything to know the nature of the discussion. It's the calls in which analysts' backs are facing the floor that are a dead giveaway it's a recruiting call.

By April, of the ten senior analysts who were in the bullpen when I started, only four remain, including Betty and Leighton. Most goodbye emails (subject line: goodbye and farewell) eulogize the individual's time at the bank where "lifelong friendships" were created and "invaluable mentorship" took place and conclude with wishes to stay in touch. Then they send a calendar invite for "celebratory drinks." Also, they CC their own Gmail account. One such goodbye email comes from a third-year analyst who makes the rounds one Friday afternoon, fighting off tears.

"Thank you so much, Bill. Today's my last day at the bank, but I had a great time working with you," she says. Never mind that I don't know her name, and I've never worked with her, though I hear she's good.

"I hope you'll come down for a drink at the Bailey later," she says. I nod, though we both know that won't be happening.

A few weeks later, Betty informs a couple MDs of her intention to quit. After three years, she realizes she doesn't want a career in banking. Her plan is to travel for six months and take time to figure out what she wants from her life.

"What'd they say," I ask as she returns from a corner-office conversation.

"They told me it would be a huge mistake for me to quit. I would regret it immediately, and I need to rethink my decision." She looks shook. Betty never sends her goodbye email. Instead, she stays at the bank. It's not so much the stranglehold senior bankers have over analysts that sways her decision, but rather the way banks treat juniors: they lure you with fantasy and trap you with fear.[1] Without exception, banks recruit students by selling them the dream: banking is the quickest way to gain access to boardrooms of the biggest companies in the world. The pay is unparalleled, and the exit opportunities are unrivalled. Think about that—they're salesmen, and the best pitch they have is to sell you on leaving.

---

[1] Not to mention the logistics of quitting—there's more paperwork to fill out when you quit than when you join.

But once you're in the machine, fear grounds you, like it has Betty. You're a pariah if you leave—"Couldn't handle the hours/pressure/lifestyle," sneer your peers once you're gone. Betty is promoted to an associate the following week and celebrates by leaving the office before midnight on two consecutive days.

Spring quickly turns to summer. Tree leaves and flowers bloom or do whatever nature shit happens this time of year, but as a banker, this shift in seasons is simply marked by fewer overcoats hanging outside cubicles and more natural light beaming through the MDs' windows. I pass most days shooting the breeze with the 7s, writing strongly-worded emails to MAKS, hitting on the female FactSet girls who make price charts for me, and deciphering the hieroglyphics that senior bankers universally use in their markups.

But progress is made: for one, I successfully master the cadence bankers use to sound annoyed when giving an explanation to a really difficult question—helps avoid follow-up questions. And I pick up helpful euphemisms: when answering a client's question to which I'm clueless, I say, "It is my understanding," rather than "I think"—makes it sound like I processed the information but was misled by faulty information, rather than the alternative, which is I didn't have any idea (the truth).

Then, one rainy Friday afternoon in June, Leighton makes the rounds in his galoshes, going cube by cube, informing everyone on the floor he's resigning to take a job at a hedge fund. He distributes gifts to every person he's worked with—to me, he gives a wireless mouse, with the caveat that I'll promise to continue working on my keyboard shortcuts. It's a deal.

Two days later, on a Sunday evening, I'm summoned to the office by that perpetually blinking red light to turn comments. The floor is unusually quiet. But when I finish up around 10:30 p.m., I hear a voice in the bullpen.

"Next thing I want to flag is cell AE 78," says Leighton as I spot him in his cube wearing his headset, the lone person in the bullpen.

"When you trace that cell, you'll see the link to the pro-forma income statement. Are you following this? I won't be here tomorrow to explain it again."

19

Capacity

John Bukowski: pls distance yourself from me

William Keenan: Did you leave a post-it on my desk with a dick drawn on it?

John Bukowski: of course…your face is torched

William Keenan: I fell asleep Saturday afternoon at the seaport on a client call that lasted 4 hours

John Bukowski: might as well been on a carnival cruise or honeymoon in oahu

William Keenan: you know what "on the cum" is?

John Bukowski: I do not know you.

William Keenan: This MD kept saying on this call Saturday. Has to do with incorporating numbers into income statement or dividend or something

John Bukowski: you have the wrong person. bye

"Hey, Ethan. You have a minute?" I say as he flashes by the forty-fourth-floor kitchen in a blur of navy blue and fake tan.

"Tee off in an hour—car's downstairs waiting for me." He glances at me, then does a double take. "Looks like someone enjoyed the weekend. Got some good color. Hit the links?"

"Was just at the South Street Seaport and fell asl—"

"I'm thinking about trying out a belly putter," he says as he spots the old Wilson putter that resides on the forty-fourth floor.

"Nice. So yeah, just a quick question on your comments for the Cornerstone deck."

"Walk and talk," he says as he starts down the hallway. I hasten my gait as he turns the corner.

"Sounded like the meeting got pushed to next week. I know you said earlier you wanted a market-updated version as of Friday's close, but since the meeting isn't until next Wednesday, are you good with us just market-updating on Monday?"

Ethan blows by his office, so I keep following.

"Gotta hit the head," he says. "Yeah, meeting is next week—" he continues. I pause outside the bathroom, but he continues speaking as he opens the door so I follow him in. "And I probably won't look until Monday night, but just market-update the book for Friday."

I can tell his level of engagement is at historic lows as I stand a few feet behind him while he unzips his fly at the urinal. Beside Ethan stands a towering VP in the group whose piss stream sounds like he's wearing one of those massive Super Soaker backpacks. In the mornings, bankers stand close enough to slam dunk their piss in the urinals. By afternoon, they're at the free-throw line, taking suspect aim.

In one of the stalls to the left of the urinals, someone is committing a hate crime.

"Look, just market-update the book. Should take two seconds, right?" says Ethan.

Excel will crash most likely given the number of comps and financial data we have pulled in from FactSet. Then I'll run the troubleshooting-utility tool, which will inevitably lead to a lengthy call with the FactSet team. Once resolved, I'll then re-paste in all the charts, graphs, and updated tables of numbers, which, in this case—since the deck is seventy-four pages, excluding the appendices—will take some time, after which I'll spend another hour tying numbers. In all, I'd say the market update will take three solid hours.

Ethan's body shivers and shimmies momentarily before he zips up.

"I can't hold your hand on this, right?" he says as he pumps the hand sanitizer into his left hand with his right elbow. After a quick glimpse of his hair in the mirror, he lets me swing open the bathroom door and we emerge onto the floor.

"Sounds good. So I'll get this updated for Friday's close, then I'll plan on doing another market update for next Monday."

"Yeah," says Ethan as he pops into his office to grab a vest. "Don't spin your wheels on this, but get the thing updated." This exercise is the definition of spinning one's wheels. "Need you taking some responsibility now."

"Will do," I say. Then, for no other reason than it's become habit, I mutter, "Thanks."

"Alright," says Ethan as he slides his arms through his vest. "First time with the new Callaway sticks." He faces me for the first time with a big smile. "Just hope they put the right grips on." He slaps me on the shoulder as he walks by me.

"Enjoy," I say as I lift my middle finger in my right pocket then head back to my desk.

"Shit," he says, doubling back and walking to my cube. He unplugs his BlackBerry and iPhone from the chargers at my desk. "Almost forgot." He tosses the wires of the two charges on the ground. After he disappears down the hallway, I re-hook both charger wires to the handles of my drawer where I keep them.

Ten months ago, this was an assignment I'd welcome, providing me with an opportunity to showcase my skills and gain familiarity with Excel, PowerPoint, FactSet, and finance in general. However, as I approach the end of my first year as a banker and have a better understanding of what I'm actually doing on a daily basis, this is the type of assignment that justifies why banks retain so few junior bankers.

> **John Bukowski:** big staffing brewing in industrials. Hear MD in office near me on speakerphone with someone

> **William Keenan:** details pls

> **John Bukowski:** Tons of chatter about needing juniors with "sufficient bandwidth"… project "will take up all their capacity"

> **William Keenan:** good grief

> **John Bukowski:** your staffer there?

> **William Keenan:** away at meeting. Think he's back this afternoon

> **John Bukowski:** man, this thing sounds horrific. "gonna need all hands on deck" says MD

> **William Keenan:** you're my eyes and ears. keep me abreast.

> **John Bukowski:** can u Just say "posted"

> **William Keenan:** k keep me abreast posted

There's nothing more unsettling than a swirling staffing. In recent months, I've done a decent job of avoiding them. The key is a combination of displaying the right stuff on my monitors, coupled with a convincing default facial expression that exudes just the right amount of despair and frustration. For me, it's this furrowed brow I've developed where a passerby might think I'm trying to calculate the WACC of a private company in my head when I'm really on Seamless trying to decide between a *carnitas* or shredded-beef burrito from Toloache. To be caught enjoying yourself, which can manifest itself in a number of ways on the forty-fourth floor, including twirling the shitty putter that resides in the bullpen or taking cuts with the baseball bat that leads a nomadic existence traveling from cube to cube, can spell disaster in the midst of a swirling staffing. It's best to hunker down in your cube and hope that this too shall pass.

* * *

"Happy, happy Monday," says Alonzo, the nineteen-year-old mail guy with a sick flattop, as he strides down the hallway of the forty-fourth floor pushing a dolly stacked with boxes. "How we doin' everybody? Another bootyful Monday afternoon." A few people acknowledge his presence with slight head nods or grumbles, but he goes largely ignored.

"Lauren?" he says pausing a few rows of cubes in front of me. "Is there a Lauren here?" He checks his sheet of paper. Seconds later, a hand pops up from a cube. He walks over. "Just need a signature here," he says handing her an electronic device and large brown box.

Lauren, a fragile-looking, bespectacled, second-year associate, with what looks like an expensive carpet draped over her shoulders, stands. "Yay! My deal toys?" she says, her hands on her cheeks.

"Uh, it would certainly appear so," says Alonzo surveying the outside of the package. "How 'bout Joel. Joel here?"

"Yo, 'Zo" I say, waving him to my cube.

"What up, slick Willy style?" he says offering me a handshake that I flub. "You know where this guy Joel is? He got a package been in mail room damn near a month at this juncture."

"He quit a few months ago. I still talk to him, so I can give it to him."

"Works for me, bro," says Alonzo as I sign for the large box.

But I'm too busy fist-bumping Alonzo to see Jack's message on office communicator. As Alonzo informs me of his new scheme to fix the upcoming basketball game at his old high school, the group staffer catches me mid-laugh as he strides down the hallway with his roller suitcase.

Getting caught laughing—that's all it takes. I'm fucked. My beet-red, sunburned face doesn't help either. Within the hour, I'm staffed on the project that by now is the talk of the floor: an IPO bake-off, which occurs when a company decides to go public and then schedules a day for a number of banks to give presentations on why they should lead the transaction. It's like a condensed, finance version of *The Bachelor*—each bank gets limited one-on-one time with the company and tries not to act as desperate as they really are. The winner gets hired and a rose, and the relationship lasts a few months.

First order of business is purchasing SPF 100. After I place my Seamless order for dinner ($24.78), I receive an email from the VP on the bake-off. He asks me to send him a PIB on the company as well as all the pitch books we've created for them in the past couple years. Cc'd on the email is the analyst on the project, a first-year whose name I don't recognize. While I've worked on bake-offs and projects like this before, it has always been with Joel, Leighton, or another senior analyst. Now I have no safety net.

My appetite subsides after my food arrives, and I'm only able to drink the three sparkling waters I ordered. As I throw away the burrito I barely nibbled, I notice the box Alonzo dropped off earlier in the day. Using the point of a pen, I tear through the adhesive tape holding the box shut, and just as I open it, I hear a ding at my computer—one new email from the VP on my bake-off:

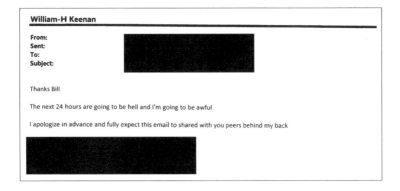

William-H Keenan

From:
Sent:
To:
Subject:

Thanks Bill

The next 24 hours are going to be hell and I'm going to be awful

I apologize in advance and fully expect this email to shared with you peers behind my back

Inside the box, I pick up one of the "Deutsche Bank Industrials Banking Group" vests, zip it all the way to my chin, and hope the banking gods help me channel my inner Joel.

20

Project Liberty

"Think we have everyone on the line," says a senior banker from the financial sponsors group. "Everyone except the one guy we need. Someone in Industrials, would you mind looping in Masters?"

"On it," I say. As I scan the MD contact list pinned to my cube, my other line rings. "Think he might actually be calling me. I'll patch him in." I transfer lines and answer my second line.

"Hello?" I say.

"Hello, Mister Keenan. This is Brendan from American Express regarding your corpor—"

Click.

I redirect my attention to the MD contact list, where I spot Masters's cell number and dial it. One ring, two rings, three rings...

"Hello?" says a booming voice.

"Hi, Rick. It's Bill Keenan. Can I—"

"Bill who?"

"Keenan—from Deutsche Bank…the associate on Project Liberty. We have the rest of the DB team on the other line. Can I patch you into the call?"

"What call?" he asks.

I can't tell if he's fucking with me or what. "The call you scheduled today regarding Project Liberty."

In the background, I hear a young girl's voice. "Enough, Natalia!" hollers Masters. "Give it a rest!"

"Should I—" I begin to say.

"I need ten minutes. Tell them to wait," he says.

"Okay. I can resend the dial-in info if you'd like. Or do you want me to call you back and loop you in?"

"Call me and patch me in," he demands. Senior bankers have an uncanny ability to refuse to dial into conference calls, instead choosing to have junior bankers call them first, then merge their call with the conference call. Aside from being inconvenient, I only have three lines and already have four seniors who want me to call them first, then loop them into the conference call. And if that's not enough, I have to adjust the volume on my phone mid-conversation, since the MDs on cell phones sound like they're talking in a bunker in Afghanistan, while the individuals in the building sound like their speaking through a megaphone.

After hanging up with Masters, I relay the news to a disgruntled group of bankers, who place the blame on me. When the conference-call participants reconvene in ten minutes, I call Masters back. He doesn't answer. Still doesn't answer after twenty minutes. Forty-seven minutes after originally scheduled, he answers, and the call finally begins.

"What are the exact goddamn words in the RFP?" barks Masters on the other line, an hour and a half into our call.

I flip to the fourth page of the "request for proposal" document, which is covered as much in the tomato sauce from my dinner as it is in yellow highlighter and red pen. "Discuss acceptable ranges for post-IPO PF leverage, assuming EBITDA and FCF growth," I say into my headset, reading the third bullet of the "valuation, capital structure, and dividend policy" section. "And again, we don't have estimates for growth so we assumed—"

"So why the hell am I looking at a page that shows *pre*-IPO leverage?" says Masters.

"Honestly, I'm not sure what page of the deck you're looking at," I say. "Assume page thirt—"

"Page thirty-one. I'm looking at page thirty-one!"

"Okay, so page thirty-one we set the stage by showing pre-IPO leverage relative to peers, then if you flip to thirty-two and thirty-three, you'll see we did the post-IPO leverage analysis and suggested de-leveraging timeline," I say.

"'EBITDA and free cash-flow generation will offset any concerns around PF leverage,'" says Masters barely audibly over the phone line, reading the title of page thirty-two. "Okay, fine...fine...and where the hell are we getting these top-line growth figures?"

"Right, so like I was saying, since the company didn't provide anything, we normalized what we have of historicals, and then, given the aggressive M&A strategy they outlined, we assumed first two projected years are in line with historicals, then outsized growth in outer years when synergies are realized."[1]

"Yeah, fine. Okay. Fine! 'De-leveraging target eighteen to twenty-four months post-IPO better aligns capital structure,'" reads Masters, again barely audibly, as I try to figure out what he's looking at now. "Alright, fine. Look, a lotta wood to chop, and everything, every number, needs to be right," he says.

I eye the electronic display on my desk phone: 10:13 p.m., the last two hours of which were spent on this call, accumulating comments.

"Will do," I say.

"And needs to be right before our 10:00 a.m. call tomorrow with the broader team. Get the analyst to resend the planner for the call, and make sure the entire ECM and sponsors team is on it."

"Sure thing," I say.

[1] To be clear, these synergies will never be realized.

"Okay," he says.

Click.

My phone rings before I even take off my headset. I read the caller ID: Steve, the VP on the project.

"Hey, buddy. Just landed. Sorry I wasn't on the call. Assume everything is clear as mud?" he says.

"Pretty much. Got a bunch of comments from Masters."

"He left me six voicemails while I was on the flight. Last three are incomprehensible, but just did a similar bake-off with him, so got a good idea of what he wants final product to look like. Just will take some time."

"We got about eleven hours—said he wants deck ready for 10:00 a.m. call tomorrow," I say.

"If you can get working on comments he gave you, I'll draft up the executive summary and the pros-and-cons list for section four. When you get the updated valuation pages, send 'em across, and I'll take a look and get you comments right away so we're not wasting time."

"That works. Thanks," I say. It's the first time a VP has offered to contribute to helping create a deck.

"Kwame still alive?" says Steve.

"Will check when I get off phone."

"Alright, buddy. I'll log in when I get home—probably forty minutes, plane's just pulling into gate. In meantime, call, email, tweet, Facebook me...whatever you want if you or Kwame have questions. Just don't Snapchat me, okay? Still don't get that shit."

"Appreciate it. We'll get going." I remove the headset and walk down the hall to Kwame's cubicle. Like most first-year analysts, Kwame is in his cube each morning when I walk into work and still there each night when I leave, regardless of what time that is. While he's learned a lot in the past year, he has yet to learn to throw his dinner away in the trashcan of whichever neighboring cube-mate has already left—the pungent odor of dumplings and soy sauce consumes his space. Pinned to his wall divider is a picture of the Nigerian national soccer team celebrating what appears to be a historic victory. It then dawns on me I have no idea how tall Kwame is—can't even remember seeing him walk down the hall to go to the bathroom. My only image of Kwame is him sitting at his desk.

"How's it going, man?" I say.

"Still having some issue with the FX-adjusted numbers. I don't see how they tie with what the company sent us. Will keep trying to reconcile them though," he says.

"You hear back from ECM or sponsors on their pages?" I ask.

"Nothing. Sent follow-up emails to both junior teams," he says.

"Alright, I'll give them a call. You were on the full call with Masters, right?"

"Yeah, on mute. He sounded pissed."

"Can you just make sure you take care of all the valuation and benchmarking comments he had? Flag anything that doesn't make sense, and I'll take a look before we send to Steve. I'm going to work on the section three comments...also, can you resend the call invite for tomorrow at 10:00 a.m.?"

"Okay. But I sent it already twice. Does Masters even look at his email?"

"I think he's too big-time to scroll through his inbox to look for an email. Just resend it so we can at least say we did."

"Will do," he says. Kwame opens up the original email he sent. It's littered with rogue semicolons. One of the drawbacks of only studying finance and accounting in college is there's a tendency to think semicolons are a formal version of commas.

The floor's air conditioner shuts off as I return to my cube, pick up my headset, and dial the associate from the financial sponsors group who covers the private equity company that owns the client.

"This is Jessica," says the voice on the other line.

"Hey, Jessica. It's Bill Keenan from Industrials...on Project Liberty with you," I say to the girl I've never met aside from a couple email exchanges.

"Yes, what's up?"

"Was curious if you have any update on timing for your pages. Masters wants to see a consolidated deck for the 10:00 a.m. call tomorrow morning," I say.

"Bill, right?" she says.

"Yeah."

"Sorry, just didn't recognize your name. First-year associate?"

"Yes."

"Assume MBA, not analyst promote, right?"

"Correct."

"Okay," she says, all drawn out like she's about to tell me how square pegs don't go into round holes. "So I have four live deals right now. I can understand you're still getting used to the role, but I will get you the pages when I can."

"Any idea on when? Like ballpark? Just trying to manage expectations, given Industrials is holding the pen on the master, and the tight timing since Masters wants to see full deck by 10:00 a.m."

"No idea on timing. Will send across when I get to it."

> **John Bukowski:** I feel like I'm digging a hole all day then filling it up

> **John Bukowski:** And sometimes I just wanna get in the hole

> **John Bukowski:** you alive?

> **John Bukowski:** I miss us.

The ECM associate doesn't even answer my call, which I chalk up as a better outcome than my conversation with Jessica.

I check the electronic display on my phone as I place my headset back on the cubicle divider: 1:27 a.m. Time has a way of speeding up at the office after midnight.

By 3:17 a.m., Kwame and I are halfway through the substantive comments we received from Masters and send them off to

Steve to review. Steve provides comments within thirty minutes; I turn those as Kwame continues working on the original Masters comments.

"Kwame!" I yell as the clock hits 4:00 a.m. on my computer. The floor is dark and silent. I throw the Nerf football I keep in my drawer across a couple rows of cubes, knocking a deal toy off one of the cube dividers—not the one I was aiming for, but still. As planned, the movement activates the overhead fluorescent lights. "Kwame!" I yell again, our side of the floor now illuminated.

"Yo!" he yells from his cube across the floor. "What's up?"

"You good?"

"I guess," he says.

"Good."

At 4:39 a.m., Kwame and I send Steve the updated deck.

At 5:17 a.m., Steve responds with comments. We turn them.

At 6:38 a.m., I save the updated version of the deck before my computer reads:

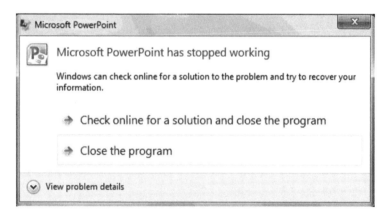

At 6:39 a.m., I say a prayer. It's answered at 6:40 a.m.

At 6:46 a.m., Kwame and I send Steve the updated deck.

At 7:17 a.m., Steve provides his "final" comments. We turn them.

At 7:39 a.m., Steve provides a couple "clean-up" comments. We clean them up.

At 7:45 a.m., Kwame finds a bust in the model. We high-five after he fixes it. Then he saves it after which his computer displays:

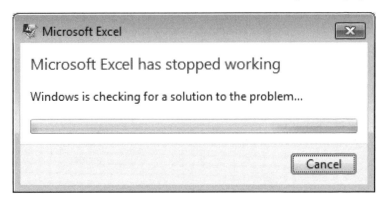

At 7:47 a.m., we realize there wasn't a bust in the model, so we revert to the prior version, nullifying the latest Excel crash. More high-fives.

At 8:18 a.m., the first admin arrives and greets me with a "good morning," to which I don't respond. Instead, I walk to the nearest conference room and cry.

At 9:00 a.m., I make a subpar joke to Kwame. It's not funny but allows us to do this thing where we mask our crying with laughter.

At 9:13 a.m., my roommate texts me: "U alive?" I don't answer—feel dead inside.

At 9:22 a.m., the sponsors junior-team sends their pages. I consolidate them into the deck.

At 9:57 a.m., the ECM junior-team sends their pages. I consolidate those as well.

At 9:59 a.m., I send out the deck to the broader team as Kwame opens the call.

"Have to drop daughter off at camp. Push call hour," reads Masters's email at 10:04 a.m.

Back to the conference room for another sob-fest, but this session is cut short by the arrival of my fellow junior bankers, who cast quizzical glances into the conference room as they arrive with coffees in hand. Phuc, his tie flung over his shoulder, peers into the room and flashes me a thumbs-up, thumbs-down question maneuver through the glass window. I give him the finger, then back to my desk I go.

John Bukowski: how bad was last night?

John Bukowski: ?

John Bukowski: you alive?

John Bukowski: Lets do dinner in conference room tngt if you can

* * *

"What if we do volume year-to-date?" says Masters, about two hours into the 11:00 a.m. phone call.

"Global or US?" asks the ECM junior.

"Global," says Masters.

"DB is number three," says the girl from ECM.

"What about US?"

"DB is number two."

"Forget volume. How about number of issues in past three years?"

"DB is fourth."

"Kill those two Chinese IPOs we show at bottom of page. If you remove them, where are we?"

"DB is first if we remove them," says the ECM girl after some typing.

"Good. Rename the table to say Deutsche Bank is leading underwriter of marquee transactions. And footnote we exclude those Asian ones."

"Will do," says the ECM girl.

"Alright, let's get these comments turned today, and I'll have one last look tomorrow."

"One quick thing before everyone drops," I say. "We sent out four options for custom cover for the deck. Usually takes a little lead time to get them printed, so any thoughts?"

The line goes silent as there's discussion about when the email was sent. Kwame sent two emails in the last hour with images of all four covers attached.

"First one is no good—too sterile looking," says one of the senior sponsors bankers, his first contribution to the entire project.

"Agreed," says Masters. "Too much black, and the test-tubes are off-putting…who designed these?"

"Industrials team," I say. "We sent out an email a couple days ago to the team asking for ideas but never heard back, so Kwame and I tried to use images from the company website to—"

"Second one is no good either," says Masters amidst grunts of agreement from other senior bankers on the line. "Looks like the guy is holding something that says 'toxic.'"

"Believe it says 'non-toxic,'" I say. "But I understand—"

"Last two are fine," says Masters. "Let's do fourth. All good with that?" He's met with a series of yeses.

"Good. Fourth one it is…one with the globe," says Masters.

"Just to confirm," I say. "Since we sent out two emails with different ordering, you're talking about the one with the globe that's sitting on the grass with the windmill in the background?"

"No…no windmill," says Masters. "One with the smiling Asian guy holding the globe."

"Got it," I say. "We'll get it printed."

I haven't been home in thirty hours. And aside from nodding off a few times at my desk, I haven't slept.

But there are comments to turn. After reconvening with Kwame and getting clarification from Steve, I do my best to steady my shaking hands and spend the next six hours buried in Excel and PowerPoint. Around 6:00 p.m., I hear someone yawn, then mutter, "Fuck my life." It takes me a second to realize my headset is on and it's Kwame's voice on the other line. He called me a few hours ago, but evidently neither of us remembered to hang up.

"You hangin' in there?" I say into my headset.

"Kind of. Can I go get some lunch?" asks Kwame. I check the time on my phone—6:05 p.m.

"Yeah, Kwame. Go get some lunch."

* * *

"Dude, you look like shit," says Jack as I enter the small conference room with my bag of dinner.

"Haven't slept in forty fuckin' hours," I say, slinging the bag of food onto the table. "Why do you always wear that stupid thing?" I say.

"What thing?"

"That bullshit Barbalu vest. You're becoming one of them."

"Barbalu? That's the Italian place that blacklisted you 'cause you complained about the number of meatballs. This is Barbour." He runs his hand down the front of his dark-blue quilted vest.

"You look like a real banker douche," I say.

"I got news for you. I am, and so are you, so might as well dress the part."

"Your call," I say tearing open the stapled brown bag containing my dinner. "All I know is I didn't eat lunch today, and I've been fantasizing about this meal since this morning."

In the first year, dinners at the office with other junior bankers were a forum for us to discuss what the job appeared to look like from the outside. We'd reassure ourselves we were in a great position, the best position, and thus collectively we could take pity on everyone else. Viewing ourselves from an outsider's perspective was the only one that mattered. Looking within was too daunting. By year two, the charade is over.

I reach into the bag and pull out a plastic bottle of Poland Spring water. My jaw clenches and a rush of uncomfortable heat cascades down my body. Then I remove the pasta dish and see red tomato sauce plastered on the plastic cover.

"You gotta be fist fucking me!" I yell. I drop the container of pasta back in the brown bag and fire it across the room at the wall.

"Jesus!" says Jack. "What the hell is wrong?"

"I ordered a sparkling water, not this bullshit Poland Spring. And Alfredo sauce on my pasta. It's a simple fuckin' thing and they can't get it right!" I slam my fist on the table.

A stream of red tomato sauce slides down the far wall as I swipe my right arm across the table, sending the bottle of water flying.

The room goes silent.

"I think I have a couple Pellegrinos at my desk," says Jack. "You can have 'em."

I sit down in the chair across from him and put my head in my hands. I can feel the tears coming. Then I feel Jack gently place his hand on my back.

"You just need some sleep, man," says Jack after a minute. I lean up, removing my hands from my face.

"Gonna be here all night again," I say, leaning back in the chair and taking a deep breath.

"But it'll be over after that. You'll recharge, and it'll be fine."

My BlackBerry buzzes. The red dot blinks. I leave the room and return to my cube.

"Call me now," reads the subject of the email from Masters to me—no one cc'd. I dial his cell.

"This is Rick," he says after two rings.

"Hi Rick. Bill Keenan. Just saw your email," I say. I can feel my hand holding the receiver shaking.

"The forty-fourth floor needs to get engaged in this process. You hear me?" Unlike the earlier call, which was punctuated by shouting and barking, his voice is now measured and sinister.

"Understood," I say.

"This is a simple fuckin' exercise. You're disorganized. The call today was a catastrophe. Your incompetence reflects poorly on me."

"I apologize if I wasn't—"

"I don't need an apology. Just get it done."

21

Sell-Side Sunrise

"Got any good hashtags?" asks Steve as he stands by the glass window of the nearly empty forty-fourth floor, turning his phone from portrait to landscape mode. The bright orange sun emerges on the horizon over Long Island. With outstretched arms, Steve focuses his camera phone on the sunrise and snaps a pic.

"Wait to post it until this afternoon," says Kwame from his cube amidst the perpetual chatter of his keyboard. "You'll get more likes."

"This one goes right to the wife, guys. Need evidence I've been at the office all night and not at Sapphire." He snaps another pic, admires it, then pockets the phone and returns to Kwame's cube, where I sit propped beside one of his monitors.

"Homestretch," says Steve as he posts up behind Kwame's chair and eyes the near-final version of the bake-off deck on Kwame's computer. "How many times did Masters change the comp set?"

"Lost count," says Kwame, hammering away on his keyboard as he conforms footnotes and ensures all slide titles are left-aligned perfectly.

"Went from six to eight to seven back to eight. Then we split the eight into tier-one and tier-two comps. Then scrapped that, went back to seven, then six—same six we started with," I say.

"Sounds about right," says Steve. "How we looking, Kwame?"

"Like ten minutes. Just need to go back through and re-paste a couple charts as pictures since labels got messed up." Steve smiles at me, conveying equal parts relief and befuddlement. He has a way of communicating subtle thoughts without using words. Like the first time he asked me a substantive question in person and I stumbled through an incoherent response. He gave me a look like I was the type of person who appears like I should know more than I actually do. But he never made me feel badly about it. We always worked around it. Hence, Kwame.

"I'm going on a quick food run to Duane Reade," says Steve. "You boys want anything? Beef jerky? 5-hour Energy? Red Bull? Sixty milligrams of Adderall?"

Steve returns ten minutes later with a plastic bag full of snacks, just as Kwame changes the file name of the bake-off deck from "Project Liberty bakeoff_v58" to "Project Liberty bakeoff_vF." Steve takes one final look before giving Kwame the green light to PDF the final version of the deck and email it to the DB team.

"You're a beast, Kwame. Now go the hell home and get some sleep." Like most analysts, Kwame lives within spitting distance of the office. As he's told me, it's quicker for him to get to his apartment across the street from the forty-fourth floor than it is to get to some places within the actual Deutsche Bank building.

Kwame, with his shoelaces snaking the ground beside him, shuffles down the hall to the elevator, his suit jacket slung over his shoulder, his Oxford shirt untucked on one side.

Steve eyes a small stack of books—*Den of Thieves*, *Liar's Poker*, *The Art of War*, and *Barbarians at the Gate*—in the adjacent cube. Like most things in banking, they're there for optics—look about as read as the textbook I bought for Science B47: Cosmic Connections, a class I took pass/fall spring semester of senior year. "Can you imagine if people knew what corporate finance was really like?" says Steve.

"I feel like only a fiction writer could show this world, what *really* happens here," I say.

"Don't sell yourself short. These models you guys crank out, these decks...some of the best fiction there is." Steve smiles. "This your first all-nighter?"

"First double all-nighter," I say.

"You did a good job."

"Kwame did most of the numbers," I say, not to deflect praise but because it's true.

"MAKS or a robot can do that stuff. Half the job for an associate is making sure phone calls are productive, everything is organized, and shit gets done...and the analyst doesn't die—it's about seventy percent of the job as a VP. And that's harder than crunching any numbers."

Despite the sleep deprivation, the absence of stress since finalizing the deck buoys my mood. "I'll be honest, Steve. I had a mini-breakdown last night—couple tears involved." It's the first time I've admitted something like this to someone more senior than me at the bank.

"Just one?" asks Steve, looking at my sideways. "When I was an associate, we had a friggin' designated conference room for crying—tucked away on the far side of the floor away from the MD offices."

I shake my head and smile. "Any advice on how to get through banking?"

"Yeah, don't do it. Get out now."

"Must be something keeping you doing it," I say.

Steve removes his iPhone from his pocket. "Absolutely. Three reasons," he says before showing me a picture of him with one arm around a young-looking boy while the other hand cradles an infant bundled in a pink blanket. Got three big reasons I'm doing banking. Right there."

"Third on the way?"

"Third reason is the mortgage I got on that house in the background," he says. Steve eyes the picture of his two kids, smiles, then returns the phone to his pocket. "When I started as an analyst, I told myself I'm out in two years, since I had no reason to stay. And I was out after two—went to business school. Then I met a girl there. A year later, we're married."

"Pretty quick," I say.

"Was starting to lose my hair, and I was punching way above my weight with Kristy. So graduated from business school with some debt. Figured I'd go back to banking after school for a year or so to figure things out—pay's good, already knew how to do it. Then we did the kid thing right away and all of a sudden, I'm here playing slapdick with you and Kwame."

"Speaking of which, last night...or maybe night before, forget, but I went to the bathroom at like 3:00 a.m. and heard someone in the handicapped stall playing slapdick with himself."

Steve smiles. "I was a second-year analyst and was walking home after a brutal night—think it was actually an IPO bake-off too—there was this homeless couple who set up shop right at the end of Pine Street under this overhang and heated grate. Saw some movement as I approached them—real dark since it was like 4:00 a.m.—and as I walk by, I see they're having sex. Weren't even fazed when I dropped a couple bucks in the plastic cup they left out."

"That's horrifying," I say.

"What's horrifying is that it reminded me of how long it'd been since I got laid. Here I was some hotshot banker, and the only action I got was a weekly over-the-pants HJ at Sapphire on Saturday nights from some Siberian stripper who couldn't string together a sentence in English."

Our BlackBerries ding simultaneously. We dig into our pockets. "Fine with deck. Need ten copies printed. Deliver to my house," says Steve, reading the email Masters sent to the team. He lowers his phone and looks at me. "Thank fuckin' God."

"We're still waiting to get the custom cover printed, but should be done by this afternoon, then we'll print and deliver to his place in Greenwich."

"Appreciate it, bud. I fly out tonight. Believe Masters's flight is early tomorrow, so just make sure the books are delivered tonight once the covers are ready."

"You got it," I say.

"Go get home and catch some Zs."

As I walk down the hall around 7:30 a.m., nearly every MD is in his office, working the phones, generating more staffings and sleepless nights for the juniors. But for now, I'm heading home, fantasizing about a warm shower and creeping under my bed sheets, which haven't been washed since I was home for Christmas.

* * *

"Bro, you moved on me," says Alonzo when I return to the office and my new cube later that evening after a few hours of sleep. He spots me on his walk down the hall. Every few months, about a third of the junior bankers swap cubes in the bank's attempt to ensure people get exposure to as many of their fellow bankers as possible.

My new spot is tucked deep in the back corner of one side of the forty-fourth floor. Not only are my days of subconsciously monitoring everyone's bathroom duration over, but more importantly, neither of my monitors is visible to anyone on the floor. Plus, I no longer have to contend with the image of the dread-inducing staffing sheet tracking my every move. It's a highly coveted cube, and quite frankly one that I don't deserve, but so we bank on.

As I unpack the cardboard box filled with all my stuff, Alonzo scrolls through his electronic device.

"Who you like tonight in the game?" I say.

"Yanks on the móney line," says Alonzo as he tilts his device for me to sign. He checks the packages on his dolly. "Shit, I musta left the box on your old desk when I went to the bathroom. Lemme go grab it." He makes a move, but I stop him.

"Don't worry about it. I'll get it later. Don't think it's anything important," I say.

"Deal toys?" he asks.

"Probably," I say.

"Yo, what the hell are those things? It's like every box I deliver here, people be asking me if I got their toys."

"Just these stupid little things we buy ourselves after we finish a project."

"Why wouldn't you just pocket the dough instead of buying a toy?"

We bump fists, then I catch up on my emails as I hear Alonzo say, "Happy, happy Hump Day," to an unreceptive sea of bankers before he and his dolly disappear from my new view.

My BlackBerry emits the low-battery warning beep. After plugging in my power strip, I dig through my cardboard box of belongings but can't find my BlackBerry charger.

William Keenan: u snake my bberry charger?

John Bukowski: I tried to that one time but you marked it with those stupid pink dots and caught me. I'd have to be moron to try and steal it again

William Keenan: k. someone took it though

John Bukowski: wasn't me...how's new digs?

William Keenan: good, earned this spot with my relentless work ethic and now celebrating with Californication marathon. Swing by if you'd like to be part of viewing party

John Bukowski: bake-off done?

William Keenan: finished deck. Waiting for custom cover. Print tngt. Bake-off tmw

John Bukowski: still wearing your stupid DB industrials groups vest?

William Keenan: yes'um. Still wearing ur stupid barablu vest?

John Bukowski: si

William Keenan: would love to continue this conversation, but I gotta go do some investment banking

An email from the reprographics team alerts me that the bake-off decks, complete with the customer cover, are printed and bound and ready to be picked up on the forty-second floor. I race down the back staircase, pick them up, and flip the ten decks, ensuring everything has been printed correctly—coloring, tab dividers, table of contents, and so forth. All looks good.

Typically, junior bankers will use the DB courier service to deliver books to an MD's home. After putting the decks into a box, we usually affix a piece of paper with instructions for the driver including the address of the destination and a note requesting the driver to call our cell to confirm delivery. At the bottom, we'll typically put any additional instructions like: "DO NOT RING DOORBELL!!!!" or "PLEASE HAND DIRECTLY TO NIGHT DOORMAN."

But this isn't just another deck. With no room for error, decks like this need to be delivered directly by the junior banker. But I ain't sitting in traffic on I-95 to and from Greenwich tonight.

He picks up after two rings. "What's up, Kwame," I say into my headset.

"Hey, sorry. I'll be in the office in ten minutes," he says through a yawn.

"No rush, man. Books are printed and flipped. In a box on my desk. Can you deliver them to Masters tonight?"

"Yeah." Shit rolls downhill in a hurry in banking. MDs push it out at the summit and analysts wait at base camp with no hope of ascension.

"Thanks. You have his address, right? It's in Greenwich. His flight is early tomorrow morning and could be rush-hour traffic so just want to make sure we don't wait too late."

"I got it. I'll order the black car now."

> **John Bukowski:** before you leave today, I need a written explanation on your shoes

> **William Keenan:** what's wrong with them. They're good

> **John Bukowski:** you got them andy dufresne shoes

> **William Keenan:** who dat?

> **John Bukowski:** are you insane? Unreal Shawshank redemptions reference out of me

> **William Keenan:** joke was too premeditated anyway. Saw you make a note of it at your desk earlier today

> **John Bukowski:** nevertheless, it's good movie and good reference

> **William Keenan:** never saw it. Worth me watching?

> **John Bukowski:** yes

My eyes instinctively track over to my email after I hang up my headset—no new emails. It's 6:37 p.m. A spurt of dopamine courses through me as I consider the prospect of leaving work before 7:00 p.m. and the possibility of not eating a Seamless dinner at my desk for the first weeknight since I can remember.

No need to duck out the back stairway, walk down to the forty-third floor, then elevator it to the lobby. Leaving for the day at this time is so inconceivable, I can exit the normal way—I'll be the junior heading to the lobby to get his dinner from the Seamless guy or going to the gym for a quick workout.

Exiting 60 Wall Street, I fake a phone call to avoid talking with an associate who joined with me and whose name I forgot. With a lowered head and my hands deep in my pockets, I book it west to William Street, then north until I hit Maiden Lane, at which point I finally raise my head and check my phone: 6:52 p.m. The evening foot-traffic in the financial district is humming. In the glow of the enchanting metropolitan twilight, a flurry of women in yoga pants carrying Whole Foods grocery bags and men clad in a variety of suits, from custom-made to Men's Wearhouse, churn through the city streets. Everyone walks with purpose, which serves only to highlight that my purpose is confined to the role I play (and fake) on the forty-fourth floor. It's the same trap I walked into when I played hockey and allowed the game to define and dictate who I was and how I felt on a minute-to-minute basis.

I check my BlackBerry—still no emails.

I have no idea what to do with myself, so I watch *Shawshank Redemption*. It brings me to tears.

Then I order the same shit I would've ordered if I was at work and am mildly pleased with myself when I confirm the $24.89 order.

* * *

"Books delivered—left on front porch," reads the email from Kwame to me later that night. After enjoying a rare weeknight on my couch, dividing my time equally between *Seinfeld* reruns and not "liking" Instagram pictures that I like, I get to bed early.

After a frantic few days of stress-inducing mornings, afternoons, nights, and back into mornings that can wreak havoc even on superlative hairlines of individuals like myself, I close my eyes and feel that sense of accomplishment that follows any difficult period of time.

When my bladder wakes me at 3:36 a.m., my left arm reaches instinctively to my nightstand to grab my BlackBerry. I stumble, bleary-eyed, to my bathroom. As I take aim at the bowl in the darkness, I see the familiar red light blinking. I enter the password, incorrectly at first. The second attempt unlocks the phone just as I reach down to flush. "Twelve new emails" —but that's not what scares me. It's "eleven missed calls" that terrifies me. I check the caller ID: four from Masters, four from Steve, three from Kwame.

I return to the email inbox on my phone and look at Masters's latest email. "Where the hell are books???" Then Kwame's email to me: "Call me ASAP! I don't know what happened. I left books on porch." Then I see Masters's first email: "Why did you deliver a box of deal toys to me?"

My boxers are around my ankles when I realize how fucked I am.

22

Terminal 5

"I'm in a cab *en route*. Got the books with me," I say holding my BlackBerry to my right ear while the box of bake-off decks sits to my left.

"I promise I left them on his porch. Exactly where I've always done it when I deliver to his house," says a distraught Kwame.

"I screwed up. I moved desks earlier and forgot to tell you. The box on my old desk was a bunch of deal toys. The box on my new desk had the decks. Did you get the flight info?"

"JFK—6:17 a.m. departure. JetBlue, terminal five," says Kwame.

"Can we pass this guy? Left lane is open. We're in a right-turn-only lane," I say to the Uber driver.

"Did you try Masters?" says Kwame.

"Called him twice—no answer. Sent him an email telling him I'll meet him at airport with books."

"You know what he looks like?"

"Behemoth guy, angry default face," I say.

"And bald," says Kwame. "Can't miss him."

"Need you driving with some urgency." I lean forward, addressing the Uber driver as we cross the Brooklyn Bridge—4:23 a.m. read the neon-green digits displayed on the dashboard of the car. One would assume commuting in the wee hours of the morning would be quick, but it appears the perpetual construction on the Van Wyck Expressway kicks into high gear right around now.

"Can you check if there are any more flights?" I say to Kwame. "If I can't find him at the airport, I might have to just fly there."

"I'll take a look."

Traffic is bumper-to-bumper at exit one on the Van Wyck, with only one lane open. By exit three, the second lane is open, and by exit six, we're screaming down the left lane, passing Queens in a blur all the way to JFK.

The Honda Civic screeches to a halt at the terminal-five departures drop-off. I snatch the box of decks and haul ass to the JetBlue curbside check-in desk as the sun pokes its first few rays in the horizon.

"Masters," I say. "Has a Rick Masters checked in for a 6:17 a.m. fli—"

"Not authorized to—" begins the guy standing next to the desk. I sprint by him and inside.

And that's when I spot Masters at one of the check-in kiosks.

He turns, boarding pass in hand, and our eyes meet. I lift the box of decks slightly as if to say, "Here they are." He walks toward me, and without a word exchanged, he takes them nearly mid-stride before continuing to the security check-in line. The last image I have is that of the linear scar on the back of his head stretching from ear-to-ear, a relic of a now-abandoned attempt to salvage his hair.

My BlackBerry buzzes on the ride back to Manhattan—new staffing. I figure I'll have just enough time to shower and throw on my suit once I get home, then back to the office.

The skyline of Manhattan comes into view as I sit in the thick of the rush-hour morning commute, horns honking and arms flailing out of windows. At one point, I think I spot the Deutsche Bank building, then I realize I don't give two shits.

I can't help but smile when a new email pops up on my phone—the receipt for my $94.78 Uber ride to JFK—and I realize that, at least this time, I'll be reimbursed.

* * *

The bake-off goes well. Too well—DB is selected as the lead-left bookrunner. The term refers to the location of where the bank's name appears on the prospectus, which is the official document filed with the SEC outlining the transaction. The bank on the farthest left (and usually in the biggest font) is lead-left. It's responsible for nearly everything (creating roadshow/marketing materials, drafting offering documents, leading diligence sessions, and so forth) and is thus rewarded with the best economics. There are a couple "active" bookrunners (including the lead-left bank) that handle the majority of the deal, while another group of banks act as "passive" bookrunners and do next to nothing. Their role during the brunt of the transaction consists of dialing into phone calls, announcing they're on, then going on mute. As the deal nears closing, their role consists of jamming the newly issued stock down the throats of their clients, but this is more of a sales and trading and capital markets job, so the corporate finance team doesn't participate much.

As a junior banker, getting staffed on a deal as a passive bookrunner is the dream. It goes on the staffing log as "IPO" with no mention of the bank's role. You could literally go through an entire week without doing a single thing, except maybe dialing into a diligence call if you're working on a deal as a passive bookrunner. On the flip side, every week as a lead-left bookrunner is like drowning in a bag of shit—not even your own shit. Which brings me to where I am now.

"I bet you guys can see him from Kwame's desk," says Steve over speakerphone as I stand behind Kwame, who's seated in his cube, a PowerPoint file open on his computer.

244

I arch my back slightly, tilting my head even further, and catch a glimpse of Masters, who sits in his office with the door closed.

"Yeah, I see him," I say.

"Okay, I'm gonna try him again. Keep an eye out," says Steve. I crane my head again as Steve puts our call on hold and dials Masters.

"Hear it ringing," I say to Kwame, who remains tucked into his cube. "He's looking at the phone...okay, definitely sees it and hears the ring...and he's back to looking at his computer."

"Any movement?" asks Steve as he comes back on the line.

"I could hear it ring," I say. "Definitely went through, but he's looking at his computer still," I say.

"Would you say he looks pissed or just disgruntled?" asks Steve.

"Somewhere in between," I say.

"Bill, how much would I have to pay you to walk into his office and tell him to answer our calls?" says Steve.

"A hundred Bitcoin," I say.

"I'd do it for fifty Bitcoin," chimes in Kwame.

"Shit, maybe I should just put my life savings into the crypto market," says Steve. "Where's Bitcoin trading—"

"Wait...I think I see movement to the phone. Looks like he's dialing," I say as I spot Masters stretch his arm to his desk phone.

"Yep. Dialing me," says Steve. "Will loop him into our call." Moments later, Masters is on.

"You got Bill and Kwame on the box," I say after Steve conferences us in.

"Management wants these pages this afternoon, so need to turn quickly," Masters says as his greeting. "Page two...multiple on the Tronox deal looks off."

"We double-checked the calculation and get one-point-four times book value," I say. "Cross-checked with equity research and they have same—"

"It just looks wrong," says Masters.

"Alright," I say, "So should—"

"Page three...need pie charts on end-market exposure for each segment."

"Rick," says Steve, stepping in before the call spirals out of control with unreasonable demands. "We've looked into the segment exposure, and we don't have the data. We can put place holders or list the end markets in bullets, but we don't have the percentage breakdown."

"Put placeholders," says Masters. "Where are we at with the benchmarking pages? This needs to be right and need it in the next two hours."

"The guys are finishing up the analysis. I'm going to review in next thirty minutes," says Steve.

"Fine. And we need that standard benchmarking page with all companies in sector," says Masters.

"We'll get it updated and slot in," I say.

"Fine," says Masters. "That's it." Then he hangs up.

"Kwame, Bill, you guys still on?" says Steve.

"Yep," says Kwame.

"All clear on those comments? Don't worry about that multiple. It's right—leave it."

"Think we're good," I say.

"And just make sure that standard benchmarking page has the full set. Masters will check that page and get all sorts of rattled if it's not complete."

"Will do," I say.

The "standard benchmarking page" of which Steve speaks is a clusterfuck of numbers—in this case, 535 unique numbers on a single page. While not overly difficult to market-update the page, it's M&A activity that creates headaches for juniors on "standard" pages like this. If a company makes an acquisition or sells a division, the financials and multiples need to reflect the new company. This is known as the *pro-forma* entity. Finding the data to *pro forma* a company is a witch hunt, and even when there are publicly available figures, you're dealing with imperfect information.

Oftentimes, we'll reference prior decks we've done for a given company. Everything is archived, which means I've been able to sift through decks from the 1990s, when Excel and PowerPoint weren't even used. These decks from the '90s had 50 percent of the information that comparable decks have on them now. I can only imagine what decks looked like in the '70s, or if there were any decks at all. With the computing power of the programs we have now, coupled with the innumerable resources we have access to (FactSet, MAKS, and so forth), senior bankers can demand juniors slap every number in the world into a deck and see what the client gravitates to, instead of putting thought into the deck beforehand and thinking through what could be important. So we'll run fifty-seven sensitivities on growth, forty-nine model scenarios, and throw a zillion pie charts on a page, and hope something grabs the client's attention—your classic "throw some ramen noodles against the wall and see what sticks."

> **John Bukowski:** let's rip down to Florida for some golf this weekend

William Keenan: what?

> **John Bukowski:** got eyes on a 2:09pm flight from LaGuardia on Friday

William Keenan: you realize there's no chance of that happening

> **John Bukowski:** yeah, but fun to at least fantasize a little

William Keenan: get in early evening Friday, play a twilight 9 before a late lobster dinner, then 36 on Saturday

> **John Bukowski:** can you give me a pity LinkedIn view, haven't had any in like 3 days

William Keenan: if you give me your leftover fries that are in the fridge

John Bukowski: leftovers command a premium—pity view plus message

After knocking out some of Steve's text comments, I return to Kwame's cube.

"How we looking?" I ask.

"All done except the benchmarking page. This guy," says Kwame tapping a company's logo on the screen, "bought a performance-materials division recently, and I'm having trouble finding details on how they financed it."

"Think I saw a presentation on their website that shows shit on it," I say.

"Yeah, but it just shows pro forma EBITDA," says Kwame.

"Do we know the multiple they bought it for?" I ask. Kwame nods. "So we can back into the target's standalone EBITDA, then multiply by acquisition multiple to get enterprise value for them. Then we can just make an assumption that they used seventy-percent debt or something." I pause, wondering if that makes any sense.

"But Steve said Masters looks very carefully at this page," says Kwame as he rifles through various PDF documents and websites in search of detail on the deal.

"There are five hundred and thirty-five fuckin' numbers on the page," I say. "And we have thirty minutes to get this out. Just hardcode the assumed-acquisition debt and you can even write in note, 'As per Bill.'"

"No," says Kwame as he turns in his chair and looks at me, his face full of concern. "If I hardcode, it will screw up the flow of the page when we update it. I need to understand this."

Like most tasks on this job, my philosophy is get it done now, and maybe later try to understand it, if there's time or interest. Not sure I have much of either these days.

23

Happy Fourth

The summer takes on a rhythm of predictability that borders on bliss, or as close to bliss as one finds inside an investment bank. The lows are low and the highs are sometimes lower.

I lose track of the days. My only touch point is listening to brief elevator conversations on my way up to the forty-fourth floor each morning—Monday and Tuesday small-talk consists of recounting the prior weekend's happenings. By Wednesday afternoon, conversations turn to discussions on upcoming weekend plans. There's a perpetual longing for weekends past or weekends to come. In banking, no one wants to talk about the present.

The majority of my time is spent creating the roadshow presentation, which the company will use to market itself to potential investors. Mornings are spent turning the client's comments, while nights are spent turning Masters's comments. After completing Masters's comments each night around 2:00 a.m., Kwame and I send the updated deck to the client, who typically provides comments by 9:00 a.m. Kwame and I get into work around 9:30 a.m. and turn those comments, finishing by early afternoon, after which we send the deck to Masters for his review. He sends comments around 10:00 p.m. And the cycle continues.

"Get any sleep last night, boys?" Steve asks on the bad nights, when he sees our emails sent out in the early morning hours. He's not apologizing. After all, he isn't the reason we stay up all night. But simply acknowledging the fact that Kwame and I spend most nights at the office is just enough empathy we need to chug forward.

Those of you chronologically inclined may notice there's a gap from early afternoon to 10:00 p.m. The never-ending stream of pitch staffings continues through the summer and eats up some of this free time, but I do an admirable job of dumping most of that work either on my analyst or my friends in Chennai, where my requests to the MAKS team no doubt are responsible for India's outsized GDP growth.

Some afternoons, I head home and take a nap; other afternoons, I sit in my cube and Netflix and chill; and occasionally, I'll just sit there and guzzle water, inducing pee and forcing me to get up just so I have something to do. Like most of life, these periods of boredom are punctuated by bursts of all-out panic when Masters or the client see a number that "makes no sense" and Kwame and I scramble to make sense of it. Masters makes weekly cameos at the office, typically on Tuesdays and Thursdays, instilling low-level terror in Kwame and me each time he storms by our cubes. The pit stops are always of the same nature—he has instructions for us and doesn't want a paper trail.

Every couple weeks, we receive "good" emails, news of "reinforcements" coming from M&A. Translation: more senior bankers from the M&A group are hopping on the bandwagon to get credit for the deal. While seemingly harmless, the addition of each new senior banker means another MD who provides comments on books, another MD who barks orders on calls.

Periodically, it's imperative to recalibrate one's idea of boredom. All transactions require participation by lawyers to help draft SEC filings and other black-and-white documents with tiny font.

Redlining legal documents involves lawyers marking up documents and telling you how DB is getting fucked by whoever we're negotiating with, when in reality, DB is really getting screwed by the lawyers, who bill hourly.

On days when we head to Midtown to the law firm we work with to draft the red-herring prospectus, I'm reminded why I didn't go to law school—aside from my shitty LSAT score. Spending days at the law firm debating placement of semicolons and constructing incomprehensible sentences makes life on the forty-fourth floor of DB feel like Saturday night at a bachelor party in the mirror room at Club K5 Relax in downtown Prague. Staying awake during these drafting sessions should be reflected in junior bankers' bonuses.

* * *

"They're starting," says Kwame. The first loud bang is followed by a succession of louder bangs.

I join Kwame in the corner conference room that overlooks New York Harbor and watch the red, white, and blue July 4th fireworks sparkle, dance, and explode across the dark summer sky.

"Blows working on the Fourth," I say.

"This transaction will look good on our résumés, though," says Kwame. Nearly every analyst has an eye on a buy-side job even before starting banking. Landing one of these highly coveted jobs requires relevant deal experience, though. Thus, the most motivated analysts are typically driven by the desire to leave the bank before they even start. It makes me wonder if the job encourages mediocrity for those who aren't sold on the buy-side exit.

In the distance, Lady Liberty stands, lit in her perpetual salute to freedom, as the vibration of the BlackBerry in my pocket reminds me of the freedom I lack: Project Liberty summons me.

"Masters?" asks Kwame as he turns, trying to read my face for an indication of how much longer we'll be in the office and if he'll be able to make the party in Tribeca he's been talking about.

"Yeah," I say scrolling through the comments. "Not too bad, actually...but he's still hung up on the EBITDA charts for the Laminates Division."

"What's his comment?" says Kwame. "We checked it six times—numbers are right."

"Says 'numbers look wrong still,'" I say, reading Masters's comment verbatim.

Here is the chart in question.

The numbers are right—they're from the client. What Masters doesn't like is the absence of stratospheric growth. As you most likely won't recall, since you're skimming over my periodic financial tutorials, credit investors salivate at charts like this—steady, consistent EBITDA numbers over time. All they care about is that the company whose debt they purchase can service the interest payments. But equity investors (like the ones we're marketing to on this deal), they're interested in the dream—the through-the-fuckin'-roof growth. For reference, here is a chart from a prior IPO roadshow deck I worked on.

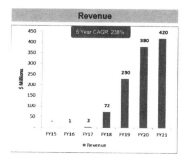

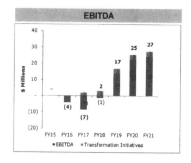

Now *those* are IPO charts. Part of me felt like I was committing a crime when I input those projections into Excel and saw the final charts on a roadshow presentation—honestly, there may be a crime in there. If it's not already abundantly clear, the projected financials, as provided by the company, begin in 2018. Your run-of-the-mill, 238 percent, five-year revenue CAGR should get that issuance ten times oversubscribed.[1]

"What the hell does he want us to do?" I say.

"Got an idea," says Kwame. He disappears to his cube as I work on some of the other comments. Fifteen minutes later, Kwame sends me an email: "Look better?" I open it:

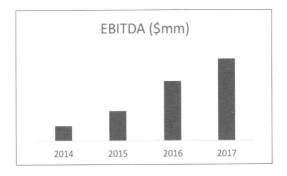

William Keenan: looks money. Where'd you get new numbers??

Kwame Adeyemi: same shiznit. Messed with scale

We turn the rest of Masters's comments. "Looks right," he scribbles in red pen above the updated chart on his final markup before we send the deck to the client. (See charts next page.)

And this is why Kwame earns his new spot in the bullpen, where he moves the day before we begin the roadshow.

---

[1] As of the date of this book's publication, the company in question has not hit its projections.

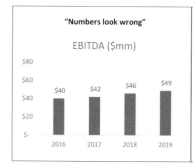

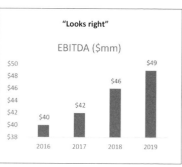

24

Lollipop at the Roadshow

"You gonna eat that or what?" I whisper to Kwame, who sits next to me at the round table in the Tivoli Room at the Essex Hotel in Midtown Manhattan. Kwame pushes his untouched cheesecake in front of me, and I dig in as our client's CEO stands in the front of the room next to the projector and hits the small device in his hand.

"Now, I'm really excited about this slide," he says. I remember making the slide—wasn't quite as exciting, since I had no fuckin' clue what Polytetrahydrofuran was when I was creating lollipop charts on its end markets. "With our best-in-class NXT additive packages and exposure to high growth..." continues the CEO as I zone out.

The tables in the back of the room are full of bankers. To my left, Kwame checks his LinkedIn views on his iPhone. To my right is an analyst from Citigroup, who is scrolling through his fantasy baseball lineup. To his right is an associate from Citigroup, who is taking notes that no one will ever look at. Masters and Steve had to leave early to meet with another client.

The table to my right is occupied by the JP Morgan IPO team. How do I know? The six of them wear matching fleece vests that, when the collar is up, reveal "JPM IPO team" embroidered in white. The banker who threw a fit because his gluten-free meal took an extra fifteen minutes to be served whispers into the ear of his colleague before they share a chuckle, then both pretend to read the prospectus.

Bankers attend these roadshow presentations to fill out the room, usher the management team from the urinal to the sink, and swing our dicks around when presented with the opportunity. In the front tables, listening closely with paper and pen in hand, are the potential investors—a smattering of hedge fund managers, mutual funds guys, and really anyone who drops a business card in the glass jar at the check-in desk. Security isn't tight, despite the CONFIDENTIAL warning stamped on every document. In fact, as I polish off my third piece of strawberry cheesecake and wash it down with some fresh-brew coffee, I think how one could enjoy free, sumptuous meals and bone up on the laminate industry if one simply knew the location of the roadshow presentation.

A collective chuckle returns my attention to the projector, where a clip from *The Graduate* plays, in which Dustin Hoffman's character is brought outside by some douche dial-tone and told with a finger in his face, "There's a great future in plastics." The company's CEO thought the clip might be a nice way to add levity to the presentation. I remember not really understanding the scene when I first saw the movie freshman year in college, then laughing at the scene when I watched the movie fifty times senior year—fuckin' Mr. McGuire.

Not as funny these days.

The key to a successful IPO is marketing to long-term investors. This helps ensure the stock doesn't tank immediately after going public. Ideally, management (and bankers) convinces these investors the stock is a solid long-term investment, which reminds me of the old investor adage: "Be right and sit tight." Not to be confused with the investment banker adage: "Be wrong and blow Dodge."

"With that," says the CEO, clicking the slide-switching device, "I'll hand the floor over to our CFO—" The screen goes black. The CEO walks to the computer and futzes with the mouse. "Looks like the computer died. Guess we won't get to the financials section." Boy, is he lucky, 'cause the EBITDA adjustments for this company are something else—we'll get there.

"Think we might as well open it up to some Q&A then," says the CEO as he returns to center stage, scanning the first few tables.

"Shoot," says the CEO, pointing at a bespectacled guy whose arm pops up.

"Can you talk a little bit about how you view the vitality index in conjunction with the new product roll-outs you've discussed, specifically in the additive segment, where you project over seventy percent of your NTM revenue will be generated?" He turns slightly after concluding his question as if to gauge how impressed everyone is. No one looks at him.

Like most of his peers in the industry, the CEO uses a wily combination of folksy charm and intricate knowledge of the industry to sound knowledgeable and to answer some questions with eye-popping detail when in the company's interest, while parrying other questions and diverting his answers toward the company's outperformance in some other category. I learned early on there's no point in really listening, since I can't tell the difference between the two. "Great question, and glad you asked it," says the CEO after most questions.

But not all.

"Is there a question here?" asks the CEO after a well-heeled hedgie with slicked-back hair concludes a monologue outlining some correlation between feedstock prices in Europe, utilization rates in the US, and the price of raw materials in Asia. It's like the kid in high school who reels off esoteric information in class, spewing a bunch of jargon just to show how much he knows, but never realizing that *this* is why he has no friends.

"Let me rephrase," says the hedgie, after which he repeats the same statement except inverts the sentence and instills some intonation at the end to make it sound like a question.

The presentation ends as it began—a smattering of light applause from those at the first few tables, while those in the back tables scroll through their BlackBerries, oblivious until front-row people stand.

There are handshakes, side conversations, and judging eyes throughout the room as I walk to the buffet table to snag a few chocolate-chip cookies for the road.

"Bill Keenan," says a man's voice behind me accompanied by the weight of a hand on my right shoulder. I turn around and see an MD from Morgan Stanley who I met during the recruiting process.

"Brendan," I say, remembering his name since it was the same as one of my favorite NHL players when I was a kid, and our conversations during recruiting revolved around hockey. "How are things?"

"Won our semi-final game last night at the Piers," he says. "Finals this weekend." Brendan took his men's-league hockey games as seriously as his job. During recruiting, he invited me to play with his team. The game started at 11:15 p.m. at Chelsea Piers on a Tuesday. I wanted a job, but not that badly.

"Any goals?" I say, vaguely remembering him telling me that he was a "playmaker."

"Two assists...plus-three rating," he says shrugging with humility. Brendan is one of the few senior bankers I met during the recruiting process whose ego wasn't on full display at every event. He seemed like a decent enough guy. "You know, I saw your name on the WGL and remember receiving some emails from you over the last couple weeks on this deal. Quite a transaction, huh?"

"Definitely an interesting situation with the restructuring and Chapter Eleven they recently went through," I say.

"Very unusual dynamic with the OTC situation," he says, lobbing it back to me. We both avert our eyes and scan the room, then, with just a moment of brief eye contact, we communicate to one another that we've reached that threshold of how much we really know about what's going on.

"Well, look. You have my email. Let me know how things progress at DB, and if there's anything I can do. And of course, we could use a ringer in the finals this weekend." Brendan does a stickhandling motion, after which we shake hands. He disappears in the crowd of suits now mingling in the banquet hall, while I wrap two more fresh-baked cookies in a napkin and pocket them.

* * *

The roadshow moves west the next day—Chicago, Dallas, Los Angeles, then to Boston and finally one final presentation back in NYC. No private jet, but Kwame and I do get those seats with extra legroom and are allowed to expense the cost of in-flight Wi-Fi. As the presentations progress, the CEO's planted jokes are crafted to precision, so much so that by the time we're in Boston, there are a few people who laugh at them. And it's uncanny how the computer battery dies right before the presentation moves to the financial sections and explanation of EBITDA adjustments—almost as if on purpose.

The deal prices at the high end of the anticipated range and is oversubscribed, both indications of a receptive and eager investor base, in conjunction with well-executed marketing. The company goes public a few weeks after Labor Day and initially trades at a premium to its peers. But after the initial buzz wears off, the stock tanks as the initial IPO investors take profits, and more sophisticated investors analyze the stock and short it, driving its valuation down. Much of the decline can be traced to the adjusted EBITDA the company (and bankers) used to market the company.

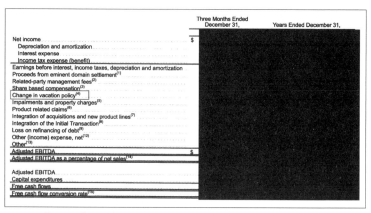

Appendix II of Prospectus—page 18

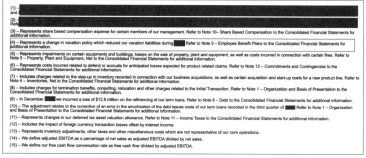

Appendix IV of Prospectus—page 20

Vacation Benefits

In ▇▇, the Company amended its vacation policy for U.S. employees to no longer allow for the carryover of unused vacation into subsequent years. The impact of the amendment was to reduce selling, general and administrative expenses in our Consolidated Statement of Income by ▇▇▇▇▇▇

Appendix III of Consolidated Financial Statements—page F21

"Change in vacation policy" doesn't tell us much. So we head to the footnote the lawyers buried in another appendix in the prospectus. Footnote four literally provides no further detail on the adjustment, aside from redirecting us to yet *another* footnote in a *separate* document. So we now sift through the appendices of the financial statement, where we find our answer: the company has reduced its expenses by no longer allowing employees to carry over vacation days—quick and easy way to bump the adjusted EBITDA figure right before going public. The adjustment is never questioned through the entire deal. And while the stock appears to trade down on an EV/EBITDA multiple relative to peers, if you don't give the company credit for that "change in vacation policy" add-back, it trades in-line with peers. But while the company's management must scramble to please shareholders, we bankers have already collected our fee.

So we bank on.

25

Back-Pocket Materials

"You're no longer a total fraud," says Ted as I pass his cube. "Congrats on the deal."

"And you're no longer an associate," I say. "Congrats on the promotion. What're you doing to celebrate?"

"Uninstalling PowerPoint," says Ted. Then as an afterthought, he adds, "And saying 'EBIT-D-A,' instead of 'EBITDA' on client calls."

And this is the essence of the irony in banking. What makes a good junior banker is in direct opposition to what makes a good senior banker. Successful junior bankers take orders without thinking, crunch numbers, and keep their mouths shut. Successful senior bankers are salesmen, "high-level" thinkers, no longer in the weeds. The only number they care about is the fee on the deal, and more often than not, they're running their mouths all day. Thus, while some skills you develop as a junior—like numbers analysis—are useful, the evolution from analyst to salesperson explains why so many senior bankers possess those affectations that accompany most people who have to feign charm.

I'm also certain any newly promoted MD sits in on a seminar outlining how to be synthetically important: join a non-profit board, some bullshit committee, and a "really special" country club, all of which are required to discuss at the beginning of conference calls.

In my old cube, next to Ted, sits a new associate who just joined the bank. Fresh off of training in London, he sports one of those manicured beards that are popular in your second year of business school after you secure a full-time job offer. Word around the office is he gave a senior analyst a markup on his first staffing and had the analyst do all the work. Ted hasn't spoken to him since, and he now goes completely ignored when he enters the bullpen in search of help. I give his beard one more week and his tenure at DB a couple months.

Things change as a second-year banker. As a first-year, when I walked around the office, I saw two categories of activity on my colleagues' computer monitors—finance or fuckin' around. Now, as a second-year, my senses are heightened. All I need is a split-second glimpse of one's monitor to identify exactly what they're working on. It's no longer finance or fuckin' around. Now, it's an assumptions tab of an LBO model, a stacked-column chart for an IPO deck, operational benchmarking for a CRM memo, or *Curb Your Enthusiasm* season four, episode two.

Tactics employed to feign being busy become more sophisticated: when the staffer makes his daily, unannounced trip through the cubicles of junior bankers, I tap the volume control button on my desk phone, causing it to emit the same sound as if someone were calling me. I rip my headset from the cube divider: "What's up? Fuck, alright, I'll get in the model and figure it out." More often than not, that sentence, delivered as the staffer passes, is enough to avoid a staffing for one more day.

Even my communication skills and language evolve. Instead of asking an MD, "How was the meeting?" I ask him, "What was the tenor of the meeting?" It's verbose and exactly what bankers like to hear.

My ability to navigate through files, spreadsheets, websites, and documents on my computer without the crutch of the mouse borders on wizardry. Requests from seniors with vague, incomprehensible demands are no longer met with gut-wrenching panic, but instead a small chuckle, followed by a shake of the head, then a plan of attack, which usually involves a senior analyst and an email to MAKS.

This progress doesn't go unnoticed. Emails from recruiters at buy-side firms, boutique investment banks, and business development teams at corporations flood my LinkedIn account and Gmail inbox. All start something like this:

> Dear WILLIAM,
> Please find details of the following vacancy, which I hope you are interested in. I trust your confidentiality and discretion in this regard. I have hand selected you for this opportunity and sincerely believe you would be a terrific candidate for this role….

Then there's the LinkedIn message from a recruiter at Goldman Sachs: "…and your background suggests you just may be Goldman material." I consider writing a book on account of this.

But none of these opportunities interest me enough to pursue.

Despite increased confidence, the work piles up and has a way of humbling you. I see as many sunrises as sunsets through the fall and into the winter, a result of fewer junior bankers and a hot market that allows senior bankers to push clients into doing something—refinance debt, make an acquisition, go public, go broke—anything that will generate a fee. I'm pulled in fifteen directions, one of which is back into Ethan's office just before Christmas.

* * *

Beep.

"You got Ethan and Bill," says Ethan. Our relationship has progressed in the past year. At the recent Christmas party, after the MDs and senior VPs took turns hitting on the female analysts, we played Pin the Tail on the Analyst. Using a face card comprised of headshots of every junior banker, MDs picked a junior banker's name out of a hat, then were required to put a sticker on the face of that person. Not only did Ethan correctly identify me, but he put his arm around me and slurred some encouraging words before retreating to the bathroom to heave.

The small, red bulb illuminates as Ethan hits the mute button on the PolyCom SoundStation speakerphone device in his office. "Senior associate, huh?" he says to me. "Couple deals under your belt. Got a nice new suit, shoes all polished." A few more junior bankers announce themselves on the line. I look at my outfit—literally the same shit I was wearing from head to toe when I first sat in Ethan's office on day one.

Beep.

"Arthur's on," says the MD from lev fin.

"Second year gets me senior status?" I ask Ethan.

"Absolutely."

Beep.

"Sorry we're a little late, guys. You got Rob and Marshall here," says our client who's engaged us to reprice their Term Loan B, a relatively painless transaction in which companies can lower the overall interest rate on their debt.

Ethan unmutes the line and is about to speak, when Arthur jumps in.

"Robby! How we doing? Anything planned for the holidays?" says Arthur. A smile emerges on Ethan's face as he points at the speakerphone device and re-mutes the line.

"This shit is always good. Arthur loves this guy," says Ethan to me.

"Heading to Banff with the family," says Rob.

"Good for you," says Arthur. "Good for you. Should be some fresh powder there."

"Single-digit handle on the weather out there. That's without the wind and at the base of the mountain. Supposed to be some polar vortex rolling through Christmas week too. Unfortunately, I don't make the rules in my house. I just follow 'em," says Rob.

Arthur emits a forced laugh over the line as Ethan's excitement grows. "Just getting started," whispers Ethan to me.

"Now they have a direct flight from Boston to Banff? Assume Calgary?" says Arthur.

"Fly to Toronto, take a toboggan to Winnipeg, then Iditarod to Banff," says Rob as Arthur lets out a laugh reserved for the type of clients you need.

"Shouldn't be hard for Santa to find you up there," says Arthur. "What's on your Christmas list?"

"Employment," says Rob. "You up to anything for the holidays?"

Ethan, with the line still muted, points with both fingers at the speakerphone device. "This'll be good."

"Shooting out to Vail with the family," says Arthur. "Been doing Christmas there last few years. Kids like to ski. The wife likes après-ski, so we all win."

"Wife's family's place," says Ethan to me as he makes a yapping gesture with his hand.

"Great place to recharge the batteries," says Rob.

"Working vacation for me, but should be nice to get out of the city—hope to get a couple runs in," says Arthur. Ethan makes a double jerk-off motion with his hands and looks at me. I have no choice but to force a smile and pretend it's funny.

Ethan unmutes the line. "I thought you hit the half-pipe on your snowboard, Arthur," says Ethan, followed by some laughter on the line. "Rob, Gary—appreciate you guys jumping on the phone with us. Just wanted to give you an update on where we're at," continues Ethan before he briefs them on the deal and confirms their meeting at the end of the week. I jot down some notes, and given there is no VP or analyst on the deal, these are notes I'll actually look at, not the fake type I usually take.

The conference call ends with a few more lame jokes about skiing.

"All good with what I need for meeting Friday?" asks Ethan.

"Got it," I say. And I'm not lying.

"How's shit going otherwise?" says Ethan. "Couple years under the belt."

I'm so caught off the guard by the question, I don't even think before responding.

"Don't really think this job's for me," I say.

"Hey, I don't think this job's for me either," says Ethan. A glaze of desperation passes over his face, and for a moment, I pity him.

His phone rings. He eyes the caller ID. "Fuck me," he mutters before picking up the receiver. "Arthur, what's shaking?"

I leave the office.

* * *

"I'm quitting," says Jack as he stands over my desk. It's how most Monday morning conversations start after a long weekend in the office.

"What happened now?" I say as I work on the deck for Ethan's meeting for the re-pricing transaction.

"Got staffed on a sell-side and my analyst just told me he's gone next two weeks."

"That kid who ends every word with an 's'?" I say.

"Yeah," says Jack.

"Shit, he's good, right?"

"The best. He told staffer he has to leave country and go back to Korea for two weeks to renew his visa or some bullshit. But I know he's got a PE job lined up and is just looking to get in as much vacation as he can before he quits."

"I don't have any analyst on my deal," I say as I hit the F12 key on my keyboard to save up a version.

"No," says Jack. "I don't like this, not one bit—when you're all contentedly slapping the keyboard with confidence. I need you sympathizing with me right now, not feeling good about yourself."

I delete the "v23" in the Save As box and replace it with "v24."

"I shouldn't've come over—big mistake. Let me know when you're as miserable as me," says Jack as he leaves my cube.

"Will do," I say.

When I send the updated deck to Ethan Wednesday night, his comments are light, which I suspect has something to do with the Redskins already having clinched a playoff berth. I'm able to print the books around dinner time and have them couriered to his house on the Upper West Side around 10:00 p.m.

Friday morning at the office is quiet. Ethan confirms he received the decks and is on his way to the airport.

> **John Bukowski:** I'm drowning over here. You still in good mood?

> **William Keenan:** sorry. Yeah, v good. Printed deck last night. Looks like smooth sailing today

> **John Bukowski:** k bye

A first-year analyst, a small Indian girl, pops up from her cube with a concerned look plastered over her face. She does a slow 360-degree turn as if in search of someone, then disappears back down into her cube. While I haven't worked with her yet, I know she's smart. I remember interviewing her prior to her internship and asking her to walk me through a DCF valuation. Her response was so thorough that I jotted down notes for my own benefit. Her head emerges again from her cube, though this time just high enough that I can see her eyes, but it's all I need to see. I pause my episode of *Curb* and meander over to her desk.

"Hey, Riya. How's it going?" I say as I casually approach her cube.

"I think I'm in trouble," she says. "I just got a call from lev fin telling me I need to do the credit model, and I really don't know what I'm doing."

"You're investment banking," I say with a smile that goes unnoticed. My attempt to alleviate the pressure she feels falls flat.

"You have an associate on this with you?" I ask.

"He's away at a wedding. And I just got the call from lev fin. They had told us they would handle it, but they just told me I need to do it." The pitch of her voice increases, and it's as though the pressure literally pushes her down in her seat.

"Sounds about right," I say as I lean over her shoulder and take a look. "Can you hit F2 on cell D16?" I say. She does.

"I just can't figure out how they're getting to this EBITDA number since it doesn't tie to the cap table," she says.

"Go to the cap table sheet and F2 the LTM EBITDA cell," I say.

She uses the mouse to switch sheets. "Oops…shoot," she says as her finger hits the F1 key. "I'm sorry." She fumbles to use her mouse to close out the dialog box that pops up.

"Have quick fix for that if you want," I say.

"Please!" she says.

I remove my keys from my pocket and in one fluid motion, shimmy my house key under the F1 key and pop it out of the keyboard. "Won't have that problem again," I say.

"Perfect!" She looks at me with the look only a struggling junior banker can convey.

Before she hits F2 on the cell labeled 'LTM EBITDA,' I already detect an issue. The cell is highlighted bright yellow, and the number is in size fourteen, dark blue, italicized Calibri font. This is the Excel equivalent of finding herpes.

"Looks like it's hardcoded, which is weird. Check the note," I say. "Shift F2."

"As per DS email," she says reading the comment.

"There's our issue—looks like a legacy number. It should be linked to that other EBITDA figure we were looking at. And what you can do is turn autocolors on—Ctrl Alt E. Autocolor will help you identify if the cells are linked or hardcoded."

"You're a lifesaver," she says, swiveling around in her chair after scribbling down some notes on what I said.

"Not a problem," I say.

"I know I shouldn't say it, but I feel like I'm so far behind with the Excel and PowerPoint and everything," she says in hushed tones.

"I promise I was light-years behind you. You have no idea." My BlackBerry vibrates in my pocket. It's Ethan. "I gotta take this, but let me know if you have any other issues.

"Hello?" I say as I plug in my headphones to the BlackBerry.

"It's Ethan. Look I'm just flipping through the deck. Need some back-pocket materials for the meeting."

"Like a page of their historicals?" I say.

"We need to show these guys an LBO model."

"Okay," I say sort of as a question as I return to my cube and take a seat. "I don't remember us ever discussing the model on the call."

"We didn't, but I know these guys, and they're gonna want to see what it looks like. They got a bunch of PE shops interested in acquiring them and we need to show them different scenarios… like what we did for that last Dow deck." I want to jump through the phone and strangle him with the cord.

> **John Bukowski:** I got a gift from the banking gods—just got a "pencils down" on my deal. I feel like a bajillion bucks.

"Okay, to be clear, for Dow, that was three separate debt structure scenarios, all with different sensitivities around entry and exit multiples and pricing," I say, recollecting the nightmare deck from a few months back.

"Do same thing," says Ethan. "I'm not trying to create work, but this needs to be done. Don't we already have a DCF up and running for these guys? Can't you just do an F9 refresh and get the LBO model?"

> **John Bukowski:** A/S/L

> **John Bukowski:** I'm swinging by with gusto. Let's jerk around.

"Slightly more involved than that. We had an illustrative DCF from last quarter, but all with hand-wavy assumptions. It's far less detailed than what we'd[1] need for the LBO."

"Well good news is my flight's delayed forty-five minutes. So still have like five hours or so before the meeting to get this done and send. I can print the pages at their office."

"Alright," I say. My head drops into my hands. No analyst to help with the model. No VP to check to make sure it makes sense. Just one associate with an unrealistic timeline for another bullshit request.

In the cube to my left, I hear the contented slap of the Enter key, the type reserved for when you PDF the final version of a deck.

"Also check to see if these guys got any NOLs," says Ethan before hanging up.

> **John Bukowski:** let's go celebrate with slices. My treat. You can even get the gross one with the weird sausage

> **John Bukowski:** losersayswhat

> **John Bukowski:** U cummin??

> **William Keenan:** I'm quitting

> **John Bukowski:** yes!!!!!!!!!!!!

---

[1] *I'd*

26

Power Struggle

The balance of power on the forty-fourth floor is all off.

"Walk me through a DCF," instructs Phuc as he leans back in the large leather chair at the head of the conference-room table.

Liz, a college sophomore dressed in a pantsuit most likely purchased for the occasion, shifts in her seat as she consults the notebook in front of her. I eye her résumé again, her most recent work experience listed as a counselor at Camp Timber Lake. Impressively, she's been able to construct a series of sub-bullets outlining her financial responsibilities at the camp, mostly relating to the canoe budgeting.

"I don't think we need to get into technicals, Phuc. This is just an informational interview so Liz can get a better understanding of what it's like here on a day-to-day basis," I say.

Phuc shrugs. "But Liz, I'd still recommend you bone up on basic accounting and valuation methodologies, because some bankers won't be as nice during the interview process."

Liz nods and makes a note. If she's able to sufficiently impress the five or six junior bankers she meets today, Liz's name will be passed onto the group staffer, who will make sure she gets priority during the application process. This only ensures that she will at most receive a first-round interview for a summer internship. This is the beginning of a months-long, wildly overcomplicated interview process, culminating in a super-day, when she'll spend six hours meeting with senior bankers whose only goal is to ensure she'll be a competent and obedient workhorse.

The fact Liz makes it to the forty-fourth-floor conference room without having to call or email anyone in the minutes leading up to the interview is grounds for, at minimum, a summer-internship role. Most banking groups across Wall Street are located on floors only accessible by an ID card, but more importantly they have an outdated contact sheet next to the phone that hangs on the wall by the floor's locked, glass double-doors. And if you think the occupants of the cubes near these doors are going to open the doors for a young-looking, lost soul, you haven't been reading carefully. Just because everyone in those cubes was at one time that person lingering outside the door with no clue how to gain entrance doesn't mean they're going to help.

It's odd being on the other side of the table, metaphorically. It's even odder to be literally sitting at a conference-room table. But when prospective interns arrive each Friday, junior bankers rule the roost, if only for a fleeting moment.

My BlackBerry buzzes in my pocket. I remove it. "We've listened to your feedback," reads the subject of the email. The body of the email explains a new initiative to shorten pitch books—twenty-five pages maximum. This all stems from a feedback meeting junior bankers had a few weeks back. What the email doesn't mention is parameters on restricting the length and number of appendices in books or back-pocket materials. All in all, nothing will change. Before I can get too worked up, I realize I'm now the douche checking my emails during an interview. I slide the phone back into my pocket and re-engage.

"Before we go, we want to make sure you have a chance to ask us any questions you have about banking, or our group, or anything in general," I say. While I know it's not realistic, part of me wishes she'll ask the question that most prospective interns have in their heads but are too scared to ever ask: What is investment banking?

"I'd like that," says Liz as she flips to another page in her notebook where she's written down a list of questions. "Is there a recent deal you worked on that stands out? And what made it unique?"

Phuc has this one teed up, given he undoubtedly asked this question a couple years ago when he was in the same position as Liz. We all did. As Phuc unloads a barrage of information about his most recent IPO, which weeks later will be so poorly executed that the group doesn't even buy deal toys for the transaction, I watch Liz force herself to take notes, feigning spellbound rapture as she takes cues from Phuc's intonation. Wall Street pays a premium for students who are motivated, smart, and have no direction. Banks are marketing geniuses, selling tentative students on the notion banking is an unrivaled launchpad, a stepping-stone for nearly any career imaginable, while ensuring those students hell-bent on a career in banking that there's a straight shot to MD if they join.

"Any other questions?" asks Phuc after he finishes outlining the mechanics of his deal. Thank God she has questions prepared, like I did. If you have no idea what the job entails, formulating questions is difficult.

"What would you say are the most important attributes of being a successful junior investment banker?"

I don't have firsthand experience, nor does Phuc, but that won't stop him.

"Time management is key. Good soft-skills are important, but knowing your technicals is just as vital. And a strong work ethic. That's not to say we don't have fun. It's definitely a 'work hard, play hard' mentality," says Phuc. At the holiday party, he took a shot in two sips. "And one other thing—you should focus on your negotiation skills. They're a banker's biggest asset. I use them all the time on deals." Phuc looks at me for corroboration. The only thing Phuc has negotiated is deal-toy terms, and he failed there too. I can't even bear to look at him. Instead my focus remains on Liz as she does the dance, allowing Phuc to own the room. I want to tell her that important skills include the ability to jam a million pie charts on a single page and figuring out how to manipulate assumptions to get to a final-output number, like knowing the answer to a test but having to show your work to get full credit.

The small trash can in the corner of the room catches my eye. Earlier in the week, I stood in an hour-long meeting for a deck on which the senior MD in the M&A group haphazardly scrawled a markup, then promptly and inexplicably tore up the papers and trashed them as he concluded the meeting. I spent the back half of the morning on my hands and knees with my analyst, rooting through the trash trying to piece together the markup. I want to tell all this to Liz, but I don't. Instead I remain silent, not perpetuating the illusion of banking like Phuc, but doing nothing to dispel the façade that enables banks to recruit otherwise intelligent students to join in masses each year.

As we wrap up our interview, Liz graciously accepts the second business card Phuc hands her, despite him having tossed one on the table in her direction at the beginning of our meeting. After ushering her out, I run into Ted as he exits the elevator.

"How was it?" I ask as we walk to his cube.

"Normal bullshit," he says. Each month, DB holds an internal symposium for junior bankers in the large auditorium in the building's basement.

"What was the topic?" I ask. Ted removes his tie and suit jacket then sits at his cube.

"Climbing the DB ladder," he says.

"Any tips on how to do it?" asks Bart from his cube.

"Simple," says Ted as he rises from his chair and bends over.

The new associate who occupies my old cube and finally shaved his beard pops up like Whac-A-Mole. "Were there any materials from the meeting?" he asks.

"No," says Ted as he tosses the spiral-bound deck titled "Climbing the DB Ladder" into his trash can.

As I return to my cube on the other side of the floor, I hear the unmistakable squeal of Phuc.

"You gotta be kidding me!?" he says as he looks at his computer, then puts his face in his hands.

Balance on forty-four is restored.

27

Let Us Pray

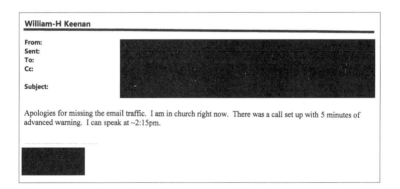

William-H Keenan

From:
Sent:
To:
Cc:

Subject:

Apologies for missing the email traffic. I am in church right now. There was a call set up with 5 minutes of advanced warning. I can speak at ~2:15pm.

G enius! I file away the excuse given by the senior associate in the M&A group as the Sunday morning call continues. DB has been retained by an industrial-engineering company to provide financing on an acquisition they're making, as well as buy-side advisory services.

"Looks directionally right," says Barry, an MD in the M&A group, as he reviews the accretion-dilution page in question.

"Do we need that secondary analysis with the price-to-tangible book figures?" asks the M&A analyst.

"That's a nice-to-have, not a need-to-have," says Barry. "Let's keep pushing forward to section two." I perk up at my desk and unmute the line. While section one of the deck was the M&A team's responsibility, section two was done by me. "Look," continues Barry, "the good news is we're all busy, so let's be thankful for that. Bad news is, we're gonna need to make up a ton of shit for this meeting, and we don't have much time."

That's where I come in. Our client is suffering from cold feet and wants us to provide further evidence that this is a strategically sound, and financially reasonable acquisition. While the M&A team has done most of the work on this transaction thus far, the Industrials group (me) has been brought in to provide "industry expertise."

"Add the gas companies for comps on page twenty-two," says Barry. "Easy for me to bullshit around them." In the background, I hear kids squealing with delight.

"Got it," I respond as I sit in my cube and hear Phuc squeal in his cube across the floor.

"On the multiples-over-time page," continues Barry. "Let's add a box in a key message, showing broker estimates for each comp. Show mean and median for two years ago, one year ago, and current. That'll help corroborate some of our other points we have in the exec summary."

"To confirm, show all those data points for every comp on that page, including the addition of the gas comps on page twenty-two?" I say. Sometimes, restating the asinine requests help an MD register the amount of unnecessary work it takes to perform the task. Sometimes.

"Yep," says Barry. "All of 'em...shouldn't be difficult. You can probably do one of those FactSet things and pull all the data in at once."

"I can definitely use FactSet to pull in the current estimates, but the others will have to be spread by hand. Happy to do it, just want to flag that it will take some time, and I know we're trying to get this printed by early evening."

"How long?" says a voice I don't recognize.

"With the additional gas comps, I'd say two hours, maybe three."

"Great. Let's do two hours," says Barry. "This trade is happening at ten to twelve times. That's just a fact, so our client has to accept that." At five-hundred million of EBITDA, Barry provides a valuation range between five billion and six billion dollars.[1] "Also, reminder to everyone this is no longer Project Sox. CEO is a lifelong Cubs season-ticket holder, so we're renaming it Project Cubs. Make sure that's a global change in this deck and all subsequent correspondence with the client."

"Got it," I say.

"Alright—page twenty-three." He pauses as I brace myself. There are a ton of numbers on this page, all of which are my responsibility. If an MD smells blood, he first loses faith, then he pounces. I mute my line, mutter a few encouraging words to myself, then say three Hail Marys. The goal is quick, decisive counter-blows to every body shot he throws:

Barry: Cap structure pro forma for new unsecureds?
Bill: *Unmute.* Yep. *Mute.*
Barry: Cash balance looks high—we sweep the proceeds from recent sale of air-handling biz?
Bill: *Unmute.* Swept 'em. *Mute.*
Barry: Are the secured notes pari to the term loan?
Bill: *Unmute.* Yep. *Mute.*
Barry: Double-checked?
Bill: *Unmute.* Yep. *Mute.*
Barry: Triple check it.
Bill: *Unmute.* Ok. *Mute.*
Barry: Is the revolver cash flow or an ABL?
Bill: *Unmute.* Yes. *Mute.*

---

[1] That's one billion dollars of uncertainty based on Barry's industry expertise.

Barry: What?
Bill: *Unmute.* ABL. *Mute.*

The line goes silent, but I hear him thinking.

"Chris Cornell from Soundgarden died?" says Barry. "Christ, he hung himself…don't get me wrong, I'd love to jump out this window, but I got clients that need me. And this window doesn't open. What was that song they had, big hit in the mid-'90s?"

"'Black Hole Sun,'" I say.

Barry half-sings a few lines from Soundgarden's 1994 hit, "Black Hole Sun."

"Great tune," says an unidentified voice on the line.

"DB stock at fifty-two week low?" continues Barry. MDs have a tendency to work in spurts, especially on internal conference calls when they're in front of a computer at their homes. "Do we buy more here or sell and cut our losses?"

"Double down," says an authoritative voice. Bankers have no issue advising companies on how to invest billions of dollars but are more often than not at a loss what to do with their own money. Hell, I can't even do my own taxes.

"Someone send me the website where we register to pre-clear trades," instructs Barry. "Alright, let's get back to the deck. Page twenty-four—who's the dyslexic person who made this page?"

Amen.

28

On Thin Ice

The rattling of the buckle on his Gucci loafers is the trigger. On a good morning, when it's relatively quiet on the floor, I have ten to twelve seconds. I type "NH" into my web browser—it automatically populates to "NHL.com/devils"—then I tap the Enter key. Recent scores are on the top banner, while highlights and news stories are just a tap of the down-arrow key away.

But it's jumping today on the forty-fourth floor, and my time is tight—seven seconds max. Two taps on the keyboard by my index finger, followed by one from my pinky, get me to the Devils homepage. "Devils: 5, Flyers: 2" reads the top banner displaying last night's score. "Hall-Star Performance: Taylor Hall Hat Trick Propels Devils to First Place in Metropolitan Division" reads the headline.

The rattling crescendos as Dick, one of the most senior bankers on the floor, turns the corner and barrels toward me, an ear-to-ear grin on his face. His wispy white hair, what's left of it, sways above his head like one of those inflatable things you see outside car dealerships. And the hair sprouting from the bridge of his nose is rivaled only by the clusters formed on his ears.

"What'd I tell you?" he says, his bushy eyebrows raised in anticipation of my response, as he posts up in the cube next to mine. He has a face that's constantly on the verge of laughter, looking for some catalyst to set him off—doesn't even have to be words. I shake my head and put my hands in the air, to which Dick belts out a howl that grabs the attention of the juniors in neighboring cubes.

"I know, I know," I say. "But Hall's gonna cool off eventually. Can't keep up this pace."

"Third hat trick already this season," says Dick with the air of someone who contributed to Hall's torrid scoring streak. "How 'bout the second one though? I mean, what a goal. How many times have you seen that?"

I tilt my head back, and sort of shake it as if recollecting the goal. Then, turning my head slightly toward my computer, I tap the down-arrow on my keyboard and catch a glimpse of the next headline: "Watch Hall's Dazzling Penalty Shot."

"You see a guy like Datsyuk make a move like that on a penalty shot, but honestly didn't think Hall had those moves. Know he has the speed, but incredible hands," I say, improvising.

Dick caught wind of my hockey days about a week into my internship. Since starting full-time, I've been happy to keep up the charade and do the dance a few times a week, for no other reason than it's a nice distraction from the monotony of the rest of the day.

"I told you," says Dick pointing an index finger at me. Behind him appears Xun, a third-year associate who stands five feet in heels. Unnoticed by Dick, who has commandeered her cube, she waits patiently before realizing it's a fool's errand. She grabs the mug of green tea on her desk and disappears around the corner.

"Watch the whole game?" asks Dick.

Questions like this make me wonder what on earth senior bankers think happens once they leave the office at 5:00 p.m. Did I watch the whole game that started at 7:00 p.m. the night before?

Surprisingly, I didn't. No, last night from 7:00 p.m. to 2:00 a.m. I was parked in my cube, balls-deep in Excel, tears in my eyes and Bolognese all over my face.

"Caught the last couple periods," I say.

"I was there—have seats right on the glass behind the Devils goal for first and third periods, think I've told you that—and let me tell you, never heard the Prudential Center as loud as it was after that win. Think this could be their year."

"Not if my Rangers have anything to say about it," I say, causing Dick to howl once again in a paroxysm of unhinged delight.

"They're in the cellar of the Eastern conference!" he roars.

"Lots of hockey left," I say. I don't give two shits if the Rangers make the playoffs. I can barely name four guys on the team. I'd go as far as saying part of me hopes they *don't* make the playoffs, since of the four Rangers whose names I know, one was my teammate in pee-wees and routinely stole my black tape, for which he'll never find forgiveness.

"Have a big M&A deal coming down the pike and gonna get you on the project. Think it'd be a good experience and chance for you to get exposure to my industry," he says. Dick works in a niche sector, covering companies that lease assets.

"Terrific," I says mustering up as much enthusiasm as I can for something that I know will ruin the next few months of my life, conservatively.

"It'll be a good bullet on your résumé," says Dick as his eyes drift up and out the window behind me.

"Congrats on that Triton deal, by the way. Saw a big piece in the *Times* or maybe the *Journal*," I say. "Sold it for nine times?"

"Nine-and-a-half, fully synergized, bottom of the cycle," says Dick.

"Is there a case study on it? Would love to dig in, see a little more of the nuts and bolts," I lie.

"I'll have the analyst pull something together by COB tomorrow and send it over to you."

"That'd be great," I say, wondering which analyst's night I just ruined.

"Alright, I'll keep you posted on when we get started on this new trade." He taps the top of my cube twice with his hand, then turns around. After a couple steps, he pauses, takes a fifty-percent golf swing, checks to see if he's on plane (he's not—way inside), then resumes his walk. The rattling of his shoe buckles grows fainter with each step, drowned out by laughter from unheard jokes in the bullpen.

On Joel's last day at the bank, I handed him the sheet of paper that has the name, title, and picture of all senior bankers in the group and asked him to highlight each banker I should try to avoid. While staffings for juniors are based on available capacity, there are ways to align with certain MDs as time goes on and steer clear of others. Joel considered the list, removed the cap of the highlighter, did a bunch of head tilting and finger tapping on his nose, then delivered essentially a neon green piece of paper to me two minutes later. Not only was Masters's name highlighted, but so was his phone number (cell and office) *and* picture. Dick's name was one of the only names not highlighted. "Pretty reasonable to work with. Rarely throws juniors under the bus," I remember Joel saying. "Horrific breath, but you learn to acclimate when you're in his office."

> **John Bukowski:** you working with the vice chairman who has massive office?

> **William Keenan:** yeah, guy loves me. just talked to him

> **John Bukowski:** what'd he say

> **William Keenan:** said he sees a lot of his younger self in me. told him I saw a lot of my older self in him

> **William Keenan:** and those were the lowlights

> **John Bukowski:** I could hear you over-laugh at his jokes all the way from my desk

Part of Dick's reputation of being "reasonable" can be attributed to his seniority. As a vice chairman, Dick is one of the more senior bankers in the whole corporate finance division at DB. While younger MDs scramble to impress clients with *War and Peace* sized pitch books, Dick has been known to show up to client meetings with no deck at all, simply asking his juniors to send him the company's latest financials.

What's a vice chairman, you ask? You're not the only one. Responses I've gotten from fellow junior bankers when I inquire range from "big, swinging-dick banker," to "old guy they're trying to push out," to "thought leader who doesn't bring in any business," to "show pony." The truth most likely lies somewhere in between. I remove the list of senior bankers that Joel highlighted, eyeing the small pictures of each MD. There is a sizable contingent who refuse to update their pictures, sporting a conservative comb-over, of which only a horseshoe of hair currently remains. Then there's the guy whose picture looks like it was taken with a selfie stick in the bathroom, but what do you expect from someone who covers a sector called "Materials?" However, the pictures aren't the best part.

"Managing Director, Co-Head of Diversified Industrials, Americas" reads the title of one MD. "Managing Director, Head of Aviation, Global" reads another. By categorizing MDs by sub-sectors and geography, every single MD in the group is either the "head" or "co-head" of something—must make the business cards look better. In fifth grade, I was voted treasurer of my class despite not running for the position nor having any clue what a treasurer does. The lone kid who ran for the position threw a fit, after which he was named co-treasurer by our teacher.

The official staffing email arrives the next morning—Project Litmus (M&A). My fingers are crossed as I skip the first few lines in search of what really matters—the analyst.

> **John Bukowski:** so…who is it? I'm prayin it's the one who sent you the -1,999% paydown

William Keenan: just found out

John Bukowski: tell me now. someone in bullpen or first year?

William Keenan: 'pen

John Bukowski: S**t, F**k off

William Keenan: yesssssssss

John Bukowski: name?

William Keenan: Ernie

John Bukowski: kid who dresses like Buck Showalter?

William Keenan: that's the one

It's my favorite part of winter. Ernie's gear, from head to toe, gets me up in the morning and motivates me to hustle into the office on those dark, snowy mornings that plague the financial district come December. But I have to earn it by arriving early enough to ensure I get to the office before him.

The oversized, faux-fur trapper hat—complete with earflaps—sits atop his head, often covering his eyes. The massive Turtle Fur mittens remain on his hands until he settles into his cube, though much to my chagrin, they aren't attached to his jacket. His slacks, which he sports in a variety of gray shades, are pressed and rival the bagginess of the JNCO jeans I wore in middle school. His brown loafers at one point undoubtedly had pennies lodged in them. But the centerpiece of the outfit, the reason I set my alarm ten minutes early in the winter, ensuring I beat him to the forty-fourth floor, is the jacket—vintage New York Yankees bomber, dark blue, satin starter number, dugout version. Last I checked, a used one was retailing for $500-plus on eBay, and it's not hard to see why.

On top of dressing like he just won the pennant, Ernie is a dynamite analyst.

* * *

Joel wasn't kidding about Dick's breath—it could cause the massive barges in the Hudson River outside his office to call Mayday. Luckily, most of Dick's yawns and belly laughs are followed by him leaning back in a satisfied manner, thereby increasing the distance he is from me and from Ernie, who sit across the large wooden table in his corner office.

As he celebrates one of his jokes with a howl and a recline, I look behind Dick and spot a helicopter emerging from the cloud cover, scanning the FDR and the Brooklyn Bridge for traffic. In the distance, I spot the Jones Beach Theater, where I watched my first concert, O.A.R. Dick's office is by far the biggest on the floor. An expansive trove of deal toys in assorted shapes and sizes, spanning deals over the past three decades, line the wall-to-wall glass window behind him and the top shelves of his desk. A few detailed maps of Somewhere, USA, with pushpins in random parts are taped to one wall. On his desk stand two unopened bottles of red wine. Next to them is a fancy-looking corkscrew.

Lining the outside of Dick's desk are a number of pictures of him posing with other guys who look like him, most of them at golf courses. One is a picture of him and two other guys with matching bellies posing in front of the unmistakable purple and pink azaleas at Augusta's famous Amen Corner. The trio look like the type who wouldn't think twice about taking a downhill six-footer gimme for bogey, even if no one gave it to them. The most prominent picture on his desk is of Dick and a hefty man who looks like a politician. The two are shaking hands. A small American flag is pinned to the guy's lapel, and a large American flag hangs in the background of the photo.

Next to the legal pad in front of Dick is a Hewlett-Packard 12C financial calculator. Ernie bought one his first week on the job. After failing to learn how to operate it in the first month, he resorted to using his TI-82 from high school.

The framed picture that sits directly behind the HP calculator and next to Dick's computer monitor reminds me of my first encounter with him during my internship, when we were all encouraged to schedule a time to meet with MDs and do our best to ingratiate ourselves with them. The moment I saw the picture, I knew I was in. Dick, with his face painted Devils green and red, has his arms around the shoulder of a young teen sporting a Devils hat and massive Devils jersey. Only thing missing was the big foam #1 hand. "What position does he play?" I remember asking Dick when I spotted the picture. Eli was a goalie, and I felt the full-time job offer slide securely in my back pocket by the time Dick was in tears describing watching his son play on the JV team at the state finals.

Dick recovers from his most recent laugh and slowly returns to an upright position in his chair. Ernie, hunched like many senior analysts due to the amount of time he spends typing at his desk, scribbles furious notes, though for the life of me I can't figure out what he's writing now, but I'm glad he's paying attention. The VP on the deal, predictably, is on sixteen other things, so he isn't around and sounds like he'll only be available to provide limited feedback throughout the process.

"Things should ramp up in the next couple weeks. We'll need to send our preliminary views to the client ahead of that call with him next Tuesday. Did you guys get the email about that?" asks Dick.

"We have the dial-in," I confirm as Ernie flips the pages in his spiral notebook and continues his copious note taking.

"Good," says Dick, tapping his desk with an open palm. "Ephraim is the M&A guy—he's the number two guy there—who scheduled the call, so let's get those pages together, then we can flesh them out when he gives us feedback on the call."

"Great," I say.

"If you can get me something by Thursday night, that'd be preferred. I'm shooting down to Florida to play Seminole this weekend...with Jim Nelson." He looks up, making eye contact with Ernie, then me as he says the name. It's gotta be the name of some famous investor, though I've no clue, and given Ernie's nose is buried in his trapper keeper, I know he has no idea either. Sure would be helpful to have the VP here.

"*The* Jim Nelson?" I say with wide eyes.

Dick nods slowly. "Good friend of mine...and helluva player—swings lefty, putts righty...scratch golfer."

"No kidding?" I say.

"You bet," he says amidst more nodding. "So like I said, get me what you have by Thursday. Don't think I should have many comments, and we'll circle up with Ephraim and his team on Tuesday."

Ernie and I exit Dick's office and post up in the bullpen.

"Lookee, lookee," says Ted, who's perched in a cube going over a markup with another analyst. "Heard you guys are working with Dick. Should be in a good spot, Keenan—only thing he loves more than golf is hockey."

"Pretty sure I saw him YouTubing videos on bunker-shot technique when we were in his office," I say. Ernie nods, confirming my suspicion.

"He'll stream security footage of a mini-golf range if he has to." says Ted. "You guys working on a leasing deal?"

"Yep," I say.

"Good luck." Ted returns his attention to the markup he's going through.

Ernie's BlackBerry buzzes. "Shoot, my Seamless is here," he says.

"I can grab it. Where'd you order from?"

"Georgio's Pizza. Thanks," he says. There's a lot of work to be done, and I'm more useful in the lobby anyway. While accounting goodwill is defined as an intangible asset that arises when one company purchases another for a premium, the most important goodwill is that which an associate builds with his analyst.

"Why don't you scan those pages he gave you," I say to Ernie. "Then, log the deal and see if we need to do KYC. Also, check the old folders to see if the financials are already spread, then try to get the model up and running over next couple days. I'll work on putting the shell of the deck together…and I'll also look up who Jim Nelson is so we have stuff to ask Dick about next week."

"Okie dokie. Sounds like a planski," says Ernie. As Ernie gets to work, I head to the lobby to retrieve his dinner.

* * *

In business school, they teach you that companies do deals for one specific reason. A month-long section of corporate finance class is spent dispelling the common misconceived reasons why companies buy or sell assets. Now, that single, specific reason slips my mind. However, I can say with unwavering conviction that whatever it is, it's not the reason any of the deals I've worked on are done. Despite what theory says or what's publicly stated as rationale, real companies with real people managing them do deals for one reason: they feel pressure. That pressure can strike from any angle. The banker's job is to sniff out its origin and double down with a cast iron clamp to guarantee a transaction closes and a hefty fee follows.

While the sources of pressure vary widely on factors like whether the company is private or public, they are generally one of the following:

1. Internal pressure to optimize performance and keep up with increased competition.

2. External pressure from favorable market conditions to finally get that once-in-a-lifetime bargain buy or premium valuation on a sale.

3. Pressure from shareholders to increase the stock price.

4. Pressure from CEO's wife/husband to put a down payment on that second or third house.

It's no surprise that most deals are viewed as failures in retrospect.

Project Litmus is a prime example of pressure coming from so many angles that the company has no fuckin' clue what it should do but knows it's gotta do something, so it engages DB "to explore strategic alternatives," which is the topic of our conference call on Tuesday afternoon.

* * *

"Have you received the materials?" asks Dick once everyone is on the line.

"Not yet. We have a firewall system that sometimes causes a delay when receiving attachments from external email addresses," says Ephraim, the head of M&A for the client and a former banker himself. And while that may be true, Ephraim doesn't have the deck, since I haven't sent it yet and instead am scrambling to make last second edits that Dick emailed me minutes ago.

"Should be coming through any second now," says Dick. "Bill sent them a few minutes ago." I double-check the final change on Dick's email, attach the document to the email I've already saved in drafts, and send to the group.

"Yeah, sent a few minutes ago," I say. "Would assume you should get it any second now."

A minute later, the email arrives in their inboxes.

"I think the purpose of this call is to walk you through our analysis of strategic options and gather some feedback on a few areas," says Dick. He then quickly walks everyone through the first five pages of the deck, which consist of high-level, useless information. Slides six through fifteen are number heavy and more in the weeds.

"Just going back to slide six for a second," says Ephraim. "If we can take a look at the far-right column, where you outline the pricing for the various pieces of debt. I follow the TLB," then as a side note, Ephraim says, "Interesting you guys think there are three yards of risk in the bank market."

"That's based on information from our colleagues in levera—" I begin to say before Ephraim interrupts.

"I got the senior secured piece, and ECA, but can you help me understand how you arrived at the private placement coupon?"

"Bill, you want to talk Ephraim through how we arrived at this? I think we're trying to be holistic about our approach here. And again, guys, these are purely illustrative, given we don't have fulsome data. Everything in brackets is preliminary," says Dick for the fifth time.

"Understood," says Ephraim. "Bill, could you opine please?"

This is the issue with being in an industry-banking group. You inevitably "hold the pen" on all documents, whether it be a model or a presentation. You're responsible for every goddamn word and number, even if you had nothing to do with it. The page they're looking at outlines the various debt markets they can tap into to finance an acquisition, and given the nuances of each market, DB has specific teams that cover each market, but no one from those teams is on the call.

"We consulted our structured credit team, who advised us on the pricing here—" I say.

"But is that private placement tranche priced off treasuries or LIBOR?" says Ephraim.

"Good catch," chimes in an unidentified voice of someone who works for Ephraim.

"Well, we show it based off LIBOR for consistency sake, given the other tranches of debt on this page are priced off LIBOR," I say. "We actually footnoted—"

"Right, but am I correct in stating that the private placement debt should be priced off treasuries and not LIBOR?" says Ephraim.

"As I understand it, yes that's how it's generally done. But again, just to make it consistent, we showed pricing off LIBOR for all tranches. And the spread we show reflects that discrepancy, so the all-in cost is the same. The footnote—"

"Got it, got it. Not quite apples to apples here, but fine. We can move on," says Ephraim.

Wasting five minutes every three pages to let the client feel smart is worth the eventual fee, I guess.

"Looks like you're showing LTV of seventy-five percent with blended costs of five percent, is that right?" continues Ephraim.

"Correct," I say. "And we think that's the most aggressive leverage, given the capacities of each market. With more detailed fleet information, we can be more precise, but that's as aggressive as we think we can go."

"I like eighty percent LTV and four percent blended cost," says Ephraim instructively.

"Let us circle up with our ABS and bank-debt colleagues and come back to you on that," says Dick. "I think we can be creative around this and get you what you're looking for." It's this type of bullying from the client that brings banks down.

"Can you also provide an analysis on two other scenarios—if we issue ten years versus five years for those notes?" It's like the grown-up version of those SAT questions: "Two trains leave the station at the same time. One is traveling at eighty miles per hour heading due south, and the other is traveling at 105 kilometers per hour heading due north." I always wished the trains would just collide.

"We'll do that," says Dick—of course "we" means "Bill."

"Page seven," says Ephraim. "Fifteen percent? SG&A...fifteen percent? Is that right?" He's looking at the 14.6 percent that has a green circle around it and is the SG&A cost as a percent of its sales of one acquisition target we proposed.

"What's management doing? Dreadful," says Ephraim.

"Not if you work there," chimes in Dick to a chorus of laughter.

"I really like that number," says Ephraim. "Very interesting," he says slowly, drawing out the word "very."

What gets Ephraim wet is the potential to vastly reduce costs if they buy this company—realizing synergies, in banker vernacular.

"Can definitely rationalize headcount," says Dick, indicating that the easiest way to reduce costs is to fire employees. It's a douchey euphemism, like when people who attended Harvard say they went to "a small liberal-arts school in Cambridge." Incidentally, I went to a small liberal-arts school in Cambridge.

"Absolutely," says Ephraim. "We could definitely optimize that cost structure."

"It's a one-plus-one-equals-three deal in my eyes," says Dick.

After outlining the various acquisition opportunities, we dive into the considerations of a sale. There are North American buyers, Asian buyers, European buyers, strategic buyers, and financial buyers—you name it, we show 'em a buyer salivating at the thought of buying their company, though the (lack of) bids may tell a different story.

I can feel the call wrapping up.

"Look, guys, I think you're thinking about things the right way and asking the right questions. This was really helpful," says Ephraim. "Appreciate the work on this."

Now, the moment of truth.

"What would be great is if you could flesh out—" continues Ephraim. I slam the table. I know Ernie is in his cube and will copy our marching orders verbatim. And what I also know is that asks from the client are far more painful than those from an MD.

"...so my guys will make sure the data room is up by COB today, so would be great to see all those scenarios by end of the week," concludes Ephraim.

"Shouldn't be a problem," says Dick. And it won't be for him, since he won't be spending the next three days in the office grinding on the analysis.

"Appreciate the quick turnaround. Enjoy the rest of the week," says Ephraim.

29

Sold

"What the fuck's a Super Puma?" asks the panicked voice on the other line as I answer the call. It's the associate in lev fin who's working on the deal with us.

I scan through the data room that one of Ephraim's minions set up for the deal. The data room is a secured folder set up for every deal and considered a "data dump" for obvious reasons. Companies will upload everything from their historical financials, to legal documents, to granular detail bordering on the absurd— including dietary restrictions of independent contractors. It's up to the bankers to sift through and figure out what's important. I open the file detailing the company's assets, which takes into account a number of helicopters, including a model called AS332 Super Puma. I remember spending an hour Googling the different models.

"Assume you're asking because of those metrics we show excluding the Super Pumas?" I say.

"Bingo."

"Pretty sure they're the horseshit choppers they can't lease, so on our call Tuesday we decided to exclude them from the asset base," I say.

"I guess that makes sense, but we're showing the capital structure develop over time, so would those assets be less horseshit in future?"

"No clue. Let's assume they're horseshit indefinitely," I say. "And footnote it."

"Works for me. Also, I know you guys have the latest version of the model. Before you send us the updated iteration, can you make sure to change the names of those final two sheets on the far right— the ones with final analyses?" he says.

I scan the Excel document. The final two sheets are titled "cash anal" and "total anal."

"Just spell out 'analysis' for both, please. I spend all day on the phone with my analyst, and it's like, 'total anal looks good, man.' I'm getting weird looks from the MD who sits in the office by me. And earlier today I heard him threaten to throw someone out the window, so trying not to be that guy."

"No problem. V-twenty-seven of the model is updated."

"Thanks. Later." We hang up.

Having spent the better part of the last two days sifting through the thousands of files in the data room, I've pinpointed the fundamental flaw facing the company—it's a shit business. It's also a shit industry and the first indicators are in the annual reports of the comparable public companies.

Any annual report littered with colorful charts, glossy graphics, and pictures of management team members wearing hardhats with crossed arms surrounded by operations employees outside a pre-school in Guadalajara with a caption expounding their dedication to social responsibility is cause for heightened concern. Like the pitch books bankers create, the fancier the pages, the worse the fundamentals. Companies with fancy annual reports are typically in trouble. You show me an annual report that's only black-and-white text, I'll show you a good company.

For our client and many of its public peers, the majority of the assets they lease are to companies who have unhedged exposure to commodity markets. This is great when those commodities are trading at premium prices, but it is devastating in the current macro environment of suppressed commodity prices with no sign of turning. Between the structure of their contracts and the niche applications of their assets, it is only a matter of time before things blow up.

My phone rings. "Ernie?" I say into my headset as I press the button on my desk phone to accept the call.

"Hello, may I speak with Mister William Keenan?" says the female voice.

"Speaking."

"My name is Tanya, and I'm contacting you on behalf of your dedicated American Express Corp—"

I hang up, remove my headset, and walk to Rhonda's desk, where Ethan is standing behind her.

"So how do I renew my passport?" says Ethan.

"You'll have to go to the website I sent—" begins Rhonda.

"Can you just do it for me if I give you the old one?" says Ethan as he places a weathered-looking blue passport with frayed edges on her desk.

"I can try—may need some more information, but lemme see what I can do."

Ethan turns around. "Lookee, lookee," he says. "Just the guy I was looking for." He removes his iPhone from his pocket. "Can I get some juice? Just need like thirty minutes."

"Sure." Ethan taps me on the shoulder as he walks to my cube to charge his phone.

"Hey, Rhonda," I say.

"Don't' tell me AmEx again," she says. I nod. "Let me look into it after I get this passport situation figured out."

"Thanks," I say to Rhonda before returning to my cube, where a worried-looking Ernie stands, a hand massaging his forehead.

"Did you see Dick's email?" asks Ernie.

"Oh boy, what happened?" I sit and open my inbox.

"He's still hung up on how we got that updated LTV of eighty percent." Ernie points to the haphazard email Dick wrote to us.

"Pain in the ass when they refuse to look at the numbers," I say.

"Keep reading," says Ernie. "He wants to see the calculation, but it's clearly not just the division he wants, since that's on the page. Assume he wants the full math, which is on a few different tabs."

"So we send him the model," I say as I read the rest of his email.

"That would make sense, but remember last time I tried to send him a spreadsheet with a calc and he got worked up and told us—"

"I don't do Excel," we say in unison, Ernie providing air quotes. Finally, I arrive at Ernie's conundrum and the explanation behind his panic-stricken expression.

"We PDF it," I say with authority.

"PDF the model?"

"Yep, PDF the fucker."

"Okay," he says slowly. "So I guess I could PDF the output tab, debt assumptions tab, debt sched—"

"All of 'em," I declare. "PDF all the thirty-three tabs. If he wants the calculation but refuses to open Excel, then we flood him with everything, and he can figure it out."

"You got it," says Ernie with a smile as he spins on a dime and returns to his cube.

It's the same story on every deal. It starts with an innocent-sounding client request at the tail-end of the call. "Just some rough math, back-of-the-envelope stuff, to see how it looks…just a page or two." Thirty-six tabs and twenty-seven versions later, some number in the model irks the MD, since he never looked at the numbers in the first place. Analyst and associate must improvise—today it's PDFing. Most days, it's not that easy.

Most days, I try to remember why I'm here in the first place.

* * *

"Got the markup from Dick," says Ernie as he approaches my cube. "And when I was in his office, Dick got a text from Wilson Winston, or Winston Wilson. Yeah, I think Winston is his first name."

"Is he on the deal?"

"No. He's the governor of Indiana," says Ernie.

"How do you know?"

"Dick told me."

"This guy have a hot daughter or something? What's the point?"

"Dick just showed me the text and said the governor of Indiana asked him when they were going to play golf next."

"So, unsolicited, Dick shows you a text from a guy just to impress you?"

"I guess," says Ernie. "Anyway, looks like most of this deck focuses on acquisition targets, which I think we already have a bunch of stuff on."

The next few weeks, we explore potential acquisitions for Project Litmus, but there are too few viable targets, and financing proves too expensive. We abandon that route and run a sale process with Goldman as a co-advisor. The CIM is drafted, and after turning comments for a couple months on Project Litmus_CIMv106, we're halfway to vFFFFFF6.[1] NDAs are signed. Management holds presentations for prospective buyers, some interested in acquiring the company and others simply interested in free food at high-end hotels. There is handholding during site visits and yelling 'cause we fuck up the hotel room booking and black-car pickups. There are letters of intent and first-round bids, then second-round bids. There are fake bids we ignore and low-ball bids we dismiss initially, then seriously consider a week later. There is mass skepticism around growth rates, but nothing that can't be solved by paying LEK six figures to generate a third-party report corroborating the

---

[1] Goldman's analyst notifies us that the Goldman logo on vFFFFFF5 is three millimeters smaller than the DB logo. We adjust accordingly.

double-digit growth rates we market. A fairness opinion is issued and is as fair as you would expect, given it comes from another investment bank. There are late nights, early mornings, and productive calls—but mainly unnecessary ones. There are tears and sighs and yawns and even some laughs, but mainly the tears.

And then. Finally. There is a sale—nine times pro forma post-transformation adjusted after-synergy consolidated EBITDA from continuing operations. A financial buyer, a PE firm. The same PE firm who sold the company four years earlier for a higher multiple.

30

Thin Mints and Tagalongs

William Keenan: you take my charger?

John Bukowski: uve asked me a million times. no

William Keenan: not the bberry one. My iphone charger

John Bukowski: still no

John Bukowski: possible INCOMINGGGGGGGGG

I pop my head above my cube, and seconds later, two pint-sized girls dressed in dark green Girl Scout garb emerge, berets propped on their heads and scarves tied loosely around their necks. After a brief conversation, they part ways, the smaller of the two heading to the far end of the cubes, and the taller one toward my end.

"Hi," says the girl, hands behind her back. An American flag patch and a number of badges dot her vest. Her smile reveals a missing top tooth. "My name is Natalia, and I'm a member of Troop 3746. My troop and I hope you'll support us and the Girl Scouts of America by buying some of the delicious cookies we're selling today."

"Who's advising on the sale?" I ask, a question she outright ignores. "What are the flavors again?"

She hands me the piece of paper she's holding, which displays the eleven flavors.

"Does your Dad work on the floor?" I ask as I scan the list. She nods. "What's your name again?"

"Natalia Masters," she says. "What's yours?"

"Bill Keenan," I say.

"Oh!" she says with a jump. "My dad knows you! I hear him yell your name at home a lot," she says proudly.

"What's your favorite flavor?" I ask. She leans in and points at the cookies set against the purple background on the sheet of paper.

"The Samoas—caramel plus coconut," she says, eyeing me. "They're the best."

"I'll take three boxes of Thin Mints."

"Those are my dad's favorite!" she exclaims.

"Actually, I want three Tagalongs," I say.

I fill out the order sheet, and she's on her way to the next cube.

> **John Bukowski:** how'd you make out?

> **William Keenan:** 3 tagalongs. You?

> **John Bukowski:** got hosed. Baker's dozen of samoas. No idea how I'm gonna unload 'em

Shrewd move selling cookies the same day the summer interns start. The group staffer weaves through the cubes, wrangling up junior bankers to attend the weekly meeting in the main conference room on the forty-fourth floor.

"Let's go, folks," he announces. "Unless it's a client deliverable this morning, you should be in that conference room." He slowly snakes through the cubes of analysts and associates.

Normally, I wouldn't go, choosing instead to dick around on my iPhone. But since someone took my charger and my phone is dead, I follow the herd of interns into the large, rectangular-shaped conference room.

On the perimeter of the room stand the juniors, interspersed with the interns, all of whom clutch notebooks under their arms. The full-time juniors, a group whose hollow eyes, shirts torn at the elbow, and slumped shoulders stand in stark contrast to the eager interns who ready their ballpoint pens in anticipation of the wisdom senior bankers from across the bank are about to impart. Within a month, half the interns won't be carrying notebooks. And by the time they start full-time, most won't even show up.

While attendance by junior bankers waxes and wanes throughout the year, senior-banker turnout is fairly predictable—those with deals recently announced show up to bask in praise and distribute "case studies" on their deals. Today's turnout is unusually big because of the new interns.

"Chicago, can you hear us?" says one of the senior bankers into the speakerphone as he looks at the projector at the far end of the room, where a group of bankers in Chicago is displayed.

"Chicago's on," says a voice on the speakerphone, accompanied by a thumbs-up from someone displayed on the projector. Boston announces themselves too.

"Let's get started," says one of the seniors in the room. "Equities, want to kick things off?"

The equity market is ripping. Let's push IPOs and secondaries.

"Folks from investment grade?" says the senior banker.

Debt markets are as strong as ever. Great time to refinance notes, reprice those term loans.

"Rates?"

Interest rates are at all-time lows. DB revised its house view of future rates down by fifty bps. The party ain't ever stopping. Let's get our clients levered to the hilt.

Blah, blah, blah.

An intern nods his head enthusiastically and jots something down in his notebook, as a senior banker reels off some jargon I've heard more times than I care to remember.

"Agile Minds Ask Questions," reads the cover of the DB folder that another female intern holds in her hand and uses as a clipboard. I tried asking Masters a question once. "Figure it out," he advised.

While interns scrawl copious notes, only pausing to turn to a fresh page in their notebooks, the full-time juniors stare absently with vacant eyes at nothing in particular—a disenchanted group, of which I'm a member.

Sitting at the large table are the MDs, directors, and a couple of gutsy VPs. There are six empty seats, and they'll remain that way until promotions are announced.

Some MDs scroll through their BlackBerries, while others flip through the bullshit market-update decks from the capital markets teams. At some point, each MD will lean over and whisper something to the MD beside him, eliciting a smile and nod. All part of the dance.

Most MDs can be bucketed into one of two categories: the large ones, who steamrolled their way to corner offices and who now relish the ability to walk slowly down the hallways, a lethargic speed afforded to them based on their size and standing in the group. Then there are the small MDs who race around the office and whose unrelenting drive makes you wonder what happened to them in high school.

Christ, these guys know a shit ton, I remember thinking at my first meeting. And they do. After twenty years doing it, one would hope they have developed some expertise. But when I look around at the MDs now, I don't see industry experts, finance gurus, and trusted advisors of some of the world's biggest companies.

There's Ethan, who, despite spending 90 percent of his day jawing on the phone, resorts to stealing my phone chargers—both of 'em—a guy who doesn't have the patience to figure out how to renew his own passport, so he has someone else figure it out for him. Ethan seems to derive pleasure from finding fuckups in decks. Turning in a deck without faults somehow angers him. He's happier when he has something to be angry about.

There's Dick, who refuses to open Excel, despite it being the foundation of the analysis we present to companies to make key decisions. And Masters, who's just a flat-out dickhead.

Maybe complacency is rampant in this place, maybe not, but there's a complacency rampant in these seniors. They're masters of outsourcing, skirting responsibility when it suits them. And the mindset funnels down. I'm as guilty of it as they are. Price chart? FactSet. Benchmarking? MAKS. Growth rates? BIS. Model? Analyst. Well, try, cry, *then* analyst.

The longer you're here, the higher you climb, and the more resources you have at your disposal. But while I'm sure some of these guys enjoy their jobs, I know many are stuck. Their ability to perform the seemingly meaningless number-crunching exercises atrophies over time as they become more dependent on others and climb higher.

After market updates conclude, Dick knobs off all the MDs in the room who closed big deals, as the interns listen in awe. "Next year's pipeline looks even stronger," he says before the meeting adjourns. "Let's get to work."

Juniors funnel out of the room first, and as I wait for the bottleneck to subside, I see more congratulatory backslapping among MDs seated at the table.

"You get your BlackBerry to work?" whispers one intern to another as we return to our cubes.

"Yeah," she responds holding it up. "Just got my first staffing email."

"Nice. Anything cool?" asks the intern.

F1 keys will soon be popped. Excel shortcuts memorized.

I shove through the meandering interns and return to my desk, where my desk phone is ringing. I put on my headset.

"Go for Bill," I say.

"May I speak with Mister William Keenan," says the male voice.

"You got him."

"Hi, Mister Keenan. My name is Jason, and I'm contacting you on behalf of your dedicated American Express team. I'm following up on some overdue charges on your corporate card. As a valued customer, you—"

"Jason," I interrupt. "I'm actually about to head out. Can you give me a call on my cell later?"

"Absolutely, Mister Keenan. Ready for the number when you are."

I remove the neon-green-highlighted sheet of contact info for MDs and read off Masters's cell phone.

"Thank you very much, Mister Keenan. Is there a convenient time to call?"

"I'm in London, so how about first thing in the morning here, which I guess would be, say, 2 a.m. EST."

31

_vF

I'd rather be at the office.

"Must be nice to get back inside a hockey rink," says Dick as he approaches me from behind. I stand in the suite we booked at the Devils' home arena, the Prudential Center, to celebrate the closing of Project Litmus.

"Been a long time," I say.

"You try the lobster? I had my guy at Le Bernardin deliver it. Best you're gonna find on the East Coast," says Dick as he tilts a can of Stella up to his mouth.

"Gonna dive in after this period," I say. Both our eyes settle on the game action. A Devils winger intercepts a pass, and a three-on-two develops. Dick taps my arm with a finger.

"Here it is," he says.

The crowd rises in unison, buzzes in anticipation before emitting a collective groan when the puck carrier decides to dump the puck and go for a line change—the right play, given it's their fourth line and the end of a long shift.

"Dammit," says Dick in a good-natured way. "Gotta get that on a net," he says looking for corroboration. A moment passes. "Skate much these days?" While I understand the effort to shoot the shit with me, I've barely left the forty-fourth floor the past few months, and while I'm certain he doesn't care, he must realize that his deal dictated my life. But it's okay. Part of deciding to pursue banking was to reset my life, pave a new path, and leave hockey behind.

Part of me considers explaining to Dick that I don't even know where my equipment is. That being at this game is in some ways devastating. That the only seat I want at this rink is on one of the benches. And that, once I quit hockey, that was it. I was done with it.

"Lace 'em up from time to time," I lie. It wasn't a clean break. I felt like Happy Gilmore on the first day of my internship—"Hi, I'm a hockey player, but I'm doing banking today."

Dick shakes his empty Stella can. "Need another?" he says.

"I'm good," I say as I raise the Bud Light I've been nursing.

A puck deflects into the stands and play stops. My eyes hone in on the Devils bench, where I watch a player cover his mouth with a gloved hand, lean slightly to the guy next to him, and say something that elicits a chuckle and a squirt of water onto the ice.

Ernie then walks up and stands next to me, holding a plastic cup containing some fizzing clear fluid and a lemon wedge.

"Uh-oh," I say. "Vodka soda?"

"Perrier," says Ernie as he pokes the lemon wedge with the small black straw. "Gotta go back to the office tonight. Just got staffed on a CRM due Friday." I shake my head and want to complain on his behalf. Ernie just smiles.

"You're a hockey player, right?" he says.

"Was one," I say.

"But I heard you played in Europe, right?" he says. I nod. "Why didn't you try for the NHL?"

"Was too good. Wouldn't have been fair for to the other players," I say.

Ernie smiles. "So were you a guy who scored goals or more defensive?" he asks with the charm of someone who genuinely knows nothing about the game.

"More of a locker room guy," I say. He turns and faces me with furrowed brows. "Like my most useful contribution was anywhere but the ice." I can tell he wants to get it, but still isn't quite there yet. "Like on Litmus—you ran the model for the most part, right? So you were the guy scoring the goals. I was more—"

Ernie tilts his chin up and nods. "Yeah, I understand now...I gotcha."

A Devils winger enters the offensive zone with speed, then cuts across the middle with his head down. A split second later, he's on his back.

"Dang!" says Ernie. "He got slammed!"

The dazed player struggles to one knee and leans on his stick to stand before skating slowly, bent at the waist, to his bench. The crowd is up in arms, but the hit was legal, and it was a beauty. As I watch the trainer lean over the player's shoulder to ensure he knows what planet he's on, I think I miss that feeling in some way. Not the pain, but knowing I can withstand it and play on. I remember the first time I got hit in Squirts. I cried, and no one gave a shit. My head shouldn't've been down skating through the neutral zone. There's something to be said for getting physically hit by your peers during childhood within the confines of a game. It humbles you in a way I'm not sure anything else can. What's really humbling though is spending the better part of your life dedicating yourself to something and failing to reach the top. It's enough to make you blindly pursue another all-consuming endeavor to help you move on. It doesn't.

During a break in the play, my eye is drawn to the white boards that line the arena that are peppered with advertisements. There's a diversified-industrials company that I did a pitch for and another chemical company that I worked on a term-loan repricing for. I wait to see if I feel something, anything—maybe pride?—but I don't. The ref drops the puck, and the game resumes.

The buzzer sounds as the second period finishes. Ernie and I navigate our way through the various conversations between management team members and senior bankers and arrive at the buffet next to one of the junior Goldman bankers, who shovels a lobster tail into his mouth.

"You guys look at the deal toy designs yet?" asks the Goldman analyst between bites. He's the type of guy who, despite being in his early twenties, looks like he desperately wants to be forty-five. I imagine his ideal Saturday night is heading to a high-end hotel bar in Midtown and hitting on 501(a)(5) accreditor investors.

"Yeah," says Ernie. "Just need to get sign-off from our seniors, but think the gray one from Altrum is our favorite."

"You excited about the new job?" I ask the Goldman kid. "Industrials-focused PE, right?" Any time shit got bad during the deal, he'd be sure to mention how he didn't care, since he had a job lined up.

"No," he says, shaking his head while chewing. "Actually, a little more untraditional route." He swallows the bite of lobster. "Small PE shop started by some ex-Goldman guys—invest in business services companies," he corrects me.

"Ernie said you have a sister who works at Goldman too. Same group?"

"She's in private wealth management."

"I should give her my bonus to invest. Feel like I'm not any better at it than before banking."

"Her clients have twenty million dollars of assets, minimum," he says.

The game remains close through the third period. One-goal leads are exchanged twice, until the Devils tie it at three apiece with two minutes left.

Above all else—talent, hard work, all that shit—success in hockey is determined by being present in the moment. It's this feeling I may be searching for more than anything else. In banking, there's little time to think (and it's generally frowned upon), but the endless tasks are merely distractions from being present. Sure, I've been lost when working in Excel models, but I never *lose myself* in the work like some of my peers do. I'm the guy operating on the fringes, just getting by and making it work. The detachment I've developed almost makes me more attractive to some MDs who feel the need to convince me how great the job is. It's that internal drive, motivated by oneself, that I've lost, but that I see in all the players on the ice, acting on base human instincts. Now my world is motivated by external factors, the need to please others. What a way to go through life. Maybe that's what growing up is. I sure hope not.

With thirty-two seconds remaining, the Devils player who'd gotten steamrolled in the second period pickpockets a defenseman, then releases an unexpected snapshot through the goalie's legs. Dick celebrates with some fist-pumps, then a howl—his breath more devastating than the bone crushing hit the guy who scored the game-winner endured.

The night in the suite ends with handshakes, back slaps, and chatter of future deals.

"My driver's here," Dick announces. "I'll give you guys a lift to the Ritz," he says to the management team.

Ernie and I wait on the subway platform downstairs, where our driver, some guy wearing goggles who steers the 2 train, ushers us from the 34th Street Penn Station stop to Wall Street. The office is abuzz when we get to the forty-fourth floor around 10:30 p.m. Ernie gets to work on his new staffing, while I head to my cube and absent-mindedly check my email.

My mind drifts to the image of the guy who scored the game-winner. I miss that feeling. A part of me never left the rink.

I'm not sure it ever will.

The forty-fourth floor is like an airport terminal without the excitement of impending travel. And I'm not talking the JetBlue terminal at JFK with the good food. I'm talking LaGuardia's sterile terminal B that reeks of old eggs and recirculates air so greasy you can taste it.

A few cubes over from me sits a senior associate, a small Asian girl who for the past few months has blockaded herself into her cube with brown boxes of deal toys. While she and her analyst wait for a pitch book to be printed in repro, I see a Zillow web page open on one of her monitors as they research the address of the MD whose apartment they'll be couriering pitch books to in a couple hours.

"Forty-five hundred square feet...on Park Avenue," says the analyst. "Absolute baller."

Ernie emails me the tombstone for our deal, a small graphic that will be placed in all subsequent pitch books, extolling the bank's deal experience. A few analysts in M&A were sacrificed along the way, but the deal closed.

It's just after 11:00 p.m. when I sling my jacket over my shoulder and head home. The lobby attendant at the 60 Wall Street station is busy chuckling at YouTube videos on his phone as I beeline through the turnstile, then the revolving door.

A breeze rushes through the towering buildings on either side of me, but quickly subsides as I turn left and walk north on Water Street.

The homeless couple who shelter in sleeping bags near Starbucks in a small, depressed enclave created by a few stairs, rummage through mounds of garbage bags stacked on the sidewalk, collecting as many bottles and cans as they can before the garbage truck's predawn arrival.

All four lanes of Water Street are unlit and appear deserted, until a set of bright yellow headlights pierces the darkness. A large SUV races south on Water Street. As it nears, the tires veer left, crossing the median, before swerving back to the other side of the road.

The buzz of the BlackBerry against my right thigh grabs my attention.

"Hey!" yells a man appearing from the shadows across the street. He runs toward a dark figure lying in the middle of Water Street. "Are you okay?" he says.

Reaching into my pocket, the horrifying, tiny red light blinks— over and over and over: one new email. It's from Dick.

I look up from my BlackBerry. I can barely make out the red taillights of the SUV as it disappears south on Water Street.

I scan the email: "Spoke with CEO on drive home from game... interested in bolt-on acquisition...put together a couple pages... good to have first thing in the morning."

Fifteen feet from me, the man helps the woman to her feet.

I turn around and walk back to the office.

The forty-fourth floor is eerily silent for 11:30 p.m. on a Thursday. At my desk, I read Dick's email in full—a doable request I can finish in a couple hours.

A few minutes later, Rose makes the rounds, pushing her industrial-sized trashcan and emptying the mini trash bins under the desks of each cube. I reach under my desk, grab my trash bin, and hand it to her. She empties it in her large bin.

"Is nice," she says as she eyes the vest Joel got everyone in the group, which hangs outside my cube.

"Thanks." I turn slightly and give it a long look. "You know someone who might like it?"

Her cheeks broaden as a smile lights her face.

I remove the vest from the hanger and hand it to her. She beams as she carefully folds it and tucks it in between her cleaning supplies. Then she's off to the next cube, reaching under the desk and grabbing the small bin, emptying it into the larger one.

By 2:07 a.m. I've finished a draft of the pages Dick requested for the following morning. The floor is dark and silent as I attach the PDF of the deck and hit send on the email. Seconds later, a notification pops up on my monitor—one new email. Bullshit or horrific?

My computer dings again—another new email. It's from Masters—"Subject: AMEX call????"

I don't bother reading either of them. They're all bullshit emails—none are horrific. They never were. I power off my computer, stand from my desk, and as I head for the exit, the overhead lights illuminate.

Shit List

I spent six months writing this book, trapped in my head. Not a fun place to be. I blame the following who contributed to my suffering: Deutsche Bank, Columbia Business School, Post Hill Press, Air Mail, Max Carter, Alice Martell, Munch, Garett Vassel, Mom, Dad.

And Graydon Carter: You not only gave me a forum to be myself, but you encouraged it. Sorry yet?